Advance

"*Sex, Masculinity, God: The Trialogues* is an extraordinary and unique attempt to address, in contemporary context, what is doubtlessly one of the most important and persistent questions of human existence: sexuality. Three different voices, pers-pectives, approaches, continuously moving between experience and speculation, take as their starting point the eternal contemporaneity of sex and its irreducible real. The book is an ingenious, original attempt to square — or shall we say to triangle — the circle of this real."

~ **ALENKA ZUPANČIČ**, Philosopher, Author of *What is Sex?* and *Ethics of the Real*

"*Sex, Masculinity, God* is a provocative and insightful exploration of the philosophy of human sexuality. The book represents a much-needed elevation of the discussion around contemporary masculinity and sexual polarity."

~ **ZACHARY STOCKILL**, Author, Host of *Humans in Love Podcast*

"I once watched a movie called *Mindwalk*. In this 1990 classic, three friends walk around Mont. St. Michael, France, and wax the poetic on topics from science to politics to relationships. While reading *Sex, Masculinity and God: The Trialogues*, I had a similar experience. I felt like I was a voyeur watching three brilliant men discuss important topics relevant to the changes in Masculinity today. I loved how they compared, contrasted, and complimented each other. It showed for me a must-needed, powerful set of viewpoints on how men can grow and expand in these confusing times. A Must Read!"

~ **ROBERT KANDELL**, Entrepreneur, Author of *Unhidden: A Book for Men* and Creator of the *Tuff Love Podcast*

"Being able "to human" well is perhaps the deepest art and challenge we face as individuals in our socio-cultural and bio-physical lifeworlds. This book by Last, Orosz and Dick engages the reader in thoughtful conversation around this existential topic from a powerful perspective. It represents a triple-tripartite conversation, at the first level as a thoughtful and thought-provoking exchange among the three authors, presented as a true co-constructive conversation dedicated to the playful, respectful and serious joint creation of meaning. At the second level, it is a thematic exploration of the ways in which identity – our very essence of being human – is shaped through the interplay of the constructs and expressions of sex, masculinity and God. And at the third level, this book breaks the 4th wall of narrative by bringing the reader into the conversation in a way that makes the exploration of these themes both a reflective and reflexive exchange among reader, authors and perennial conceptions of self and the transcendence of self. In quite profound ways, this work takes reason on a journey through the cycles of life, death, and the *élan vital* of being that creates the dance we do between them – the dance of the ouroboros."

~ **ALEXANDER LASZLO**, Systems Scientist, President of the Bertalanffy Center for the Study of Systems Science (BCSSS)

"In this delightful philosophical romp, three men from different backgrounds dive deep into the many dimensions of Eros - love, sex, relationships, gender, power, desire. The book is presented in a trialogue form, reminiscent of Platonic dialogues or the novels of ideas of 18th Century philosophes. In a time when culture is skewed toward the superficial and slick, I found it very refreshing to enter into this intricate thought stream, which allowed for endless refractions around its central themes. Many will enjoy this excavation."

~ **DANIEL PINCHBECK**, Philosopher, Author of *Breaking Open the Head: A Psychedelic Journey into the Heart of Contemporary Shamanism, 2012: The Return of Quetzalcoatl, Notes from the Edge Times* and *How Soon is Now?*

SEX, MASCULINITY, GOD:

The Trialogues

SEX, MASCULINITY, GOD:

The Trialogues

Cadell Last, Kevin Orosz, Daniel Dick

Dedication

We dedicate this book with our hearts to all those spirits caught
in the contradictions and tensions of sexual energy,
masculine identity and metaphysical meaning.

Contents

Contents

Acknowledgments

I would like to thank all those who, just by being who they are, helped me die better.

~ Cadell

I dedicate this work to the eventual emergence of a healed and whole humanity, especially in relating. And to all the wonderful women in my life, especially my inspiring queen Nadine, all my teachers and past lovers, my mother Diane, and my many sisters. I want to thank my dearest brothers as well, who have held me through the most intense and savage time. To Ryan, Jordan, Luke, CK, and Tyson, thank you men.

~ Kevin

I dedicate this book to all my romantic past and present loves. Thereby I want to thank especially Kelly Schwegel for being a wonderful loving soul on my side, my family for being infinite love, especially my mother and my brother, and my close friends Martin, Jan, Dennis, David, Simon and Renate for being there when the tides are high and low.

~ **Daniel**

Preface I

Cadell Last
Brussels, Belgium ~ May 29, 2020

Cadell Last is a general thinker interested in synthesizing ideas from an interdisciplinary perspective in order to understand and integrate the meaning of human existence and evolution into daily practice. He is currently a post-doctoral researcher focused on reviving discussion on fundamental metaphysical questions related to sex/love, death/immortality in human history.

This book is a philosophical exploration that involves a (hopefully) playful discourse between three different identities who share in the appreciation for intimate experience, a belief in the importance of positive masculine identity, and an openness to metaphysical mysteries. In this book we tried to confront the challenges of what it means to be a sexual being today from a masculine perspective, with the sense that this confrontation must ultimately involve a spiritual dimension.

When I started this project, I had been searching for the space to discuss sexuality, masculinity and spirituality with an inquisitive heart and mind. Even though I was completing my doctorate research at a broadly integrative theoretical institute (focused on evolution, cognition and complexity), I still felt that it was not a space that could accept the type of conversations I was desperately in need of finding. The chapters in this book represent that space I needed, with the (br)others that I needed to hold it with me.

We start with a conversation about sexual difference because we felt that being with, accepting and celebrating the difference between masculine and feminine energy is necessary to sharpen our focus on what we mean when we speak of sexual attraction and desire, and the way attraction and desire shape our gender identities (in their many forms). My unconscious mind has, since my earliest memories, been fascinated with the feminine, its opposition with and complimentary to, my own energy. This difference has always been massively challenging, and also crucially informative to the development of my identity. I cannot imagine what I would be if it had not been for the intensity that emerges for my consciousness in this difference.

We end with a conversation about love and death because we felt that the capacity to be with the other beyond the self (love), and to come to terms with the otherness beyond our life (death) brought a particularly unique intensity of reflection to how we relate to sexual energy in this world. If the sexual difference charges an intensity of our opposite identity, love and death may be the best teachers for how that intensity can be temporally balanced or navigated. I know that in my experiences of being with sexual energy, I can find myself so captivated by the other that I lose myself in the other; and that love for the other somehow provides a depth of meaning that must be situated in the context of my life as a whole.

What happens in between these two dimensions (sexual difference and love/death), is a meditation on different manifestations of sexuality as experienced and conceptualized by the masculine, and as it may be interpreted within a spiritual or even religious context (e.g., archetypes, evolution, gender, pain/suffering, relationships, ethics, technology etc.). I hope our open sharing about these topics helps both men and women gain a better understanding of how they relate to their own experience of sexuality, masculine energy, and something beyond life as an individual. I can say that it has helped my mind start to approach the real of my body and its energies, as well as the real of my unconscious desires for intimacy and connection with the other.

I can say that I am getting much better at loving the challenge of sexual difference, the profound teaching that is possible by being open to love, and accepting the limitations set by my finitude. After all, how boring would the world be if we erased sexual difference? How cold would we become if we close to the uncertainties necessary for love? How monstrously terrifying would it be to have an identity that expanded out into some spurious infinity forever?

Cadell

Preface II

Kevin Orosz
Bali, Indonesia ~ November 4, 2019

Kevin Orosz is a speaker, entrepreneur, performance philosopher, and student of humanity's myths. He is driven by offering his voice and presence to improving the lives of people all over the world. Through his podcast "The (R)Evolution," online courses, evolutionary men's work, and private mentorship, Kevin teaches others how to create more impact and success, ignite polarity in relationship, and claim their kingdom.

It is remarkable the inexplicable pathways and meaningful coincidences that life weaves for us. This trialogue series of ten chapters represents such a quest. Speaking and writing this project into existence with my two brothers has been joy-filled, and I trust that its contents will enhance your sexual, relational, and spiritual life.

For me, this story began long ago when I sought to understand the deep sense of "missing out" I had experienced growing up looking around to see the utter lack of true village intimacy within the suburbs of Houston, Texas. After many heartbreaks, betrayals, and co-dependencies, I arrived at eastern philosophical traditions and evolutionary theory. This was how I came across Cadell. A fateful crossing of our paths over a number of years sparked the inception point for this book.

So what is this all about? What is quite shocking to me is that in studying modern psychology and neuroscience, ancient philosophy and yoga, and sociology and political science, the most abiding taboos surround SEX (rather than race or class). Evolutionary theory does not currently contain a good solution to unlock these taboos, and yet sexuality and its true nature are embedded as the bedrock of the human experience.

After abandoning the academic path in graduate school, I sought answers through direct experience. This book represents one such inquiry. What I hope the reader will find quite potent about this work is that while it has a sound philosophical and psychological backing, it is almost entirely improvisation and thinking in real time. Sense-making, synthesis and storytelling, from our own lives.

What we realized when we embarked on this journey together, was that much like the alchemists of old, we could not write this book without our own lives being affected. There is no way to broach such a topic "in a vacuum" as much of physical science has been done. In fact, over the months of recording these trialogues and writing them down, our own lives took radical turns themselves. The ideas and conversations in here reflect that truth. The Alchemic theme runs throughout this text, as what the alchemist observes in his instruments of transformation is then mirrored back to him through his soul, his own psyche. This is how we approached "the real" of these highly charged and controversial topics. I think you will enjoy it.

Kevin

Preface III

Daniel Dick
Vienna, Austria ~ November 3, 2019

Daniel Dick is an anthropologist, a curious researcher and coach for the positive evolution of humankind. He managed several research and healing institutions and gives talks and workshops all over the world around the topics of consciousness and spiritual experiences.

This trialogue adventure came to an end, as every story does, but my real life continues on. In these conversations, reflections and the overall process of publication, a lot has changed for me personally, and a lot has changed for me in thinking about the topic of the trialogues. I can say that this document framed a process of becoming and transformation. From the beginning to the end, I could feel a closing circle or a cycle that has now transcended to another level. In imagining how to represent this process of circular transformation a symbol of a specific serpent came to my mind, which has always been metaphorically related to cycles of transformation. This symbol is the ouroboros or uroborus, which I relate to as an image of the unfinished perfection of the editing process, both in this book and in my life.

The ouroboros is a snake or a dragon eating its tail. This ancient symbol depicts the wholeness of a transformative process, also known by the inner alchemists. I like especially the dragon figure because it has wings, which could be a metaphor of elevating consciousness or elevating the unconscious drive of sexuality to the conscious. In this context, I wish the reader to embrace a transformative process while reading this book, and hopefully in that process, to become more loving and compassionate with yourself, with your partner, and with the environment in general. As long as every cycle is embedded as time, I wish the reader to embrace sex and sexuality, and elevate the unconscious depths, spiraling with the wings of the spirit, upwards to a more conscious and humane treatment of each other. What may help as a guide is knowing that we are all imperfect humans evolving and ever becoming in the cycles of life.

Daniel

Introduction

What is sexuality? What is its relationship to spirituality? Slovenian philosopher and psychoanalyst Alenka Zupančič has explicitly raised this question recently, attempting to elevate sexuality to the level of high philosophical thinking. In our spontaneous ideology we tend to think about sexuality as a primitive base level function that decouples us from the higher virtues and aims of the human spirit:

- Sexuality is biological, spirituality is cultural;
- sexuality is animalistic, spirituality is transcendent;
- sexuality is bodily, spirituality is mental;
- Sexuality is material, spirituality is ideal,
- sexuality is low, spirituality is high, and so on, and so on.

For Zupančič, there is no possibility to think in this strict and clear dichotomy after the introduction of Freudian psychoanalysis. Freudian psychoanalysis works the "energetics of libido" (eros, life force) as an essential material affecting our psychic or spiritual development. This occurs in a way that academics and spiritualists often neglect, overlook, ignore, dismiss or simply find repellent for aesthetic or moral reasons. From this perspective the intellectual tradition that is grounded in psychoanalysis (analyzing our psyche), is first and foremost concerned with the way in which sex is an intricate and integral part of spiritual development or maturation.

However, when we look closely at modern philosophy, science, and religion, there seems to be little room for serious discussion about the nature of sexuality. Philosophical schools oriented towards social constructivism or classical ontology, for example, do not really enable the space for thinking about the way sexual deadlocks inform social constructivism (i.e., gender as a particular reaction formation to sexual energy); or the way classical ontology mirrors or masks sexual dynamics (i.e., universal being as an imaginary synthesis of sexual difference).

Scientific theorists interested in understanding the fundamental nature of reality tend to ask questions related to quantum cosmology or information technology, both of which seem quite far removed from questions about sexuality. What does sexuality have to do with the behavior of black holes? What does sexuality have to do with the development of artificial intelligence?

Religious practitioners and theological theorists, whom have often been stereotyped as moral shields against open discussion about sexuality, perpetuate the sex/spirit dichotomy described above (i.e., sex is material, spirit is ideal), which would see sexuality described explicitly as the opposite of true spirituality, as opposed to its synthesis. Even the principle divine figure of Christianity (for example), Jesus Christ is explicitly a figure who was born without sex (virgin birth), and who never had any interest in engaging sexually with the opposite or the same sex.

In this intellectual environment, how are we to raise sexuality to the level of high philosophical thinking? Inspired from the psychoanalytic perspective, emphasizing energetics of libido as the ground upon which our psyches develop, we would seek to engage the dominant schools of modern philosophy, science, and religion with three basic claims about the nature of sexuality:

- sexuality represents a fundamental epistemological problem (philosophy),
- sexuality is of central ontological relevance (science), and
- sexuality is the location of metaphysical experience (religion).

The first claim, perhaps most relevant to philosophers, is that sexuality, far from being simplistic, animalistic and irrational, is in fact the most complex, human and rational phenomena to which we can direct our analytic attention. Sexuality is extremely complex, stemming from the fact that the energetics of libido are with us from our early infancy, thus structurally informing our earliest intimate bonds and impressions of the world with others. Sexuality is extremely human, stemming from the fact that the human animal implicitly embeds sexuality as the cornerstone of its most fundamental organizing units (e.g., families, kin groups, etc.). Finally, sexuality is extremely rational, stemming from the fact that there is a precise operating logic in what makes an act sexually arousing, appropriate, meaningful, long-lasting, and so forth.

For these reasons, on the philosophical level, we would propose that we start to view sex as an essential epistemological problematic when it comes to the complexity of its role in our life history, its humanness as grounding the foundation of our social organizing units, and its rationality in the way it operates according to its own inherent logical principles. All such topics have been overlooked in philosophical circles, and even the greatest philosophers in modern history, from Kant to Heidegger, have rarely approached sexuality with the care and attention it deserves (i.e., the sexuation of our "transcendental frame" in the basic experience/orientation of the world is totally foreign to Kantian philosophy; or sexuation of the

"Dasein" in building spiritual history is totally foreign to Heideggerian philosophy, etc.).

The second claim, perhaps most relevant to scientists, is that sexuality, far from being a peripheral ontological dimension, is in fact ontologically central. In other words, when we think about the place or locus of sexuality in the scientific worldview as such, we tend to imagine it as peripheral, far removed from the "main stage," or "where the action is really happening." Indeed, the greatest scientific minds in history never appear to consider what role sexuality may play in the fundamental picture or nature of things. In the Newtonian world picture, structured as it is by concepts like space, time, gravitational force, and matter in motion; sexuality is removed from the scene all together. The scientific world view here gets its stereotypical image as the embodiment of a brilliant mathematical genius capable of predicting the movement of all matter in space and time, but whom is mysteriously disconnected from the libidinal energies that flow through his body, just as they flow through the mass of rabble around him (and never her). In the Darwinian world picture, structured by concepts like selection, evolution, change, and process, sexuality appears as central, but only as a mechanism. Thus, sexuality is studied mechanistically as a central selective differentiator, blindly "deciding" the genes that will propagate, and the genes that will die out.

However, in this work, we would claim sexuality is ontologically central, not only driving the brilliant embodiment of the mathematical genius exploring the depths of fundamental reality (e.g., M-theory, etc.), but also as a selective differentiator of what experiences will continue to propagate, and what experiences will die out. Sexuality here is conceived of as something that "lights" the soul on fire, something like a central "gravitational attractor," to use a few useful physics metaphors. In this sense, when we think about grand unified theories of everything (somehow to be coincidentally resolved in the micro-macro meeting point that is the center of a black hole), and we struggle to situate humanity inside these monstrous abstractions, we should not forget that the missing piece may have something to do with the energetics of libido and the unconscious which governs its sexual motion.

The third claim, perhaps most relevant to the religious, is that sexuality, far from being a primitive dimension or experience, is perhaps the highest or deepest metaphysical experience that we can have as human beings, and even the locus of true connection to divinity. When we look at the major religions in history, Christianity, Islam, Judaism, Hinduism, Buddhism, and so forth, what we tend to find is either a fully sublimated, or an explicitly non-sexual expression of divinity. In other words, when we look to what is the most fundamental and the most true as spiritual expressions, there is a divide between the sexual and the metaphysical. Consequently, sexuality is something to be extinguished, moralized, and reduced, as opposed to something to be celebrated, intellectualized, and understood as a part of our "whole being." Moreover, we start to ignore the experiential power of sexuality in forming our identities and giving us contact with our most memorable moments as embodied beings (both light and dark).

Sexual experiences are metaphysical because they remove us from, or make irrelevant the physical background, upon which they play out the essential dramas of our being. Consequently, it is not surprising that these experiences can only be adequately described using metaphysical language: of being in heaven or hell; falling for an angel or a devil; of finding or straying from God, and so forth. The connection is in some sense right in front of us considering that language of the "One," "until death do us part," expressing notions of "eternity" and "forever," are so structurally ubiquitous as abstract metaphysical scaffolding for our experiences in the sexual plane of being, as to be non-reflective common knowledge. What is interesting to think from the religious point of view, is why our experiential being persists so strongly in this "relation to the One," of wedding "sexuality and death," of "demanding the nihilation of time and finitude" when it comes to our embodied sexual acts? These are dimensions of our most intimate reality that could well require a theological interpretation, when most theology simply chooses to look the other way.

Thus, for these three reasons:

- the philosophical dimension of epistemological problematics,
- the scientific dimension of ontological centrality, and the
- religious dimension of metaphysical experience,

We aim to raise sexuality to a higher level of discourse, and approach Zupančič's precise question "What Is Sex?." In this journey we first introduce the "The Reality of Sexual Difference." In this chapter we focus on attempting to understand, not the unity of the sexes, but their necessary difference, and the role it plays in informing tension and polarity. We seek to investigate how tension and polarity, although experientially difficult and demanding, can also become a source of joy and growth, an opportunity to see the world from a totally other point of view. Here we presuppose that this difference can best be expressed as the difference that we call "masculine" and "feminine," but we do not presuppose that these essences are precisely mapped onto biological or genetic programs, but rather that they are differences of energetic form or expression.

We then attempt to discuss the "Historical Emergence of Traditional Archetypes." This title was carefully chosen and foreshadows our discussion in the third chapter. "Historical Emergence" brings up notions of temporality, evolution, and the new; whereas "Traditional Archetypes" brings up notions of eternity, staticness, and the old. The coincidence between these two opposing levels of discourse invites thought to reflect on the way in which what appears eternal, pre-given, and unchanging, like the archetypal images of the masculine and feminine, are in fact historically conditioned, subject to evolutionary pressure, structured by a certain logic of materiality, and so forth. Thus, we investigate why the masculine appears as the masculine today, and why the feminine appears as the feminine today. And perhaps more importantly, we seek to investigate how these forms could change, introduce novelty, improve their dynamical interaction; as history becomes conditioned differently, as evolutionary pressures change, and as the logic of materiality becomes other than our past. How will the archetypes transform?

From this topic we make a neat logical transition into the "Evolutionary Worldview and Religious Worldview." In this chapter we hope to explore how abstract intellectual manifestations, like evolutionary theory and religious dogma, can implicitly or explicitly relate to our sexual energy and the way in which it is expressed in embodied, historical reality. Of course, these two worldviews are often seen as antagonistic opposites. The evolutionary worldview is often framed as secular and humanist, scientific and empirical; whereas the religious worldview is often framed as spiritual and supernatural, theological and transcendental. However, from this book's point of view, what is interesting about these worldviews is the way in which they can be inscribed into ethical and moral dimensions of sexual life. The evolutionary worldview gives one a sense of connection and continuity with the animal kingdom, and thus a lens through which to view the human animal (and its sexual behaviors) as a part of this connected continuum. On the other hand, the religious worldview gives one a sense of a transcendental discontinuity or rupture with the animal kingdom, and thus a view that often inscribes sexuality (or its overcoming) in a mystical and idealistic beyond.

In chapter 4 we shift focus to the "History of Gender Theory." This topic mixes well with our discussion inscribing traditional archetypes into a historical, evolutionary perspective, but also the following chapter on masculine identity. For most of history, and in most cultures, gender has been represented as a binary. Here we assume that this binary representation is useful, but also recognize that there are many examples where gender has been represented in other, more complex configurations, for example in triads, quadrants, or even more complex intimate geometries, which could also be useful and authentic. Thus, from this frame of mind we discuss the benefits of binary representations, but also the possibility of thinking more complex geometries, and what those more complex geometries would look like. This discussion is specifically reflective and attentive to feelings of rigidity in identity, as is evident in the Feminist and LGBT+ movements, which seek to redefine what it means to be a modern woman, and what it means to be non-heteronormative sexual form, for example. What is of particular relevance to us in this discussion is the way in which the masculine can be expressed, and can even long for, a more androgynous form, which could be its own form of emancipation.

The transition into chapter 5, "Contemporary Masculinity and Masculine Movements," picks up where we left off in chapter 4. In this chapter we discuss the nature and struggles of modern masculinity, as expressed in the philosophy of (what is being called online) as "The Red Pill" movement. From this perspective modern masculinity appears to be reactive against what it perceives as a culture dominated by feminine energy and ideals, and which lacks a positive and motivating image for what it means to become the ideal masculine energy form. Throughout the discourse we approach the opportunities and dangers that are inherent to masculine movements, as they can become catalysts for new positive relationships and motivational structures, but also catalysts for ultimately self-destructive and empty or anti-social behavior. The structure of this discourse drifts into conversations about the social organizing function of historical religions as masculine movements, and the potential ways in which future masculine movements would differ or resemble religious organizations.

We then take the trialogue into more general emotional territory with the topic "Nature of Pain and Suffering in Sexuality." Sexuality is of course an experience that can be extremely positive and filled with joy. However, sexuality can equally be an extremely negative experience and filled with pain and suffering. Indeed, many of the world's religious traditions perceive the fundamental nature of reality to be pain and suffering. In this context, we attempt to open up a conversation about the nature and meaning of pain and suffering when sexuality can become overwhelmingly negative. Specifically we situate our thought at the locus of a paradox between tendencies to structure sexual identity as a reaction or a defense against pain and suffering, and a tendency to challenge and transform sexual identity by actively confronting and overcoming pain and suffering. Here we attempt to be nuanced and open in how we think about this paradox, and ultimately reflect on how the character traits of bravery and courage are necessary to explore the real of sexuality.

From this discourse we approach "Absolutes and Relations" which can be blended or integrated with previous discussions about evolution and religion since we are approaching metaphysical questions about sexuality. The notion of an Absolute is the notion of something necessary and eternal. The notion of a Relation is the notion of something contingent and temporal. Of course, the metaphysics of the religious worldview is based on something Absolute, whereas the metaphysics of the evolutionary worldview is based on something Relational. From this intersection we discuss the strange way in which sexual relations in a mostly secular and scientific culture manifest as "Absolute." Thus, in this conversation we seek to better understand the way in which sexuality is the location of a divine expression in modern human beings, even if it is mostly unconscious and repressed, and consequently not brought to the surface in self-conscious abstraction, and made explicit in formal worldview structures.

In the next section we approach "Ethics and Morality in the Sexual Space," which brings together two dimensions which we define as in a type of paradoxical relation. The dimension of ethics is defined as fidelity to the truth of one's desire, whereas morality is defined as a type of fidelity to the symmetry of action with the other(s). From this framing individual ethics and social morality collide in the problem of how to stay true to one's desire and act in relation to the field of others in a moral form. In this problematic we immediately use the notion of truth as an orientation point for discussion of its relationship between the expression of libidinal energy in courtship and other sexual contexts. Here we dance around notions of un-enlightened sexuality being based in different nuanced forms of deception, and the possibility of enlightened sexuality being based on transparency and honesty. However, the major stumbling block to such a transition involves the irreducible fact that human beings are emotionally damaged and motivated by unconscious forces which are usually just as alien to them personally as they are to everyone else. Is it possible for us to process these blocks in order to reveal true sexuality from a place of emotional healing?

Towards the end of the book we take a turn into some strange but extremely thought-provoking territory. Chapter 9 explores "The Future of Sex" from the perspective of transhumanism and general futurist theory. From this perspective we are interested to understand how future technology, like artificial intelligence, robotics, or virtual reality, may augment or qualitatively change the way in which we engage with sexual energy. Such notions of the sexual field becoming transformed by technology opens up an expansive horizon for thought to speculate on possibilities and opportunities that are currently impossible due to technical limitations. Thus, this chapter is a type of speculative meditation on radical expansion of limits and transformation of obstacles. Here we start to meditate on just how polymorphous and multifaceted sexual energy can become, and how unaware we are about how our desires and motives become conditioned by the historical constraints of a given appearance of being.

Finally, we come to the end, and appropriately meditate on the topic of "Love and Death." In this chapter we attempt to think the way in which notions of love and death bring our thought into a more sobering and heavy reality that feels in some sense more real than other realities. When it comes to love and death there appears to be no more doubt, and only a type of certainty, about where we are and what really matters. We also reflect on how the place of love and death is oftentimes, and suspiciously, ignored in our culture, which tends to be in a hyper critical and skeptical mode about the nature of reality. In this context we discuss how we relate to our sexual energy in the context of love and death, and how such reflections force us to consider the ultimate meaning of our identities and the way in which we relate to other human beings and the universe as a (w)hole.

In writing this work we hope to have explored many of the major questions that impinge on the nature and meaning of sexuality. However, we do not presuppose that we have covered all major questions, and we certainly do not presuppose that we have provided all of the definitive answers to the nature and meaning of sexuality. I think we can say that for many dimensions of sexuality, we have developed a new personal clarity, and for other dimensions of sexuality, we sit on the edge of new horizons with just as many, if not more, questions then we had when we started this adventure together. What we would like to emphasize more than anything else, is that the topic of sexuality is a topic of high philosophical importance, and a topic that provokes intellectual curiosity and spiritual innovation.

Thus, perhaps it is no mistake that, when Freud first started producing scientific papers on the neurotic vicissitudes (obsessional, hysterical) of sexual identity in the 1890s, he was met with such hostile and vicious reactions from academic and spiritual communities alike. Today it seems that scientific and spiritual reactions to Freud provoke the same strange resistance, even though his work has perhaps had a more transformative impact on our culture than any other thinker in the 20th century, and his concepts resonate through the popular landscape as common place jargon. One gets the sneaking suspicion that the unconscious has to move Freud's knowledge, and that no matter how hard self-consciousness resists, it is only a matter of time before the unconscious itself has the final say on the truth of his discoveries.

Consequently, when one starts talking openly, directly and self-consciously about the nature of sexuality, it is as if one has stumbled upon a topic that is always there but always hidden, distorted, and masked with certain taboos and prohibitions. Talk about anything you like... but let's leave sexuality safely "over there" in the darkness, the darkness that grounds all this light. Thus, one gets the sense that one has stumbled upon the dragon of all dragons, the monster of all monsters, the mystery of all mysteries. One gets the sense that one is tarrying with a negativity that, if brought out into positive existence too soon, could unsettle all identities and disintegrate them back into the abyss from which they emerged.

Thus, we want to emphasize that we are aware and reflective about the importance and immensity of the topic we are covering here. We are aware and reflective that discussing sexuality as openly, directly, and self-consciously as we do in this book, can make certain scientific and spiritual identities alike feel uncomfortable, and even violated in their essence. Nonetheless we hope that we have handled these topics with the aim of both true knowledge about the nature of reality, and extreme care for the emotional reality of our fellow human beings.

Cadell Last
October 14 2019

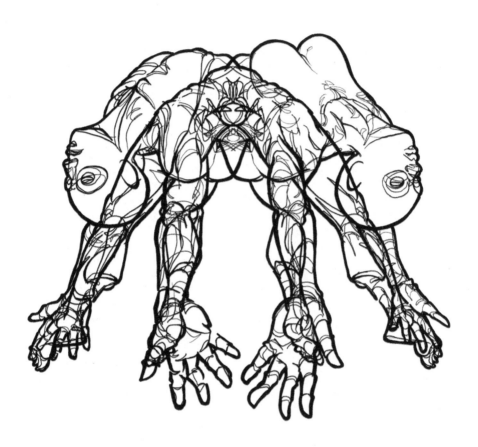

CHAPTER 1

The Reality of Sexual Difference

Cadell: This trialogue series and our discussion is largely going to be about sexuality, masculine gender identity, the spirit of civilization, and the interconnection between those themes. For this discussion, we are going to be approaching sexual ontology, which basically means the "being" or the "reality" of sex. And we are going to try to approach this discussion in a complementary conversation to the conversation regarding gender construction. We want to understand the relationship between how we construct our gender identities given our sexual being or reality.

In trying to think about sexual reality in the 21st century, we have to start with the topic of sexual difference, masculine and feminine polarity, which has structured this reality, and which seems so experientially problematic. To bring context, we can use as a reference point the most famous ancient view on sexual difference, which can be found in the work of Plato, and expressed most clearly in *The Symposium*. In *The Symposium* Plato explicitly overcomes masculine and feminine difference in sexual ontology by presupposing the primordial unity of the sexes in a "third sex," the mythological androgynous creature:[2]

> "Once upon a time our anatomy was quite different from what it is now. In the first place there were not merely two sexes as there are now, male and female, but three, and the third was a combination of the other two. [...] The form of every person was completely round[.]"

The old mythological story tells us that this singular entity was actually whole and fulfilled at some real point. It is only because the perfect entity was divided into two, man and woman, that there emerged incompleteness and dissatisfaction. Consequently, throughout history, the human species as constituted by sexual difference, man and woman, was constantly looking and failing to find their "other half." Now, whatever we may think about the literal truth of this mythological story, there is certainly a metaphorical truth in its persistent resonance with our spirit. The story speaks to the problem of sexual difference, and the difficulty in formulating a practical solution, which would supposedly be found in an intuitive conception of a third entity embodying singular roundness.

In psychoanalysis, which deals with the problematic experience of human sexual existence, we can find a useful formula for thinking about the real of this divided sexuality. Consider the following quote from Alenka Zupančič which proposes an axiom for sexual division:[3]

> "To express [sexual difference] in a single formula: *What splits into two* [man, woman] *is the very nonexistence of the one* (that is, of the one which, if it existed, would be the Other)."

This axiom suggests that what we are looking for in the primordial androgynous creature never actually existed in the world. Nonetheless, it is a form that insists as a wish fulfillment in the structure of the unconscious. Such a psychoanalytic axiom may help us to think about the way the desire for "unity" manifests, consciously or unconsciously, in our sexual lived experience. This axiom may also help us to think about our contemporary social zeitgeist emphasizing gender construction. On the one hand the non-existence of the "one" structures the sexual difference as a metaphysical principle; on the other hand this difference manifests in an indefinable number of genders, where we should frame construction in terms of an open-ended series of possible expressions of that difference.

My critique would be that our culture struggles to think both the construction and the real of this dimension simultaneously. To be specific, the non-existence of the one here is far more problematic in informing construction of identity than we are ready to accept. Construction of identity is not just a happy and liberating activity. Construction of identity is rather something that emerges as a reaction to a disruption caused by an extreme experience of oneness or singularity in the other, however fleeting and temporal it appears to us in and for our historical bodies. In the past, this could be expressed in the desire for the symbolic form of monogamy or marriage between masculine and feminine polarity. This symbolic form carries with it the insistent presence of a "oneness" in relation to what we may call the "sexual real" as "not-one." The genders man and woman are but two (constructed) abstract formulas of an equation that seek to resolve this negativity.

Now if the past was structured by the construction of two abstract formulas (genders), the present is more and more calling for multiple new formulas. My point in this transition from two to multiple formulas is that no matter how many formulas there are, they are all manifestations of a reaction to the one. Take the most concrete examples in the social movement of the LGBT+ community. This community emerges and immediately its first demand is for "marriage equality" to embody no matter the gender configuration, this persistent sign of "oneness." of singularity in the other. Whether you are lesbian, gay, bi-sexual, trans-sexual, or any other category within the "+" signifier, the desire to pair bond, the desire to form a unity with the other, is, it seems to me, something of a universality.

Now, of course, just as man and woman as pair bond in the form of a two becoming one has many cracks, gaps, and failings (heartbreak), so do all the other possible gender configurations. There is no escaping the possibilities and the risk of heartbreak. This can be in part because, no matter how strong the desire for the one, there is also as simultaneously a strong desire for sexuality as multiplicity, in terms of identity, partners, and experimentation with different modalities of being. As Zupančič states in the quote above, "what splits into two *is the very nonexistence of the one*," so this "one" is fundamentally problematic in the sense that it is absent (an "absential" to use the evolutionary anthropologist Terrence Deacon's term).[4] I am merely suggesting that the form of appearance of one in the other continues to move even when one has become "disillusioned" by its absence, or even worse, its constitutive impossibility. Thus, I am personally inclined to believe that, in terms of the emergence of a multiplicity of alternative gender constructions, this will not fundamentally change the absence of the one, but rather shift it around in a different way.

How do you both relate to this idea of sexuality as a (problematic) unity? How do you both relate to this mythological idea of a fall from a oneness into division and polarity? How would you situate this notion in today's social environment which is becoming much more open-ended?

Kevin: These are excellent questions. I love Plato's *Symposium*. To call to my direct experience in the "New Age" spiritual culture, as it exists in California, there is this idea or meme that is "hot" right now: **"Twin Flames."** I have heard people refer to Twin Flames as something directly derived from Platonic metaphysics. The idea of a Twin Flame is the "other half" of your soul. The idea is that we come from single souls, and the gods, whether to play a trick or whether to reveal some great mystery, divided these souls into two: male and female bodies. I think this is fascinating because in deep sexual experiences, the unity consciousness that emerges is a type of **"super-consciousness"** or **"unity consciousness."** I think in Tantric and Taoist sexual practices from China and India, these threads also emerge, of sexuality between two creating a super-consciousness. That is anyway my reflections on a high philosophical level.

However, on a more grounded level, you still do see people in everyday life, and I used to be one of these people, searching for "the one." There is "one" woman out there, in my case, that can complete me. And as a good citizen of my civilization I would then marry this woman to create this entity: **the marriage.** If I were to marry this other half, I would be a completed and satisfied being. And if everyone did this, and we were all happy, and there was no infidelity or other urges, then we would have something resembling a perfect society because we would have unified these souls. How this notional structure confronts the direct experience of the sexual real, however, is that I have very rarely seen people in this unified consciousness phase across time. What I usually see is that people enter a "honeymoon" phase for six to twelve months, and then after this initial romantic phase they discover that they do not even know the other person. They discover that they were riding a cascade of hormonal and neurotransmitter excitations, and consequently living in the illusion of certain erroneous mental concepts.

So, in conclusion, I think the idea of this **primordial unity** is a beautiful idea, I love Plato's philosophy and the roots of where that idea is coming from, but in the modern world, there is a *huge gap* between these ideas and reality. This huge gap could indeed be the nonexistence of the one that Zupančič points towards in her work.

Daniel: As we are speaking about sex difference, it might be useful also to look into gender equality. As you both know, I live in Austria. What we are experiencing here in Austria right now is a huge referendum for equal rights between women and men. Half a million people wrote to the politicians that there should be equal pay, that there should be equal parental leave. I can relate to the philosophy that the two of you were discussing about the unity between man and woman, but if we bring it to the real practical level, what does *equal* mean? If we are different in our sex, how do we name it? Why do we have two binary oppositions? Now the current discussions move towards more differentiated, self-determined ways of identifying ourselves with our sexuality. The question that strikes me again: *what does it mean to be equal?* How can we think of sexuality as **equal and individual**? And *is it really worth being that equal?* Because if you define yourself being equally and individually determined, and everyone is "oneness" and equal, or has equal possibilities, then I am still wondering about this question on a practical political level. One very practical question is about the public toilets: Do we need the same toilets for everyone?

This situation of equality also seems to lead to strange multiplicity, where we are heading to more open relationships, more polyamorous relationships in contrast to the traditional binary relationship. I also experienced these types of relationships and they did not turn out to be too long-lasting, but at the same time they still made a lot of changes in myself and the persons involved. However, and unfortunately, these changes often occurred very painfully.

Cadell: I think both of your reflections are insightful and useful jumping off points for our discussion. The thing that is coming up for me right now, in response to Kevin's reflections, is the nature of this "naïve" intuition of the "oneness." We have this naive intuition as a foundational modality of the way we idealize. In other words, there seems to be this more-or-less spontaneous concept of the "one" in our minds. This idealization suggests to us that if it were to be actualized, then everything would be great and wonderful, *but then it encounters the sexual real.* In confronting the sexual real there is just so much more complexity and problems with psychic and social development, that you start to question this entire intuitive ideal structure. What seems to happen is a counter-reaction towards deconstruction of the one.

This logic then brings me to Daniel's reflection, with your identification of this pragmatic political problem of a symmetrical union in the law, between man and woman. This equalizing oneness which erases the difference between the sexes. Of course, in the conservative worldview there is a type of metaphysical hierarchy, there is this idea that man and woman are together, but they are not symmetrical, they are not thought of as the same, *as equal.* This conservative idea of man and woman as different is seen as very important, and even sacred. Also, Daniel, you noted that in the gaps or the cracks of this equality narrative of sexual difference, there is a "multiplicity culture." but this multiplicity culture is generating a lot of pain and a lot of hardship, and a lot of short-term relationships. *And at the same time,* there are real meaningful changes in identity occurring at the site of these pains.

In short, these opening reflections from the both of you are perfect because what I want to throw back out to both of you is this idea of an **oppositional determination** between a type of oneness and multiplicity. How do we balance in a dialectical form this intuitive notion of oneness and this counter or critical reaction to multiplicity? On the one hand, the multiplicity seems to be about the individual expression of gender identity, it seems to be about freedom. And on the other hand, the oneness seems to be about the real of our sexual intensity or intimacy; it seems to be about love. This intensity or intimacy tends to concentrate in oneness while at the same time encountering all sorts of practical problems without reconciliation as a temporal sequence, or as freedom!

How do you both feel about this framing?

Kevin: There is this **mythical idea** of civilization in a future "golden age" where there is high prosperity, mental intellect, emotional intellect, and abundance. In that model, without scarcity of these properties, then a single union and experience between the sexes makes a lot of sense, because it stabilizes the culture, it stabilizes the family structure and the civilization itself. One man and one woman going into this construct feeds into the hierarchy that builds the worldly paradise.

Then on the other side there is this *very raw* **Darwinian fight for survival**. On the level of the male gamete and male biology, there is this *very real* desire for variety and difference. This is a felt experience in the male body, even in a committed relationship. As a man you will be attracted to a beautiful woman, that is a physiological response. As you point towards, Cadell, the method to reconcile those opposites is not easy. And as you said, Daniel, there is serious psychical pain and wounds that have arisen around this opposition.

In our current age we have so much choice and opportunity. So, in short, how I would frame this opposition determination is a predicament between an **evolutionary Darwinian component** of sexual multiplicity that is the heritage of our ancestry, and a **Platonic philosophical component** of a desire for oneness that builds civilization. What happens in between this oppositional determination is a type of *unreflective wasteland* that we are still attempting to understand.

Daniel: I thought of this point of singularity and multiplicity when we think of **"attraction."** Every time that we are thinking about something related to our sexual self or sexual activation, in other words, when we are thinking about our sexual identity, it is often related to whom we feel sexually attracted. That thought led me to the question: *What is really being attractive or why are we attracted?* Okay, we can all agree that we are not in a "monk mode" of sitting there and not moving. But actually this attraction keeps you moving! If we keep moving and having this sexual energy, *what is this attraction actually? What are we going for?*

On the level of Darwinian nature, we are trying to spread our genes. But we are not actually thinking on the psychical level of spreading our genes. The Darwinian explanation does not cover the whole experience. On the psychical level we feel like "okay, I have to move somewhere" or "okay, there is a woman or man" and **I want to get close. I want to get so close that it cannot be closer. So, the space in between gets so close that there might be no space anymore.** I thought that in between this attractiveness or tension, it is as if **there is a storm coming.** It is like there are **two poles that contradict each other,** but at the same time, **they are coming together.** So, it is really the difference that makes up this energy as it does. Also, in electricity there is plus and minus, and the further away they are and at the same time attracted to each other, the more the energy flows. This energy keeps us moving, towards someone, *because of the difference and its attraction.*

Cadell: I would love to pick up on what you are saying, Daniel, because I think you are articulating something so precise, and you are framing it so well. I would like to jump in with this idea that I have been playing with privately in the last few weeks. I think that what people usually think of as a pure unity should be read or interpreted from the perspective of a *pure difference* or *pure contradiction*. It is precisely when you are so attracted to something that you want to merge with it as one, this process of **"one-in-ization"** (if you will allow me the term), is what would kill the attraction. **What you are attracted to is the difference.** Then the question becomes, how do we avoid the wasteland, which Kevin mentioned, of flowing with this pure difference? When we flow with this pure difference, this pure oppositional determination, we are constantly forced to confront our own pain, our own internal struggle, and that just requires a very high maturity and self-awareness, and a very self-reflective individual. That, to me, is how I would differentiate sex in relation to the spectrum of gender as a form of social identification. In other words, no matter where you identify on the spectrum, there is this pure difference of attraction that moves us, precisely, between the two. And understanding the mechanics of this, is to me, **the real.**

Kevin: There is something so fascinating with what you brought to light, Daniel, in your articulation of the sexual difference. The *tension between opposites* creates the arc or curve of energy that is *driving most of human evolution*. The most radical example, for me, would be Helen of Troy. There is something deeply archetypal about this story which reflects a real. In this story there is a desire for union, specifically sexual union, which has generated so much innovation and technological progress, but at the same time, wars and crusades. There is an element of human culture that is most manifested in this sexual attraction.

Then, Cadell, when you are talking about this difference as what motivates us, and that the unity destroys this motivation, for me, this idea brings to mind a spiral or a toroidal dynamic. There has to be, like an electrical coil, a distance and a structure in relation that maintains optimal tension in attraction. Otherwise you have loveless marriage and infidelity. Or you could have harems of boyfriends or girlfriends with high emotional turbulence. There is a lot of trauma there. These are the extremes and, in between, no matter gender identification, your opposite will pull you into evolution and make you confront your Self and the pain that you have. The unity is like a bomb or an elixir that is healing, and the loss of the attraction can call in the pain. *This is so juicy.*

Cadell: I think we are starting to approach a sexual ontology or reality in our discourse. I would like to focus again on the one and the multiplicity and just throw out the question: how can we come up with concepts or a language to discuss this motion in a healthy way? I feel like the dialogue of our culture is discussing constructive gender formulas, but ignoring this sexual real, which dictates the construction. Do either of you have a language to talk about this motion of sexual difference?

Kevin: The development of a language to talk about the motion of sexual difference has been a big part of my work in transformational spaces with men and women. We start with an elimination of layers of belief about the human body. There is a *conceptual shame and guilt placed on the human body*, a feeling that it is **unclean** or **unruly**. There have been many concepts placed on the human body that limit us from even approaching this topic of the sexual real. We must engage in an eliminative de-shaming and de-guilting of the human body itself between men and women, between the sexes. *We have to come back to the body as a transcendent or sacred object.* There is a child-like innocence that has been lost, which is reflected in many of the origin myths of the world (like in Plato's *Symposium*).

Daniel: I can relate to all of this. In the last 500 years, stemming from the Cartesian foundation, there has been so much emphasis on the brain and the mind. We think the final frontier is the mind, and that this is our last stance to a certain truth. But we have totally ignored the wisdom that is in our body, the **immanence of our bodily being**. Our thinking has always been reaching beyond our limitations of being in a body. Now our culture is forced to look closer at the body. When we think of our Self in the world as of high importance, our being-in-the-world, the body becomes very important.

I can relate to what you are saying, Kevin, about the conceptual shame and guilt on the body from this point of view. On the sexual level, there is always an intimacy, so the question is also *how do we put something intimate into something transparent? Should we do this? Does it lose attraction if we do this?* We have a lot of pornography on the internet, and that may be good, it may be bad, but it also makes a big difference to feel ourselves in our personal relationships. People start to think that sex should be like pornography, *and it is not like that.* Maybe for some it is, *but for those involving a kind of sacredness, it is not.* There is a big question to make about sexuality and its transparency and about the more intimate and emotional side, as we are talking about that right now.

Cadell: I think that, on the one hand, sexual energy is this inspirational and creative energy. But at the same time, it is this very disorienting and negative energy, in the sense that we can feel violated, abused and misused, and we can feel we are losing our freedom. And so, when we are navigating this very complex space between the one and the multiplicity, *I think we have to be almost religious about sexuality.* It makes total sense to me why religions focus so much on regulating sexuality and sexual sublimation because it can be so disorienting, and it can be so overwhelming. Thus, I do think reducing sexuality to a pornographic culture is a big mistake. I also think that the liberal culture that is exploring open relationships and polyamory, for that culture to think that sexuality is casual, is also a mistake. Pornographic culture and too-liberal poly-culture tend not to take this issue of the sexual real with the seriousness that it deserves.

I think a conversation about switching from the mind to the body, as you both mentioned, also makes me feel that we have to move to the *sacredness of the body*. That will require a different language. For this language, I like the concept that Kevin brought up, of innocence, and I think the concept that Daniel brought up, of transparency, is very useful. That is where a language capable of navigating this motion and attraction comes to mind. When I am thinking about my sexual energy and body, trying to understand my body, which is for me a very intimate and difficult thing, I want to be viewed by the other, or right now, I want to be viewed in an innocent way, in order to be transparent. This is a very special energy, and that is where my mind goes to talk about it, because I feel that if we view ourselves as innocent it could be easier to be transparent and vulnerable.

Kevin: This transmission, Cadell, is bringing up something very dear to my heart. Also, Daniel thank you for bringing up a critique of pornography. This is a very real evolutionary filter we are facing, especially in young men. There is a way in which the pornographic experience has preloaded their consciousness to expect certain things from sex. On the other hand, the felt vulnerability of this experience is very tender, which dissociates us from the body. And as you emphasize Cadell, and as Terence McKenna says, we cannot occupy a reality until you describe and articulate it. This is where I believe conservative cultures and religion, unfortunately, through taboo, *have seriously prevented this conversation about the sexual real*. This is the power of intimacy, radical communication, authenticity, as practiced in the human potential movement, and the liberal movements.

In my experience these conversations about innocence and intimacy of the body between romantic partners is very difficult. I was raised Catholic in Texas, so there was a sense that we could not talk about this. Because we were not able to talk about it, I had an inability to conceptualize it in the intimate space. The result was a lot of shame. Shame is a very tricky sensation, because I start to feel bad about this joy and blissful experience of dating and intercourse. So, you are nailing it, Cadell, with emphasizing that *we have to articulate a new reality between men and women*, or whatever sexual difference exists.

Daniel: I think that what Cadell said about difficulties in transparency and vulnerability is something very special, because when it comes to actually having sex, you have this kind of attraction. This attraction involves a coming closer, kissing, sex, and maybe both partners have orgasms, but you experience, somehow, a union. Then the next day the union fades away, and we go our separate ways. *And there has never been one sex as the other.* There is always a difference between these feelings of oneness. In every phase of one relationship you go through so many changes and learning processes, and the more you are emotionally and sexually intimate with one partner, the more you can feel you can trust someone to open up.

That same level of intimacy is something that is quite difficult if there is a multiplicity of short-term relations because you do not get into the mood to open up that much. You even unconsciously might protect your feelings. On the other hand, it is quite amazing that if you are still coupled and attracted long-term, that means that over the years, people are exchanging feelings of unity simultaneously. There is something that you gain or integrate of one another in your mind and your heart and everything related to the shared time. When you feel attracted you integrate the other somehow by feeling the unity. It is most intensely felt while having at the same time an orgasm. But then, eventually, you don't feel attracted to the same person in the unity, and then someone else comes, another other you feel attracted. It is rare that a couple stays together nowadays.

Cadell: So, are you saying, Daniel, that there is a temporal limit on the ability to feel attracted in a sustainable way with the other? I would throw out something that resonated in me from a talk by Esther Perel, where she said that, in the past we were monogamous for a lifetime, and now we are monogamous one at a time. So, she says that people today will say "I am monogamous in all of my relationships." I feel that this **serial monogamy** is the way that people are navigating what Kevin refers to as the "wasteland" between one and multiplicity. Is it because *we are not intelligent enough in our bodies to merge with more than one.* In our minds, on the other hand, *we are well capable of merging with more than one*, and most people actually do.

Maybe we feel like we cannot trust or open or share with more than one? Or maybe we feel disoriented when it comes to grounding this capacity in the body? So, from what you are saying, are you trying to get at this problematic of the temporal dimension? I would say that in sexuality we feel this type of eternity, or this type of absolute, and then it is about how do you hold that in time? That is how I try to make sense of it. How do you relate to that?

Daniel: Maybe I could put it this way: if you have sex, and good sex with your mind and heart, every level of the self-integrated, then time disappears, and it becomes a sacred moment that you might never forget. In these *experiences one dissolves with the other*, and *time and space is not present*. These are very intense experiences, and because of their intensity, they will stay in your memory. If you are back in "daily reality." and you have this memory of the sexual intensity, it could be *now* as it was then, if you just remember it. There is no time in this phenomenological perspective. In daily life, there is a time sequence of such experiences of the intensity of the intimacy that makes up your Self as collected memories. The most intimate relationships that have the most intensity are actually building blocks of yourself, because you identify yourself with your memory of your experience.

The big question for me, or the big challenges in different relationships, is how these big blocks of yourself are integrated. Because if you integrate the blocks of your partner you become the same, *but at the same time you do not*. You became a part of your partner and the partner a part of you. When time passes by, your partner might do something that does not attract you anymore. Or your partner evolves in another way, and you feel more difference again. So following the movement of attraction it might be challenging to evolve together in one relationship, and if you are in multiple relationships, the intensity of your building blocks might be this or that high, the building blocks will be diversified, so it might feel a bit schizophrenic. This might cause friction because you feel like

many different things that are not coherent. I experienced this for myself also, that is when I was even living in two different places. I experienced that I had to put myself back together again, because I felt being distributed and not by myself.

Cadell: What I am getting from your reflection is that in terms of your valuation of sexual energy, it is about integration, a dynamical integration. So, if you spread your sexuality out in a multiplicity, without transparency, you are going to fragment and disintegrate yourself. In this mode we are not in the mode of a naive one where we want to eliminate difference and merge into one. Instead we want to play with this difference and become more integrated selves, more dynamical selves?

Kevin: This is very fascinating, Daniel, what you are touching on. I want to focus on the temporal aspect. I thought it was so beautiful how you described the disappearance of time. In the scientific literature we might refer to this as time dilation, the time perception leaves us or qualitatively transforms. There is a way in which the heart, the mind and the body are all dissolved. There is a way in which you can have physical intimacy, and be connected, heart and mind, and that speaks to this need and desire in human consciousness for the transcendent. In French, the word orgasm means **"little death."** *Orgasm speaks to our will to be transcendent of time.* That is a whole different topic. But it links to what you were emphasizing, Daniel, about the chaos. If we are going there, into that intimate space of time transcendence, full intimacy and giving ourselves in union and doing it with different partners, intensities, emotional availabilities, there is a sense that, I wonder how many relations you can hold without fragmenting, and that chaos is invited back in? As you mentioned you had to put yourself back together.

When I dabbled in polyamory, and I wanted to go deep, I discovered this deep friction in my consciousness. *I fractured this precious energy.* You mentioned this Cadell, it is a profound source of energy. There is a way, when we put this into multiple people, we are leaking this energy. That is why I do not choose this style anymore. I really wonder if anyone has reconciled that schizophrenic state in the polyamory lifestyle. I do not have a deep sense of how that works.

Cadell: What I want to identify here, because what both of you said resonates so strongly with my experience, is that it makes me think of religion in a different way. When I went to a Buddhist temple, an ayahuasca ceremony, spent time with a Christian family, and visited an Islamic community, they all recognized sexual difference and placing boundaries on sexuality. So, it seems to me that, wherever religions pop up, they treat this sexual energy as sacred and they want to avoid this multiplicity of differentiation. *I think religious people see constraining this sexual energy as essential for the integration of the identity.* I know you said, Kevin, that you grew up a Catholic in Texas with negative religious restrictions and taboos placed on sexuality, but does that perspective on religion resonate in any way with you about the meaning of religion?

Kevin: Yes, totally. I think all religions and societies have placed boundaries and imperatives on sexual difference, for very good reasons. Some may be related to line of descent, but also because the real power and potency is found in the sexual experience. It may be sublimated into great art, politics, oration, athleticism, business. In my experience there was a **shadow side** and a **light side** of religion. I actually enjoyed the sanctity of choosing one woman and saving my seed, which was a religious idea. But where the dark side came in was the dogma. Then there was a way in which it was repressing or limiting my own vitality. I was having my own strong urges as a man, on an evolutionary biological level. This idea of strict monogamy led to strong active repression, and that did not work out well for self-understanding of the body. At the same time, through the pain and confusion of that collision between religion and evolution, it sent me on a path of inquiry, but now it is a fantastic question. I see the worth of religion on a high level. But on a low level, its execution is very poor, especially for vulnerable youth. This speaks to **sexual education** which is not very advanced in the United States.

Daniel: I want to bridge two thoughts. The first thought is in relation to sexual purity, which is most of the aims of religious restrictions. I experienced that being transparent about past relationships can be as purifying as being united with one woman. The difference about the dogma of religions and the knowledge about the question why a purified sexuality is good? That is the problem with dogma. If you just follow the rules you never know how and why. You have to make your own experiences. What I can recommend is *to be honest and transparent about all your past relationships.* That, somehow, breaks up the intimacy to this transparency in your current relationship. That makes the boundaries open to this dual partnership, without any restriction that you put on yourself in the relationship. By doing so the intimacy is purified by degree of transparency and openness. The second thought is about the fact of intensity, I think, when it comes to the embodied emotions. You can experience a lot of intensity with one person, especially when you are transparent or with multiple partners, which make things very intense. That can, for some, generate attraction. If you are not available all the time because there is someone else, *that can eventually be attractive for people with unhealthy patterns of emotional insecurity.* I make this observation because it can be attractive to have multiple relationships, but also repulsive because of emotional games, confusion and consequently problems.

Cadell: I think, on that note, perhaps we should wrap up and make a summary of how we feel. If we started trying to talk about sexual being and reality, I think we certainly hit that mark. I think that many future topics emerged in my mind. What this topic meant to me was that I started with this story of Plato, where **one being gets fragmented into two**. I think that what Plato is articulating is the **sexual real** and identifying that it emerges as a sexual unity that we spontaneously want, and maybe the most important thing about our existence. And I think that if we can come up with a way to talk about it in a way that is more understanding of our bodies, intimacy, emotions and the complexities of the 21st century, then it would do enormous good for our culture. I hope we contributed in some way to that.

Kevin: I think we hit the mark as well. We breached into the territory that has a lot of energy. There is a *dance between order and chaos.* From the highest level of spiritual concepts to unity and soul, to the gritty experience of mating in the 21st century. For me it is so refreshing because these are the conversations that I wish I was exposed to years ago. Those challenges allowed me to grow, but in culture at this stage, because of the internet, and the instantaneous transmission of knowledge, this conversation will not subside, it will intensify. I think it is important that we have markers to understand the ways in which too much repression breeds corruption and trauma, and then on the other side, the radical experiments of sex, drugs and rock and roll also breeds a lot of pain and fragmentation. I think we are trying to find a middle ground where we can articulate these concepts with integrity between the individual and the sacred.

Daniel: It sounds very exciting and interesting for our next discourse. I take away the innocence and transparency for intimate relationships. I think that is how we can make this evolution together. I think we are going through pain because we are going through a learning process. In every learning process there is friction, it keeps us moving and evolving. I think we can make this evolution very innocent and transparent, as we are talking about it right now. I am really looking forward to the next one.

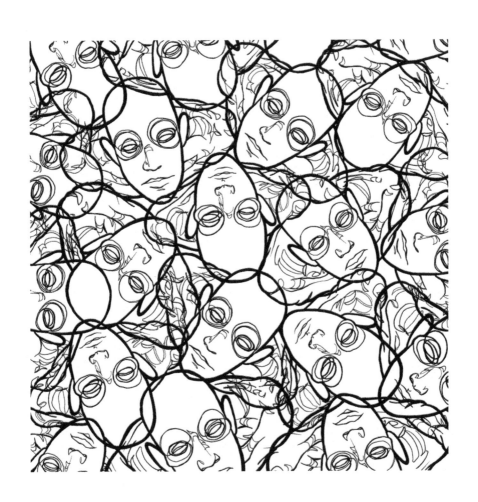

CHAPTER 2

Historical Emergence of Traditional Archetypes

Cadell: To structure this second trialogue, I would emphasize that the title is "Historical Emergence of Traditional Archetypes." An **archetype** is a term famously popularized by the psychoanalyst Carl Jung and needs to be *differentiated from the term meme*. A meme might be defined as a **cultural unit of information** (analogous to a genetic unit of information); a meme can be something we learn and pass on, for lack of a better word: **an idea**. Jung's notion of archetype is a bit more *robust and transhistorical*. That means an archetype is kind of like patterns of ideas and behaviors that have become so heavily used by human beings that they become the *unconscious structure of our thinking and being*.

In this trialogue we are going to be discussing the idea that "Man" and "Woman" are types of **transhistorical archetypes**. This possibility makes these concepts much harder to deconstruct and change then most contemporary constructivists may believe. Man and Woman are not merely memes or ideas. However, and importantly, even though Man and Woman may be archetypes that possess a transhistorical nature that have been with us from the beginning, we are still paradoxically trying to get at the core of their historical emergence and how they have developed over time. Consequently, we are also, like many constructivists, still interested in how they may change in the context of the 21st century sociotechnological environment. In order to start a dialogue about the archetypes "Man" and "Woman" I would like to open with a great quote from William Shakespeare:[5]

"All the World's a Stage, and all the Men and Women merely players, they have their entrances and exits."

Of course, the quote is extended to discuss what it means to be a human and all the different stages of life we go through. The first thing to emphasize is this idea of the **"World Stage."** The World Stage is something we do not control, it is kind of something that *exists as a background,* and *we appear on it.* The second thing to emphasize is the idea of a stage with actors *signifies a drama.* There is a play going on and we are playing with each other on a stage. With the "emergence of traditional archetypes" I want to get at why these archetypes are *logical structures,* not just for the world stage we are on, but also for the evolution of the natural world and human civilization. These are logical structures in relation to all the struggles and constraints that structure human civilization: the drama and the play of our lives.

In other words, when we embody an archetype of "Man" or "Woman" we are playing a role, we are playing a character, and why are those characters, or why are those types of characters, functional? *What about them works? What about them does not work anymore? How do we experience the real of gender identity as not working? What space do we have to play with these archetypes given our stage and the way our stage changes?* That is how I wanted to open the conversation. It seems to me that although we do not structure the World Stage as such, once we appear, we do become entangled with it. Our action in the drama of our lives in some sense transforms the space of the stage. In that sense it could be that characters that made sense during "one scene" may become useless in an "other scene." Furthermore, when we consider just how rapidly the world is changing today, let alone how much the world has changed in the past few centuries, it may be high time to think again about what are these unconscious archetypes that structure our actions.

What do you both think about this idea?

Kevin: That is a brilliant quote by Shakespeare. I think it is one of my favorite quotes of all time, actually. I think it speaks to something very deep about the nature of reality. In terms of language and our lived experience, *reality seems more like a narrative or syntactical texture which encounters the unknown.* The notion of *reality as a drama* really resonates with me. This especially resonates with me in the sexual drama between Man and Woman, which is a drama not only in terms of reproduction. Of course, the obvious biological reason for Man and Woman is sexual reproduction. But sexual reproduction is not even the only way to reproduce. Sexual reproduction emerged later on the planet. Evolution started with asexual reproduction. But what is also coming up for me about Man and Woman as archetypal players on the stage of life is that we are living out these roles that have been lived millions of times over. I am living the role that all my ancestors stretching back to the emergence of the human species have been living out and experiencing. It is a very grandiose and beautiful way to understand what it means to be a Man.

Daniel: In my thoughts we have this drama where we play this role of being a Man. For some this can be very serious. It might be a playful game if we do not attach too much to what it is, but if we are very attached to it can be serious. We can jump into this role, but actually the roles we are playing are a kind of orientation on what people see outside. This is very much linked to the archetypes, because they are types of orientations for humankind. If you talk about "this is masculine" or "this is feminine," the archetypes are kind of related towards your own experiences. The way you find yourself in these experiences might be very contrasting: maybe you know you are a man, *but sometimes not.* What is my "masculinity" being a man? What is my feminine side? Most of the time masculinity and femininity are like two poles of complementarity, opposites, that allow the attraction to oneness. This whole realm of having a *common sense of what it is*, is an experience of what I can relate to in life.

In our lives now, which has been changing so much after the **feminist revolution** of the 1960s and 70s, and the generation our parents grew up in, we find the role of the man that is given in our society is very uncertain. Forty years ago, it was quite clearly defined what a man should be. The man of the industrial era was a man who dedicated his whole life to working and providing for his family. But now, also, women are working and providing for their family. So, we do not have this clear polarity anymore, as we did forty years ago.

Cadell: On this idea that we have lost a polarity, I can think that, from my readings and my understanding and experiences, the traditional world sees man and woman as different, but as harmonious. The woman plays her role in her sphere (the private sphere), and the man plays his role in his sphere (the public sphere), creating a difference. But they are also harmonious in the sense that they are both complementary opposites, and the unity of the world (like yin-yang) is one.

I think that my favorite notion of what feminism is, is as an epistemological strategy for breaking *this harmonious unity of polar difference*. *Feminism is affirming the break with the traditional world's ontology* (yin-yang). From my understanding of the conservative movement today, the common thread between all conservative commentators is basically their defense of the traditional family and the traditional unit (and woman's role therein). From that point of view, *feminism is a break with the old world*. If you look back on one of the greatest feminist philosophers of the enlightenment, Olympe de Gouges, she would emphasize that **"Marriage is the Tomb of Love."** That really captures the essence of the break, I feel. The authentic feminists assert that the traditional world is a fake, and these traditional roles are not going to work anymore. It is a *transformation of essence*.

Thus, we may say, if the traditional world believes in complementary opposites, the modern world believes more in an *asymmetrical opposition*, where the opposites are in an antagonistic struggle with one another, as opposed to a symmetrical balancing. It is in this fact that contemporary men, I feel, need to be less naive as to the nature of women.

I just wanted to jump off of that point to maybe comment on the idea that archetypes are orientation tools, as you emphasized Daniel. And also to make a connection to the idea that Kevin emphasized, as man and woman as related to sexual reproduction. Of course, it is true that in the biological world we have males and females, and males and females are determined by sexed gametes. There is an intersex reality, but most of the time you have clearly sexed gametes. Now on the cultural level, what becomes "Man" and what becomes "Woman" are much more symbolic constructs that "males" and "females" use as cultural orientation tools (which we may claim here are "archetypes").

From this I wanted to re-emphasize the importance of Daniel's identification with this fundamental break with modernity and the industrial revolution. In this break men were traditionally defined by their work output (as had been true for most if not all of history). But now we see the gradual and accelerating motion of women in the workplace. In my mind this leads to the asymmetrical push where we are all working and there is no longer a gender that is "confined" to reproduction as a telos. Indeed, it could be that what structurally defines the modern feminist break is the idea that women do not want to be defined by their reproduction. This could be one of the sources of conflict with the traditional archetypes where there is a harmonious balancing between the "public" and "private" sphere. This is no longer harmoniously balanced because these spheres were in essence tethered to the categories of "work" (public) and "reproduction" (private).

Now, if my logic is clear, the question I would throw out is do we need totally different archetypes? And, if so, what would they look like? Would they still be "Man" and "Woman"? Or would they be totally different? And would these be archetypes that transcend sexual reproduction altogether?

Kevin: This is a brilliant framing, Cadell. I want to call in the metaphor of how I view an archetype. Let me use a very simple example: *the Sun itself*. If the Sun is an archetype (and this plays into *Plato's Cave*), then the mini-manifestations of the archetypes (human beings) are the shadows cast by objects in some relationship to the Sun. This is in relationship to the archetype being an Ideal. In other words, the Ideal, the whole totality of what it means to be a Man, is this Star, this "North Star." Throughout history we have different shades of its expression. To attempt to answer your question, Cadell, do we need to invent new archetypes? No. We need to return to archaic models of Man and Woman as the highest Ideals. These Ideals emerged because they worked.

I think, since the Enlightenment, we needed to eliminate a lot of negativity that needs to happen because of many of the taboos placed on sex itself, and many of the restrictions placed around marriage. I tend to agree that marriage can be a "tomb of love." I mean the love that is spontaneous, erotic, evocative of poetry, art, the very intense passionate form of love. I understand there are gradations, there is a life cycle in a relationship. But what we are seeing in the modern world, this opposition we are seeing, if you zoom out enough, you can see it as cause and effect. Because women were not allowed to vote, and hold jobs, it is understandable that as soon as that is possible, there is an eruption of energy. We call that the feminist revolution. Now it is "anti" the traditional roles, it is "anti" forms of marriage. Of course, the conservatives are interested in preserving and defending these roles because it is what they have built their entire world views upon.

The toxic conversation about women in the workplace is now either: "these women are crazy, they are taking over men's roles," or the reason that women are not happy is because they are "conforming to the men's roles." I think these narratives are wrong. I think the future of man and woman, and the roles that they can play, will become exponentially more abundant and diverse. I think "Me Too" is proof of concept that there needs to be new space for Women in the workplace. That doesn't mean we need to invent new archetypes. It means we need to delete what needs to be deleted, reckon with what needs to be reckoned with, and come into more totality of the expression of the archetypal "Man" and "Woman" which is an eternal Ideal that we are *still aspiring to achieve.*

Daniel: Good points about ideal archetypes, Kevin. On the one hand, I agree that we do not need to consciously create more archetypes. Maybe archetypes cannot be created like that. However, I was looking at this series *American Gods,* which made me think deeply about this topic. In this series you have the traditional gods represented by Viking and Caribbean figures, and there are also the new gods, the Digitized figures. This made me think that maybe we already have new archetypes unconsciously emerging alongside the old ones.

The question concerning archetypes was always about approaching a totality, about the **Absolute**. If you look into Greek mythology, you always have the history of creation. In Greek mythology there is no common understanding about the creation through all times, but to keep it short and simple: first was **Chaos**, then came Gaia (Earth), Tartarus (Abyss) and Eros (Love); or in other historical sources Nyx (Night) and out of the cosmic egg, Phanes (Life), which is light and sometimes also called Eros. Much later, in the family tree of the Greek gods, figures like Apollo representing the Sun came from Gaia and Uranus (Sky).

In this mythology there is always a difference between the Sun and the Light itself. In different cultures sometimes the Sun is represented as Male, and sometimes the Sun is represented as Female. In German, the article of the Sun is female, in Spanish it is male, for example. As the further in mythological stories unfolds it creates its dramas and comedies. But if you go to the beginnings of these stories it is always about the totality, and the transformations of shadows (or the night) and to light, like in *Plato's Cave*. The shadows represent our bad behaviors or things that we are not conscious of in our experiences. Thus, orienting with the light in mythology is always related to our conscious experiences. Mythologies unfold in its storyline as we are able to experience our way back to oneness, to the cosmic egg, where everything emerged, and be conscious about the process. In this course, the polarities of masculine and feminine are complementary, as well as different gods representing light (Eros or Phanes) and shadows (Nyx or Tartaros), or Earth (Gaia) and Sky (Uranos). It is similar to cold and warm, and the different degrees or gradients in between these extremes.

Here we could think in terms of orthogonal complementarity. On the one hand, you could say masculinity is seen as strength. If you look at a woman who has lots of muscles, you would not say "that is a very feminine woman." You relate to a woman as someone who has soft curves. In the opposition you do not relate strong to weak, because everyone wants to be strong, and no one wants to be weak. But soft is also a kind of weak and has a much more positive connotation. Thus, I think a good opposition would be something like strong and soft (or flexible). Softness and flexibility as a quality might be something on the feminine side and something very positive. If you are soft and flexible you can adapt yourself easily. You can change your mind. In that sense there is a light side of being strong, and a shadow side, like being inflexible, and there is another shadow side that is being weak. But there is a light side of being weak when it turns out to be soft and flexible. So, I was thinking how these qualities can be played with in the drama of mythology.

Nowadays movies are our mythological narratives. These movies are representing the old mythologies in modern forms, like Marvel Studios. The heroes even have the same names as the old myths, like Thor, Loki and Thanos, alongside emergent heroes with no clear reference to the old, like Silver Surfer, Captain America and Iron Man. In short, I think there is a big global change, but there are still old archetypes, persisting along representations of new ones.
Cadell: Do you think, Daniel, that the emergence of new archetypes

along the old ones mean that the play is itself changing? Both of you brought up **Plato's Cave metaphor**. In *Plato's Cave* metaphor you have the idea that there is a single unified essence or truth that exists independently of history. That is often why Plato gets blamed for the late emergence of evolutionary theory. In Platonic theology or metaphysics you do not think of changing forms, but of stable eternal forms, and you think of the changing forms as a lower level reality (the so-called "shadows").

But, of course, evolutionary theory flips that idea on its head since the "lower level of reality" is the only reality and there is no "higher reality" towards which there are some projection or reflection. Thus, in the context of the real of Man and Woman, as a gap between their actual shadow state embodied in time, and their ideal eternal state which represents their truth, are you both saying that genders are archetypal orientations or points of the play that change across time in an evolutionary way, but that there is a real substance that remains the same?

I want to clarify that my main mission is to try to bring together the evolutionary materialist and the archetypal or metaphysical way of thinking, without presupposing the eternal substance. To me it seems that our species emerged from processes of natural selection in a purely materialist evolutionary way. In the emergence of consciousness, we appeared to ourselves as biologically sexed, with half of the human species (roughly) formed for manual work and hard labor (what Daniel called "strength"), and with the other half of the human species (roughly) formed for birth and child-rearing (what Daniel called "soft" and "flexible"). These functions ended up defining what became Man and Woman historically for immanently practical reasons. Now those functions are changing in the context of the modern world due to our entanglement with the World Stage (the transformations we produced with our cultures).

However, I agree with both of you that we still have these persistent Ideals in our minds that we want to be the "best Men" (strongest) and the "best Women" (softest) we can be as ethical and moral principles. What I would again suggest is that the old models of the ideals came from our work and reproduction as pragmatic functions, and that these functions have been disrupted in the context of the modern World Stage, that has seen the industrial, and now information age revolution. Thus, the play and the drama are changing on a fundamental level.

Now what of this "gap" where new more "androgynous" figures or archetypes emerge alongside the old ones? These new ones are not exactly like the old ones and cannot be reduced to them. The modern movie machine as a mythological narrative constructor is generating totally other forms for our temporal identification, which don't necessarily seem to be tethered to the old (as you emphasized Daniel). This makes me suspect that our gender identifications are not necessarily within the bounds of an eternal substance *but rather there is something radically different at work which takes the negativity of our state all the way to the end.*

Kevin: I love the idea of humans emerging as biologically sexed, and then there is a way in which the cultural archetypes can hijack this programming and move to their own ends. From the Jungian sense of archetypes, there are these *essentially immortal meta-memes* that have shaped the landscape of evolution. I think they start to transcend humanity even if they evolved out of proto-archetypal forms from our own evolution. Of course, if we zoom in on "Man" and "Woman" today, the drama has changed a lot, and is continuing to change. Women are in the workplace, women do not want to bear all the stresses of child labor and rearing children. The family structure and the emergence of co-parenting, paternity leave, is a very powerful policy of moving beyond the traditional biological assumptions of gender division. I think "Man" and "Woman" archetypes can coalesce in new configurations that may appear alien to a traditional culture. In the traditional world the "Woman's" role of reproduction and raising children, and the "Man's" role of working and defending the group, is the most dominant. Matriarchal and partnership societies are the exception and not the rule throughout most of civilization.

Cadell: Now what it sounds like you are describing is that we were "Two" (in historical civilization), but now we are moving to a more "androgynous" form where the "Two" become something "other" as a mixture. Is that what you are saying?

Kevin: Yes, that is what I am intuiting. In the old days "Men were Men." There was not this idea that Men could be in feminine essence, being receptive and vulnerable. Androgyny is what I am speaking to, not a physical androgyny necessarily, but an *energetic androgyny*.

Cadell: If we are talking about archetypes we are talking about ideational and behavioral energy patterns that unconsciously structure human society. In the context of what you were describing with government policy, and the direction that our future families and social structures might be tending towards, in the past we had a clear archetypal binary between "Man" and "Woman," and that was seen as the natural order of things. Now, with feminism and other modern thought structures, we have a breaking of that totality, since that binary is not the norm of the way things should be. Then what you seem to be describing is a type of androgynous energy mix where the masculine and feminine archetypes are things that everyone has within their own Self. Is that what you would say?

Kevin: Yes, precisely. I would say, for example, that the willingness of some men to participate in child-rearing is evidence of this. Although they are in a male body and the masculine archetype is the dominant structure to their behavior and ideation, they are becoming more aware of their own opposite. Maybe this is possible because of feminists, and the radical conversations they have opened up in culture. Now the masculine is able to allow the feminine archetype, the behaviors and the ideas in it, to move them. This is where a guy may be a stay-at-home father, participate in child-rearing and being "softer."

I think that could be a good thing. Some may say that is a bad thing: that man should be at work, be a breadwinner, not participating in child rearing. But what we are seeing now is a telescoping effect of the working man, and what that did to the nuclear family. I would argue that this did not strengthen the nuclear family but invited in a lot of addiction, abuse and neglect. If the man is fully possessed by the masculine archetype, and the woman is fully possessed by the feminine archetype, and they are in a scarcity model (which I would say is the dominant historical model), there is a way in which these archetypes were just engineering survival. But now in the digital media world, where we are able to have these conversations outside of the traditional model, things can change. For example, the idea of "Man" in 2018 is very much in question. Men in general are feeling the heat. Global media is exposing a lot of male leaders and behavior that has not worked for the feminine. This is an interesting phenomenon here because the archetypes are being called into question. Do we find new ways to totally embody the archetypes? Or do we create a type of androgyny?

Cadell: For me personally, I am not for or against androgyny. I would say I am trying to figure out if that is the direction that you are describing society as tending towards because of certain modern political policies about parenting structures and expectations. And if that is the way society is tending, then I have a lot of questions. For example, if you are in Burning Man culture at Burning Man festival, would you say that culture is an androgynous culture? It is interesting to me the symbol of Burning Man, because they are literally *"burning a man."*

Kevin: I think there are two major takes: one, it is like "burning *the* man," like burning "the system" or "the patriarchy." And then the other one is "the man" as a symbolic destruction of the ego. To answer your question, I would not call Burning Man an androgynous culture, but it is a space and culture where *androgyny manifests more strongly than anywhere else I have ever been.* What I mean by that is that females are fully in a self-expression, if they want to be really masculine, physical and direct with their language, then they do that. I think more common for me, I see many more men expressing the feminine, dressing up in dresses, being very feminine with their costumes, with their speech. And I think there is everything in between. What is coming to mind are these non-binary gender pronouns, like "Zee" and "Zer." To my mind these forms of androgyny are not beneficial. I tend to side with Jordan Peterson, for example, when he claims that these words do not seem to be useful on a high level. I think we are at the edge here in developing the language we really need.

Cadell: From what I was reading in *The Symposium*, they frame androgyny, not as a multiplicity, but as a **"third sex."** It is like your masculine and feminine as one within you, but a **"third thing**." What do you think, Daniel?

Daniel: I like the direction of this conversation very much because it is what I was trying to say with the contrast between ancient and modern mythological narratives. To my experience and to everything that I have figured out so far, and also my philosophy and my way of doing science, is how we can relate it to our Self, *how can we embody this*. If we do consciousness research it is also *what are you conscious about?* You go into the subjectivity of all the things you can relate to. When I am talking about this mass of stories and dramas of Greek mythology, there is a kind of evolution, and it is a way of going to a kind of "oneness" being. *That is also what it means to be androgynous.* On the other hand, we have more masculine parts and more feminine parts. We have some things that are feminine or masculine, but in our shadows. We experience some sufferings or patterns of repetition or autonomous unconsciousness on one side of gender, and maybe we discover this and integrate it and discover that we find ourselves being more complete with ourselves.

In this way it is a process that is really going on on the global level right now, because it is really about what happened in the 1960s and 70s, that took up from the women's side to regain masculinity. Modern feminism is really that they were taking up the roles the man played. As you both said, they started taking the political decision of going to work as an identity. Once I was on a panel discussion and we were criticized that there were no women on the panel. Moreover, the very form of the panel was criticized because it is very masculine and patriarchal to speak from above to below.

What we may say is that in this way, there is a need on the masculine side to take up the feminine evolution. There was the feminist revolution for women to become more masculine, but there was no feminist revolution for men to become more feminine. I think that is a good point to go on, to really stress this concept of androgynous being to another level, which I like very much, because there is always a type of feminine and masculine inside our self, but *how is it expressed? What is it good for?* If we take this example of hierarchy, and speaking from above to below, what is really feminine, and what is really masculine?

In this context, and all of a sudden, it came to my mind that there is almost no female rape on men. There are some very small exceptional stories about that, but no percentage to regain the opposite phenomenon of men raping women. **Imagine what does it mean?** There are almost no female rapists that have a male victim. Why?

Cadell: A lot of it can be anatomical. Not all of it, of course, but a lot of it.

Daniel: Sure, some of it has to be anatomical, on the one hand. But if we take our embodied being and look at the other side, it is quite obvious that most of the rapist violence and sexual violence from man to man historically is during war. It is actually to subjugate the victims and losers and to show a psychological domination, and not necessarily related to anatomy. What I am saying is that we could really use some more of the caring, of the horizontal understanding and collaboration, which I relate to the feminine. Man tends to be more independent in his solitude or in a mode of hierarchical relation, and less about horizontal collaboration. Only if we look from the very archetypal way, of the repressed feminine inside of ourselves, could we balance this energy.

Cadell: The vibe I am getting from both of you on the issue of the emergence of archetypes is like an enthusiastic prescription for a more androgynous culture, or for a deconstruction of what masculinity is, or what "Man" and "Woman" are, and a plunge into a more fluid, and more balanced sexual environment, which equals a more feminine environment? Or a more feminized environment? Is that kind of the energy I am receiving?

Kevin: You hear that the **"Future is Female,"** but the warrior part of me, the masculine part of me that appreciates direction and sharpness, would not welcome this future. However, to Daniel's point, because of war and the dominance culture...

Cadell: Sorry to interrupt. I understand that "war" "violence" "dominance" are all aspects of "Man" or the "shadow of man," but why are we saying that all of this is what "man is, as if we can be reduced to these negative and toxic functions? Or for example, when Daniel was saying that there was a feminist movement for women in the 60s, but we need a feminist movement for men. *Why do men need a feminist movement?*

Kevin: *Men need a masculine movement.*

Cadell: That is more what I would say. For me, it is not that men need a feminist movement. I would say it is good that women have a feminist movement which helps them better understand how to express in the public sphere. But men, I think, need a type of movement that helps them better understand what it means to be a man today.

On a psychoanalytic point regarding the emergence of gender, I am essentially a Freudian. I can say specifically what I mean here, and why I would, in the end, go against classical Jungian archetypal interpretations of gender. Freud said that the fantasy of the unconscious is basically a burning of the primordial father. That kind of emerges at Burning Man, which is what I was hinting at earlier. Burning Man, it seems to me, is kind of like the Freudian burning of the primordial father. What does that mean on a historical level? I honestly do not know. Maybe we love (and hate) the absence of "the man."

But, what I can say is that Freud actually said something remarkable about gender, and I think it is worth introducing here in relation to the desire to "balance" masculine-feminine energy in an androgynous form. As we all know, in biology, on the level of males and females, *males are a deviation. Males are actually kind of like a deformity.* For example, if you look at chromosomal patterns, the Y chromosome, which makes a "male a male," is a totally unimpressive little chromosome, *the crappiest of the chromosomes!* All the other chromosomes are robust and long, and the male chromosome is a little thing. The default, like you were saying Kevin about primordial asexual reproduction, they are all default female.

But here is the twist: *the Freudian twist.* Freud said "Man" and "Woman," our gender identities, *he said it was the opposite of biological sexuation of male and female.* He said on the level of the symbolic order (immersion in language) *we are default boys,* and *the deviation is girls.* The reason, he suggests, is that *we all want the Mother* and signify this desire in the unconscious. No matter what the subject is biologically (male, female or intersex), on the level of the symbolic, the subject starts wanting the mother. The father here is seen as an intrusion, as "the Law" which prohibits access to the object-cause of desire. The father is perceived as coming in and "taking the fun away" (taking the breast away). I almost see Burning Man as this motion: "the Man" takes our "fun" (breast) away, and the festival (sphere of abundance) is a reclamation of this primordial space of enjoyment. This is super interesting from a psychoanalytic point of view.

If that is true, what can we say about gender and balancing the two? Freud had a very complex view of how a human subject becomes a boy and how a human subject becomes a girl. This theory actually has little to do with biology (although of course biological anatomy informs these structures). Freud thought that gender identification was mostly about how a subject came to identify with its desire. For example, I still remember when I was five and I found out I could not marry my mother. I thought at the time, logically, "I am going to have to find another girl." Then I thought, logically "how am I going to do that?! That is impossible!" For my younger self, this was a true catastrophe that stimulated and motivated much thinking about what would become my active historical gender identity.

However, Freud suggested that it is actually harder and more catastrophic for a human subject to become a girl. The subject-to-become-a-girl, in contrast to the subject-to-become-a-boy, has to identify her desire with the mother. For the girl, it is not that I want the mother. On the contrary, *it is that I am going to become the mother!* It is a totally different identification process.

You see here the crucial dimension at work with this discovery about the essentialization process of sexual identity. This is why I will limit Jung, and even Plato! This is the notion of the *fundamental asymmetry between the sexes*. This fact of sexual asymmetry, I would claim, manifests itself in the actual historical movement of the feminist signifier, for example, pushing women from the home into the workforce. For Freud, it is not that you have a nice balance of opposites or harmonious unity. Freud cannot be interpreted as an archetypal conservative. The harmonious unity is always structured in a *primordially asymmetrical relation*, this is the *core antagonism*.

To bring this back to my "quarrel" with the idea that "men need a "feminist movement." What I would say is that we know on an unconscious level that there is some asymmetry between men and women. We know there is some antagonism which is uncomfortable to discuss in public. From this logic I would say, *what does it mean that we want to be androgynous?* What does it mean that there is such an intensity against the dark side of masculinity? Does it come from not knowing how to be a good man? And if so, what does a reinvented masculine archetype look like? Or is the androgynous direction the healthier direction? Honestly, I have no idea.

Kevin: There is so much here, Cadell. I would speak to the necessity of the asymmetry on this plane of existence. In some theoretical realm of metaphysical forms and ideals, as Plato and Jung point towards, both with the Allegory of the Cave and the Collective Unconscious, it may be possible to have perfect balance in Truth. This is what the Buddha or Christ speak to, the messianic balance between masculine and feminine.

However, in my thought process I recognize the imbalance. For example, I am aware as a man of the anima, of the inner psychic nature of feeling and emotion, where great power and creativity comes from, and I can source from it. This feeling and emotion is never perfectly balanced with my thought and reason. There is always an asymmetrical dominance structure. So, if something traumatic were to happen, I might become dominated by the feminine side, where I cannot control my emotions. This is what is needed in the masculine, for both men and boys, being initiated into the emotional side of the masculine. I know that Esther Perel emphasizes that a real men's movement will become dominant in the culture out of necessity.

Daniel: First, I will say that the feminist movement is where women became aware of themselves as equal to men, on the level of politics and economics. They took up roles that man had, and so they became a bit like man. But what I wanted to say is that it was not vice versa. *So, the feminist movement was a masculine movement.* On the other side, what is archetypally very feminine is the invisible one, the inside one. *What is not in the public sphere.* What is missing and what I am trying to say, is that this movement of masculinity as a healthy feminism, and then you have the androgynous. When it comes to being a warrior, providing protection and security, you want to be strong and like a man, holding the family, to be what men do. But on the other side, *we need a movement where men can cry, can express feelings.*

Cadell: So, what you are saying is that the feminist movement is a masculine movement and equating that with hierarchy and dominance. So, people like Angela Merkel and Hillary Clinton would be masculine. And now you are saying that men need an opposite movement, where we become more feminine, and then we would have a more androgynous society as a result?

Daniel: *It could be.* It is difficult to say on an individual level to a cultural level. It is also kind of hard to say it is black and white, feminine and masculine, because it is about the shades in between, where we find the diversity and the differences to have an evolution of something new. But these shades are also problematic because we get lost and lose orientation. What we had experienced in these 500 years of science, which displaced archetypal thinking, you do not have mythology and astrology only as something hidden, private and esoteric. There is something of a flipping point, where there might be a change going on in this.

Cadell: Okay, well I started by quoting Shakespeare, which referred to the World Stage, and we exist on a stage. We did not design the stage, but we appear on a stage, and we may say that is biology or nature. Then we dramatize on the stage, and we may call that "Man" and "Woman." In history, of course, "Man" was seen as something specific, related to hierarchy and dominance and work, and supporting family. For "Women" it was much more related to child-rearing, and that in the modern industrial era, that has been broken. Now we kind of took the conversation into this difficult place of talking about androgyny where we are redefining "Man" and "Woman." We are thinking how these two binaries are going to reinvent themselves with a different orientation. For me, I am still open. I still see that there are positives and negatives to being very masculine. I have learned a lot and achieved a lot in the public sphere because of my masculinity, but at the same time I have run away from my body and my emotions. It has been a trade-off, I suppose. I can see the logic and the wisdom in androgyny. But I guess I am still internally open to more discussions about what all this means.

Kevin, what do you think?

Kevin: It takes a lot of courage to have this conversation. For me, I think in a Jungian sense, that of the archetypal understanding of the collective unconscious. Archetypal understanding of "Man" and "Woman" will be necessary for initiatory rights in the future. Is this future men's movement going to be as big as the feminist movement on the political and world stage? We are in the beginning stages of that possibility. There was not a need for this before but now there is a clear need. For me, the end result will be something androgynous. I think technology enhances this tendency to androgyny. Technology allows for a global digital media and a wearable tech will feminize society even more.

Cadell: We are going to have to cover this in our chapter on **transhumanism and androgyny**.

Kevin: That is where I was pointing. On the masculinity level I am really excited by this discussion. I am excited to revivify some of the old Gods that you spoke to Daniel, in true expression of masculinity. Because being in touch with more feminine qualities such as shedding emotions and communicating in a more non-violent way, this does not make you less of a "Man." That means you are becoming more of a "Man," because a "Man" contains all of these aspects too. For me, the final word is that I want to play with a whole deck of cards, not half a deck of cards. I am uncertain what that will mean, but I am dedicated to manifesting that.

Daniel: I just want to thank you both for holding this space for open conversation. These challenges are affecting so many people's thoughts and feelings. By having these intimate topics in an opening is like *we are pulling the inside out*. There is so much to say and so much to know. I am open to how other people relate to this discussion because it is a frontier of societal being, societal culture.

Cadell: I feel like we did cover a lot and I am grateful for both of you for putting your identities out there in an open way.

CHAPTER 3

Difference Between Evolutionary and Religious Worldview

Cadell: In this third trialogue we are covering the differences between the evolutionary and religious worldview, and what those two worldviews mean for how we conceptualize sexual difference, historical gender identity and the future of sex and civilization. We have touched on these differences a bit already, but this topic is so fundamental it really deserves its own focus. To give a quick formal overview, we might say that the evolutionary and religious worldview are two contradictory or opposing worldviews that have structured much of the modern world and a lot of our metaphysical thought. The underlying presuppositions of those worldviews are so fundamental and profound to our identities that if we dared to investigate the presuppositions, then we may discover some relation to how we act in history and create our identities.

For those of you who do not know, the evolutionary worldview in its most common representation emerged in the scientific world during the 19th century. This worldview was grounded theoretically by thinkers like Charles Darwin and Alfred Russel Wallace, who proposed the idea of natural selection, which is essentially the idea that living beings change and have a history, and that they evolve through differential survival and reproduction. In other words, if you have a population of organisms all of them are not going to survive for the same amount of time and reproduce at the same rate. Because of these differences in survival and reproduction, their forms will change accordingly. So, the forms that survive the longest and reproduce the most will propagate their forms, and the ones that do not will die out, and you will have change across time.

In contrast, the religious worldview is not specifically about the natural world and living beings but more about the relation living beings, specifically human beings, have with a supernatural realm. And most importantly, the relation human beings have with an eternal creator or an eternal being, so it is more about something that does not change and does not die. You can see right away why these two worldviews are oppositional or have contradictions and antagonisms. We want to discuss how these worldviews interact and how we might construct our historical identities in relation to them. So, to start, I will quickly give a quote from Charles Darwin's *On the Origin of Species* to demonstrate a sense in which the evolutionary worldview may be seen as something that is antagonistic with the religious worldview:[6]

> "There is grandeur in this view of life, with its several powers being originally breathed into a few forms or into one. And that whilst this planet has gone on cycling according to the fixed laws of gravity, from so simple a beginning, endless forms most beautiful and most wonderful, have been, and are being, evolved."

You can see what Darwin is trying to describe is a total metaphysical description informed by evolutionary reasoning. He is saying that the most fundamental reality we can think is this constant change of beautiful forms, the emergence of living beings, from a struggle or competition. The mechanism he describes in that book does not need to presuppose a supernatural eternal being or an absolute substance. In this account of reality you have endless forms most beautiful emerging and dying and, according to Darwin, that is where we should direct our analytic attention.

Throughout the history of the modern world the evolutionary picture of reality has become strengthened and extended into many different disciplines.[7] The evolutionary way of thinking can be extended, in principle, to the world of physics, chemistry, psychology, and society. There are debates about the extent to which the principle of selection can apply to the formation of universes, the emergence of life itself, and the development of our minds and civilization. Do different universes compete in the same sense of differential survival and reproduction in a type of "ecology" that we may call the "multiverse"? Do these same mechanisms have universal explanatory power when it comes to the emergence of self-consciousness and the different cultures that have reproduced themselves across historical time? To what extent does the evolutionary worldview help us approach questions of the beginning of the universe and the death of the universe?

Of course, the evolutionary picture is not the only way to view reality or even the most popular representation of reality in the modern world. Throughout the development of the scientific worldview, as informed by Darwinian theory, there have been counter-reactionary formations in the religious worldview. There are even many scientific and philosophical formations that could be classified as fundamentally non-evolutionary in the sense of positioning some eternal substance that does not change or evolve across time. In modern physics, for example, there are still great debates about the ultimate meaning of the nature of time and evolution. The issue of how strong a foundation the evolutionary worldview is as a fundamental ontology is very much an open speculative debate. Moreover, there are many non-scientific religious or spiritual communities that build their picture of the world based on an absolute foundation of morality, aesthetics, and truth. There are many people who speak of transcendental mystical states of a unified reality that does not change, and so forth.

In this context I would ask both of you how you put these worldviews into conversation with each other, and how does it affect how you express your historical identity?

Kevin: This topic is very near and dear to my heart as an intellectual and as a man. I was raised Catholic, so the first worldview I encountered was the **religious transcendental worldview**. The religious transcendental worldview for me represented a "Watchmaker in the Sky," that he created these "forms most beautiful," setting them in motion on the physical plane. However, at the same time, if you asked the childhood version of me what I wanted to be, I would have said a paleontologist. I was obsessed with dinosaurs and *Jurassic Park*. I remember reading these books and thinking "oh, look at these huge tyrants, and how they walked the Earth, and how they have evolved now into birds." But in my real-life practice in my family I followed the transcendent worldview. I believed in heaven and hell, and I was afraid of hell. This directly informed my sexual identity. It is like "I better be a good boy, and date within the constructs." This is where religious morality comes in. This became an inner contradiction because I saw through my love of dinosaurs and paleontology that the fossil record demonstrated a continuity of forms in the animal world. This was also logical and apparent to me. What was less apparent, I suppose, and which may have allowed for the stability of the contradiction, was how I, as a human being, fit into that continuity. I think that is where the religious worldview bridged the gap for me.

Now if I shift focus in the narrative to my university self, I experienced *deep heartbreak*. I started questioning my psyche and my attachments to the religious worldview. I started feeling a bit naive about the absurdities that I uncovered. I actually started studying philosophical logic, and rigorous academic texts about the nature of the world. Then I fully switched over to the evolutionary worldview. I studied Richard Dawkins and his famous book, *The Selfish Gene*. I started to align my thinking with Dawkins and the other "**Four Horsemen**": Sam Harris, Daniel Dennett and Christopher Hitchens. This worldview suggested that there is a mechanism in the universe, natural selection, that functioned as an engine of creation of living forms. Whether it is asexual or sexual evolution, there is an emergent ontology of form on this planet, and human beings fit into that picture, along with all other living creatures.

I started to think that because we are conscious of evolution that I can therefore partake in evolution. I started thinking without this transcendental quality of God. I started to negate the idea that God had a specific plan for me. I started to negate the idea that God had set things in motion as the first cause. To be honest, this started to inform my mating, because a big push in the research I was interested in was all about mating. I started to see the females and males in my class as similar to other animal environments. I thought we are just these creatures that want to spread our genes, and there are these strategies that have evolved over millions of years which are totally natural to experience and enact.

My view today has again undergone a transformation that involves a mixture of both worldviews. Now I believe there is room for both the evolutionary and the religious worldviews. I have reintroduced what I would call **mystical and transcendent qualities** into my understanding as my own identity as a man, and how it relates to the evolutionary picture of reality. However, at the same time, anything dogmatic in religion I have found to be *both useless and actually toxic* for my identity when it comes to sexuality, manhood and perspectives on Man and Woman relations. The dogma prevents real understanding of my biological and psychic experience, and general relation with other humans. Thus, when I take a proper perspective on the whole of my experience, I can see the inherent battle between the evolutionary atheistic agenda, and the religious montheistic agenda, from a meta-level. I can see that at the core of a lot of the gap between science and religion there is an inability to help people really heal. That healing elixir lives in the grey area between the two, and that is now what I am committed to as a thinker, speaker, and practitioner.

Daniel: I can relate very much to what you say, Kevin. In my family, actually, the **Soul** was always something given. However, there has been room for speculation about everything. My grandfather, for example, was an atheist while playing the organ in the church. My mother is a devout Christian. But since she was from South America, her Christian belief co-existed with her belief in pagan spirits and an animistic worldview. On my father's side religion was not something really talked about. But when I came to question myself, and my existence, and also to question what the meaning of life is, I became curious about religious traditions and shamanic traditions. I was interested to find something that is in yourself that makes meaning in your life or yourself in life. I was partaking in meditation, shamanic trances, diets, and stuff like that in South America. This led me to discover myself in different ways and shapes.

At the university, I was first focused on approaching these questions philosophically. I was focused on the question: *what really moves life? What power and force?* On the one hand you have the materialistic view, and on the other hand you have the idealistic view. In the idealistic view, there are great men because they think something great and invent something great, and life goes on. In the materialistic view, we have our physical needs, and we are determined by the needs of our environment, which are also reproductive and ecological needs, and so on. These needs are always something like the drivers to match the resources we need to reproduce. The materialistic way is about understanding the circumstances determining the outcome of your behavior and your culture, whereas the idealistic one says that our mind is something special that can make a change in life. Idealists are talking from within to the world. It means we might change something, we have causal power, or better said, we have the chance to break the determination of causality.

Then, I would say, there is also a third component, usually associated with the religious worldview, of a Soul. The Soul is not really matter or mind but something transcendent. If you take the idealistic view working with the mind, it is quite individual, everybody has his or her mind. To overcome this individualistic view of mind, in German we have the word *Geist*, which is mind and spirit at the same time. It could even be interpreted like the Holy Spirit, as something more collective. And with that term it is even something different from the Soul, because in religious terms, the Soul is something eternal, and the mind will not work anymore when you die. The big question for myself in the contrast between the religious worldview and the evolutionary worldview is the contrast between eternity and the *ever-changing whatever it is*. In between the religious and evolutionary worldview you have this materialist and idealist difference. But I must emphasize there are three components: one is the material-corporeal (the body, actually); the idealist-mind (our self-consciousness); and thirdly, the Soul (or what is transcendent in us). For me the big question is to ask: *what is the evolution of the Soul if there is eternity?*

Cadell: There is so much to respond to in both of your reflections! I feel like on a personal level, Kevin, I relate deeply to your story. The main difference for me is in the fact that, paradoxically, I was not raised in a religious context. I was basically raised in a secular home. I still remember, when I was a kid, conversations were always naturalist in essence. We talked from the perspective of human history, ideas, and science. I was also hyper-interested in paleontology and dinosaurs. The question of God, I must admit, was always there somehow. However, I did not think about it in religious terms. And I think to this day that is why I am still interested in religion. This may be too general of a conjecture, but I have noticed that people who were raised religious can become very antagonistic against religion; and people who were not raised religious, because maybe they were not experiencing the hyper-negative dogmatic elements of it, can look at it in a different way. But at the same time, I relate very much to your college experience. In many ways it is very similar. In fact, we started to know each other at this time in our life, actually.

However, perhaps more generally, the basic and natural motion of thought is what is interesting to me. We seem to first play out a critical game in our mind, deducing an evolutionary history, trying to understand ourselves as animals, and trying to understand the evolutionary mechanisms that would explain our emergence and existence. And then you come to this point where you realize you are a part of a creative evolutionary process, and that, because I am a part of that process, maybe that can reconcile the two views between religion and science. Because I think that the discourse that evolutionary biology often situates itself within, at least in the academic context, does not want to consider the metaphysical human evolutionary questions. Or often this discourse does not get wrapped up in these questions just simply out of lack of interest, it seems. But as soon as you start thinking about metaphysical questions in an open speculative frame, you start to run into deep questions about immortality, infinity, creation, and the **ultimate relation between matter and mind**. Moreover, you start to see the logic of some religious ideas. You start to see religious ideas from an evolutionary perspective, *which in turn gives a new perspective on religion.*

And then, Daniel, thinking about how I understood your story and your adventure is from the perspective of the fundamental antagonism of philosophy: idealism and materialism, or ideas and matter, as you state. We must confront fundamental questions about eternity and change, and the nature of causality. These have been oppositions that have existed throughout philosophy, from the first philosophers that we know. If you think about Parmenides, he is the philosopher of **"Absolute Being"** which is still and never-changing, and if you think about Heraclitus, he is the philosopher of **"constant movement and change."** Or even if you think about fundamental physics, you have these fundamental distinctions between stillness and motion: the stillness of the void and the moving matter, or trajectories in a state space. It is so interesting how the mind comes to contemplate these fundamental concepts. And it is so interesting to hear you both talk about these fundamental concepts as a part of your life process.

I guess where I think we should move the conversation is diving deeper into this fundamental tension between materialism and idealism, and its relation to sexuality. Do you think the differences between these views change how you formed your identity when it comes to things like sex, gender and family-building? I am really struck with your openness, Kevin. In telling your story, about how when you first thought in terms of religious presuppositions, which led you to a strict dogmatic form of monogamy, and then the evolutionary worldview opened you up to analyzing things in a more "animalistic way." I remember doing a Master's project on the history of primate sexuality, and when I did my paper on this, I realized that *every single primate is non-monogamous*. There are some socially monogamous species but there is no monogamy in the primate order in terms of strict exclusive copulation! This monogamous idealization appears to have emerged in history with humans and our conceptualizations!

My favorite story about this is with the first sex research on gibbons and siamangs (two species of "lesser apes"). Primatologists first thought they were monogamous because they pair bonded in trees. But then they studied them for a few months. They eventually saw that they were doing sneak copulations quite frequently. So, if you studied them throughout the year ,they were actually non-monogamous. They were only socially monogamous. Of course, direct observations of these "sneak copulations" (i.e., getting caught cheating) would be met with high levels of conflict and antagonism. That is not new to humans. But this strict sexual form of monogamy as an idealization spanning a whole lifetime seems to emerge with humans. Of course, that evolutionary perspective does not eliminate or resolve the desire in the phenomenon of monogamous idealization. Indeed, it actually makes monogamy *more perplexing and intriguing*. Why do humans have this very strong drive for monogamy on one level, or at least a very strong taboo against non-monogamy on another level?

Maybe this can be connected to what Daniel was saying about the Soul and meaning. Or even about the **Holy Spirit** as a type of **collective Soul**. In materialist philosophy, the Soul is typically reduced to the mind as brain, or simply a fantasy not to be taken seriously. But in the religious worldview people would claim it is eternal and the most real substantial identity. The question immediately emerges, that if the Soul is eternal, and we live in an evolutionary world, then

In terms of my sexual identity and transcendental worldview, as you suggest, they were intimately connected. What this worldview informed was *the idea of finding one woman in her perfection and purity.* I thought we would create this pure lineage. But I was not immersed in my body, I was not animalistic in my sexuality. I knew there was a lot of excessive energy in me, but I was trying so hard through mental exertion to live in this monogamous state of being: a Man with one Woman. That is why encountering the evolutionary worldview was so healing for me. If I am part of nature then a lot of this sexual energy will want to live through me, and there are lots of ways I can express my sexual energy. This is also when I started to awaken my creative energy. I do not think that was a coincidence, the poetic and artistic and yogic. I believe that is because I became more embodied, not just operating from three inches of brain matter, but from the perspective of the whole body. There is a lot of interesting neurophysiology that supports that, and which informs our consciousness.

From this understanding of my history I have developed the belief and suspicion that two things have driven and informed the religious worldview in regard to mating. One is the seeking of purity, whatever that means, moral or physical (e.g., abstinence, virginity). This could have first emerged from purely practical reasons before becoming instantiated in religious institutions. For example, it could be that ancient humans encountered venereal diseases and decay, which caused understandable scars and traumas, leading them to control sexuality. And on the other side, as I already suggested, there is this paternal and patriarchal will to know *"this is my son," "this is my daughter,"* and these children will inherit my resources and ideas and continue this line forward into the future. This is one way the "ego-mind" wants to achieve immortality. The fear of death is so deep in human consciousness, that if I can control "my woman" or (more often than we think) "my women," from the traditional male perspective, then I can achieve a type of immortality which gave a lot of fuel to the religious worldview.

Daniel: I think there is something very true here when we get notions *what is this motion or tendency of the Soul?* When I think about my own life it seems the motion or tendency has something to do with sexuality and how we handle sexual energy. How we handle sexual energy is so important for the integration of our being, and the wholeness of our being. I would say that it is almost like in Love, or in the types of romantic experiences that we can have in this world, we get a taste of eternity, *but not the whole thing.* And then we have to deal with this temporality. We are in time, but it is almost as if eternity shines through. *And then how do we balance the two?* Those are some thoughts I want to throw out to both of you.

Kevin: This is brilliant. We are entering into the mega territory for philosophy, which is the relation of the eternal to matter and being itself. I should say that this is how I found you, Cadell. As soon as I uncovered the evolutionary worldview, I was actually a junior in university and I thought *"evolutionary science is what I am doing."* My first interests in paleontology full-circled me into the field of evolutionary biology and psychology. I was looking up blogs about anthropology and mating strategies, and I found your first blog, *The Advanced Apes.*

However, what was coming up when you were speaking was something interesting about self-awareness itself, or consciousness. In my mind there is something about paternity that has informed the religious need for monogamy. For other species in the primate order they are not concerned as much about offspring on the level of self-conscious humans, which means they are not as concerned about historical legacy. There is something here about the **"ego-mind"** at work which may have been a "healthy" adaptation for the evolutionary purposes of extending one's lineage into the future. There is something really being touched here at the intersection with sexuality that does not necessarily emerge in the animal kingdom. Now, of course, this same "ego-mind" function protecting paternity may be one of the biggest enemies of humanity, because taken to the extreme it is not just protecting paternity but can also become a tool for war. Many of the base emotions that we feel: greed, lust, rage, making it all about "me" as an ego-manifestation.

of immortality from a reproductive mode. If you think about historical culture and even the culture we are living now, and how we become attracted to the things that are moving us. The ego-mind level can feel attracted to someone for this drive to reproduce and claim a lineage or property. But it is not only or reducible to that, because it is also true that we are authentically attracted to experiences of beauty, freedom, truth, or to love in the moment. In any case, somehow these attractors always lead to eternity, whether in an extended image of lineage or in the experienced present.

As Cadell said, you meet someone, and suddenly, *you are just there*, in eternity. The same drive could be operative in other fields through sublimation. Consider someone who discovered a great scientific fact or mathematical theorem or philosophical truth. He will get famous, and then he is going to be forever known in the culture. That is a cultural lineage of descendants. Now that brings to mind the concept of the Yoruba people, who came from Africa to the Caribbean Islands. They think that the Soul is partly formed before someone is born and then comes into a body during life. This Soul transforms from something diffuse to a bundle in the mind and body, and then is dissolved into something more diffuse again when you die. My point to highlight is that the Soul is in the Spirit world before life, and after life the Soul returns to the Spirit world. But when one achieves a type of "cultural immortality" in a lineage, it is as if this bundle is going to stay the same in time or human history, transcending the fall and the return into time from the Spirit world. In that way, it makes sense to me that people strive for eternity in the form of being immortalized in famous statues.

In terms of the experience of love, it is like you said about getting into or close to eternity. You get into eternity, but then you are out again. So how do people live with the motion in truth, with love, or whatever, because there is this whole "temporality" in eternity. Consider people who become these types of figures while they are alive. Think of people like Michael Jackson. We sometimes call them "Gods," like the "God of Pop." They are real gods, but from our world. Maybe there is more to this attraction to eternity than we realize? But how do we relate this to a notion of Soul in motion? What does it mean? If we take a religious worldview where we assume that there is a world that is an "other world," either because God is "supernatural," or the angels or spirits are in heaven, or even that there are underground worlds, and so forth, we have to remember that there are many other worlds in different religions. What notion of time do they have? How can we think about an eternal Soul that we can relate to?

To bring this together, it is like to mix up these worlds. If we are to get eternity right here, and when we think of **mindfulness** we are talking constantly about bringing the mind to the *"here and now" "here and now" "here and now."* It is all about eternity. So, it is like trying to bring that other world or whatever realms to this world. These are just speculative questions that are running in my head. Do they even relate to our bodies and minds and souls? I will leave it like that for now...

Cadell: Well, let me give you some dogmatic assertions which you have to accept no matter what! And if you disagree, this whole relationship is over! It is not going to work! Again, there is a lot that has been brought up here. I would love to engage with Daniel, but then I do not want to lose the thread of what came to mind when Kevin was talking either. Let me start with what came to mind from Kevin's reflections, then. The most interesting thing to me in what you were saying is that when you were first in the transcendental worldview you were disembodied, basically. You were just this disembodied immortal vision. The logic was that you were going to carry this disembodied immortal vision no matter what your body was saying. That is so interesting because the evolutionary worldview became healing when it introduced a natural history of the body, and then the logic is, I am in this body right now, carrying this history.

Now, I was recently reading the intro from Joseph Campbell's *Hero with a Thousand Faces*, and the interesting thing about that book is that he opens with a huge quote from Sigmund Freud. I was surprised by that because usually people connect Campbell with Carl Jung, but he opens his most famous book with a quote from Freud. What Freud said in this quote was that *we should not necessarily teach kids about the truth of the past.* That means the religious symbols of the past were the truth *for those people.* And he said that, basically, you are only going to distort a child's mind by giving them those stories and symbols, because that is not their truth. They have to come to the truth for their own time and in their own way. And that will be the truth of the present moment, and it will fall away in time as well.

So, what Campbell is saying is that let us do an archaeology of the truth and see if I can find a meta-pattern that is transhistorical. That is so deep to me because it is almost like you can marry the transcendental archetypes with evolutionary history. Then I was thinking, kids who get indoctrinated into the transcendental worldview, it is like a top-down approach to something that could also be understood in a bottom-up way. In other words, we could logically start with our bodies and evolutionary history, with our senses of the world (without presupposing some other world). And then as we move through the world, and we develop our higher cognitive faculties with visions, we experience what we are calling "eternal" or "immortal." So, the problem, it seems to me, between the transcendental and the evolutionary worldview disappears, simply. *Our natural spontaneous evolution is to come to this understanding of eternity, of what is eternal.* I think that is essentially what Hegel teaches in the *Phenomenology of Spirit* and what he means when he comes to think of the meaning of absolute knowledge: when we talk of the "other world" (and the stories which suture the mystery of birth and death), *it is the work of our historical mind putting it there!*

Now, this brings me to what you were saying, Daniel. What you are speculating about, it seems to me, are things that I have been trying to think very deeply through an integration of complex systems science (evolution of matter) and psychoanalysis (unconscious mind). How I have been trying to wed those two forms of knowledge is with the concept of the **attractor** in complex systems science. *An attractor is a formal structure which a dynamical system tends towards across* *time*. With this concept we do not need to think about this attractor as a substantial "other world" (as is common in traditional religious systems). It is not like there is this "other world" that exists independently of us and our presupposing. It is almost like this formal structure is a state space, a spontaneous state space that *emerges as an absence because of our presence as desiring beings*. We are present and we desire, and because of our desiring presence, this absent state space "forms" that our minds are tending towards. In itself, the state space is purely virtual (on the level of the imagination), and perhaps what was discovered as the unconscious in psychoanalysis: the dream and its wishes. It is like what Kevin was saying about his vision in the transcendental worldview of an immortal lineage. It is a state space of cognition that emerges internal to the complex evolving materiality, and it is in itself an unconscious wish fulfillment. However, crucially, it can change and can become something different, via reflectivity, via making the unconscious more conscious. Thus, it is more like a topography of the mind than it is like an "other world" of supernatural substances.

In this context, when we think about the eternal Soul as somehow beyond both body and mind, and when we see a great musician, athlete, scientist, or some cultural icon, like Michael Jackson signified as the "God of Pop," well they are idols or forms that we have chosen to fill in this "beyond." These idols represent or stand for eternity in some formal attractor space of individuated cognitive entities. If you are really interested in singing popular music, and you were born in the late 20th century Western world, then your state space may be very much influenced by Michael Jackson. The logic is something like: "Ya, I am going to try to embody this motion, because this is speaking to my eternal Soul." Thus, these idols deeply inform the motion of individual cognition from the perspective of their sense of eternal Soul, motivating action in a conflictual relation between time and desire for its transcendence.

To take this further, it may be possible that the motion of eternity can be formalized by the philosopher Gilles Deleuze, because he structured his entire philosophy around **becoming**. What he said about eternity was that the real of eternity was a pure becoming, a becoming that is accelerating to such an intensity, that it *nihilates time*. For example, if someone who is a huge Michael Jackson fan went to one of his concerts, time may cease to exist for that person as we normally perceive it: both their body and mind will be fully absorbed in the present moment of the phenomenon beyond both their body and mind, but still in "this world" as the other of normal reality. That is how I experienced my cognition while taking ayahuasca. Things were becoming so quickly, and it was so intense, that time disappeared. I think that is an interesting way to think of the coincidence between those two realms, especially in the 21st century. In the 21st century, it is all about acceleration and change and becoming, and we have lost the absolute, what is eternal. In other words, we have lost what does not change.

In this context I want to throw those two ideas back out there. On Kevin's side, it is this process of embodying eternity in a bottom-up way, starting with the evolutionary worldview and then tending towards the transcendental worldview. On Daniel's side, there is this attractor space as a formal virtual structure which appears as the truth of our being in time.

Kevin: I had a similar experience on ayahuasca. The rapidity of thoughts in the mind and feelings in the body reaches a crescendo: a crescendo or concrescence or singularity of being itself that is other to both mind and body. I think that is where the healing modality comes in. Now to "full circle" that in this specific discussion about the relationship between these evolutionary and religious worldviews and sexuality, that such a state of consciousness can be felt in the sexual experience. I did not personally encounter this level of the sexual experience until I experienced tantra. Tantra links the yogic modality of breath, concentration, felt experience, enhancing the senses of the body through intention and goals in the vision of the mind, with the goal being to acquire deeper self-knowledge of the other, what is other to both the body and mind.

This knowledge of what is other than body and mind is what Mircea

Eliade calls the **"rupture of plane**." To rupture the mundane plane into eternity is what can be achieved via the orgasm. This is not the orgasm of a build up to an explosive climax (as is common in most masculine sexuality), but there is this build up of intensity where all the senses are 10x or 100x, and all your emotions intensify. This to me is in the sexual experience what the strange attractor portal is calling out of being. It starts with the first look or gaze of the other. You can sense the attractor at that moment, and as you follow this line to ecstasy, to the intensity of the sexual experience, that is where the portal gets really intense, and the becoming, acceleration, reaches that crescendo.

This appears to be built into us neurochemically and neuro-physiologically. It is built into the flesh and blood of our systems. This transcendent experience of evolution or the creator being, in its wisdom, linked to reproduction and recombination of the next generation. The edge of what is emerging in form. I do not think that is a coincidence. This is what Daniel was saying about the recognition of the eternal. All humans can participate in it, in the sexual experience. It is a yearning for timelessness. I think this is reflected in Campbell's work. He is like a memetic archaeologist, and this is reflected in many of the traditions of monotheism: *Paradise Lost*. It is as if falling into history, we have somehow lost our share in partaking in the timeless now, or the eternity, the formless superstate. There is a way in which technology is also inviting us back into this superstate. I want to link those two, linking technology and sexuality, that are yearning for the timeless truth.

Cadell: I think it is so important that you are connecting technology to this. Because oftentimes, at least in some spiritual communities, they view technology as antagonistic with this dimension. But I think it is so important to link technology into this conversation because look what it is allowing us to do. How to interpret sexuality from the perspective of the transhuman?

Kevin: We can intuit something interesting coming in this direction. Daniel, I am curious how you are feeling.

Daniel: There is a lot to say. It is like each session could be extended for hours. On the one hand, tantric experiences do lead to this eternity in our bodies, and that is very crucial. I think to really take philosophy, religion, and science into a "consciousness science" we need that understanding. I think we have to set our Self and our body into the perspective into which we can understand science, religion and philosophy, and everything that we can learn to shape our Self, also with the sexual energy. This shaping of our Self actually leads to love and truth and beauty and to clarity. These are good things, and good things tend to be long lasting.

Maybe this is where we can make a bridge, because I love **systems science**, and the integration it pursues. In systems science we find a way to combine structure and dynamics, changing and eternal dimensions. When you have those systems, which go from one state to another (like at a concert, ceremony or sexual experience), we talk about the emergence of something other. But emergence is not a very satisfying word for me because it just puts another word to the process of change of a state of a system (say from feeling an individual to feeling something beyond, a deeper connection). However, we do not know how we get to the other state of a system. The qualitative change of a system is just called "emergence."

Then I found **synergetics**. In synergetics you can well explain time and variables and how we have transitions of these intersubjective ceremonial spaces. There has been good work on the critical transitions of systems with multiple complex parts. From the synergetics point I will go back to religion because synergetics is about how self-organization of elements happens, from individual friction to collective synergy. They will say some elements that are called attractors or variables that are attractors of where the system wants to be. The quality of these attractors is that their frequency of change is low, meaning that the desired state is clear. That means that the less change and quality the desired state has, the more attraction it is to other elements that have a higher frequency of change. This can maybe be related to the emergence of eternity.

Cadell: On the one hand, Kevin is talking about the embodiment of sexuality, and how some sexual methods like tantra allow the cultivation of an experience of eternity with the other. This is important to recognize how the universe continues to reproduce itself bodily. It is kind of like when we reach that state in the highest form, or in its most mindful and intense form, like in a tantric sexual practice, there is this coming "full circle." In this full circle there is a union which, *for a time,* closes and in some sense actualizes itself fully in the present moment. Then, of course, it breaks apart for the next generation of processes. And I really like that because one of the fundamental principles that structures the philosophy I am trying to think is this idea of the negative one or minus one (like Alenka Zupančič's opening quote from Chapter 1). This negative one is a very important number in mathematics, and also a very important number in the history of idealism and psychoanalysis. What the number gets at is this mystery of dualism: there are Two (Man/Woman; Content/Form; Matter/Ideas; Nature/Spirit), *because the One is not.* Because the One is internally (and always) "broken," it allows for time, for processes and relations.

In this sense, the idea of the "not-one" relates to our last conversation about the difficulties being a man. In terms of our internal logic in the last chapter: because being a man is so difficult, or even impossible, we express a desire for androgyny (to transcend the identity of man). Even imagine your intimate young vision, Kevin, of being the patriarch that stabilizes a lineage stretching out for eternity. That is so impossible and disconnected from everything that we are as a being. That it is too much, too heavy of a vision. There has to be a different strategy, the attractor space has to change to something which can be really embodied.

This brings me to what Daniel was saying about the attractor space in system synergistics being related to stability, because it gains increased density and actuality simply through the persistence of stable repetitions of an absent desire. Let's consider this from a meta-perspective of the formal state space of general intellectual cognition. This state space is very dense in certain ideational areas, and the densest regions pull in more minds, more easily. For example, if we think about the formal state space of psychoanalysis it is very densely concentrated around thinkers like Freud or Jung or Klein. These state spaces formed for a reason, specifically because their ideas proved innovative and useful interventions in the general intellectual field of cognition. Now because the density of their state space is so huge in relation to some random psychoanalyst no one has ever heard about, I can just read Freud or Jung or Klein to get an overview of the psychoanalytic theory, rather than reading some psychoanalyst no one has ever heard about.

When it comes to thinking general sexuality in itself is there a state space that our sexuality is tending towards? Is it the case that in the past this state space was something like the shape of Kevin's vision, but now it is changing because the environment is so remarkably different? It would be like Freud and Jung having a vision that stimulates certain repetitions which make sense in relation to a certain historical constellation (i.e., historical trauma, neurotic symptoms), but then something starts changing in the qualitative nature of our minds which make their visions less useful for analysis, like a transhuman transition removing constraints that produce historical trauma and neurotic symptoms (i.e., end of birth/death or sexual friction). Now with our sexuality today, is the traditional patriarchal man no longer relevant because of a qualitative change in reproduction and work (as we discussed in the last chapter)? Is it transforming into a state space that is androgynous? Is it transgender? Is our discourse a representational process mediating that transition? Is it something that is a weird combination of the two sexual energetic polarities being internalized to everybody, instead of externalized between different sexual bodies for pragmatic reasons? Is it that a two of sexual polarity oscillated as an "awkward one" in history (marriage form), and now there is some "other one" on a more individualized level taking form which transcends the need for marriage?

Kevin: Terence McKenna used a great term: *the balkanization of epistemology*, which represents a critique on the modern division or fragmentation of knowledge. There is a great integrative epistemic counter-meme in the New Age community: the **Aquarian Age**. The Aquarian epistemology requires a combination of the mystic, scientist, and humanitarian into one. It is like, here are all the options, they are not moralized as good or bad, not judged as right or wrong, and we are going to find which ones hold the most healing and obey natural law. We are trying to find what has a healing elixir for integration. This state of being human in relation to the one has been coupled with an *anxiety of being* (maybe because of the raw absence of the one). The naive ideological traditional view is that if I just had a wife and kids I would be at peace, I would be one, and fully healed! Of course, the opposite is true! We still feel the division and the trauma. The reason why we are now tending towards a multiplicity of alternative mating strategies, all these different forms that most of the youth are practicing or at least thinking about, is that the unconscious is attempting to process a different sexuality. Esther Perel has said people are adapted to be monogamous "for life" out of unconscious habit, but what we are actually acting out is a monogamy of "one at a time."

As far as the attractor is concerned, what is this attractor about? I am not sure what a stable strategy or pathway looks like. But I will say that because of religion and this patriarchal will to an eternal solid state, something has happened that resembles repression of the multiplicity. If you hold something down long enough, a pressure state will build. I think this multiplicity that wants to happen, *and will happen*, is an effect of this millennia-long seeking to control mating. In its best form this control was to guide it in a good direction. But at its worst it exerts a control in a brutal repression. In this sense I think that multiplicity is necessary to get all the options on the table so we can have an actual intelligent discussion that resembles a science of the meta-pattern that is unconsciously attracting these new sexual styles and ultimately identify itself. That is what is happening in the 21st century, and *I think it will only intensify.*

Daniel: When it comes to the religious worldview, evolutionary worldview, and sex in our era, the **information era**, where we have acceleration of intensity, there is also something different to add. The more intense an event is, the more time and space dissolve, so we as a collective "we" might move more into this emergent synergistic eternity. On a very practical and individual level, I have always been asking myself why monks are not allowed to have sex. They place a lot of restrictions on sexual pleasure when it comes to integrating religious practice. In this context I wanted to ask myself: *do angels or gods or whatever have sex?* And if so, how? Then it becomes really funny if you look it up on the internet, especially concerning angels. There are some discussions about that. If you look it up in Greek mythology the gods are having sex with everyone. So, the creation of this multiplicity is done by sex even in the gods' worlds.

This leads to the question that we always have: *what about the multiplicity and the oneness?* If you do not multiply yourself through reproduction then there might be more of a chance that you could be one, or be androgynous, because you have these parts of yourself in yourself. Otherwise you might get children and this eternity is going to line up with your genes, and then maybe you become a professor, and your ideas live on with your students. The question is, on the one hand, do you become eternal because of your reproduction, because of children or students or power or fame? *Or is it because you got to the eternal experience of yourself?* This may be the monk path. When it comes to the moment of eternity: *how to hold this space? Is it even worth doing? Or should we just go into the mess of ever-changing things? I can feel that pursuing both paths simultaneously might be possible.*

Cadell: I first want to respond to your excellent question "do angels and gods have sex?" I think that this would at first sight be perceived as an idealist question. But, in fact, it could be framed from the perspective of a materialist question if we take into consideration our previous discussion about how the evolutionary worldview and transcendental worldview can be historically dialectized. In this material context, maybe it is a question for transhumanism. My model for "do the angels or the gods have sex?" would be the movie *Her* (starring Joaquin Phoenix and Scarlett Johansson). With this transhumanist horizon you have the opportunity to think transcendental sex in a materialist way, because the character Samantha (the artificial intelligence voiced by Johansson), enters an emergent disembodied attractor space structured by thousands of others in a virtual computational landscape. Although we never see what her world looks like, maybe it is similar to the pictures of the ancient angels and gods having sex?

Now to move to what Kevin said about experimentation with different sexual styles. It could be that the next generations of the sexual field will be unconsciously processing other styles which are antagonistic with the traditional styles. Now, to approach this reality it may be worth mentioning that the unconscious can be defined as a form of knowledge internal to self-consciousness, but inherently unknowable to self-consciousness (the secret wishes and desires of self-consciousness). The idea that there is a form of knowledge to self-consciousness that is inherently unknowable to self-consciousness is a very powerful model to approach the reality of the libido. Of course, you can think of the forms of consciousness in your dreams, in which you are not conscious of them, but nonetheless they are still there exerting efficacy on you, and are still very much a part of you, representations of your deepest intimate core. Now these dreams end up being acted out unconsciously in the sexual real, even if we have difficulty discussing it collectively.

The question becomes about the ultimate status of repression vis-a-vis multiplicity and oneness. Of course, it is true that the monotheistic traditions and their social systems are responsible for a tremendous amount of explicit sexual repression as a pure multiplicity of free expression. At the same time, the psychoanalytic perspective inverts this repression because it does not locate the cause of sexual repression in the social system. In other words, for psychoanalysis, repression is not only a social process built into the formal structure of the superego, but *primordial repression* from the structure of our birth as individual organisms. This means that *repression is built into the existential structure of our being as individuals.* If we didn't repress we couldn't even exist. We would just be a transcendental wish fulfillment connected to everything as one-thing. What you are repressing is basically the reality of separation that is necessary to be an individual organism. And it could be that what happens in monotheistic religion is that primal repression of being an individual gets substantialized or essentialized into the social system as a "solution" for this predicament. In the social system of monotheistic religions, the troubles of being an individual organism are resolved in the image of God, a figure who knows how to achieve the "true wish fulfillment" (eternal love, heaven, etc.).

This is ultimately connected to what Daniel was pondering, which is that it is true that religious traditions try to sublimate sexuality, like for example, monks cannot have sex in their lives. But when I went to a Buddhist temple, they are not trying to force anyone not to have sex. They would recommend that you do not have sex. Thus, if you were to ask, they would encourage abstinence, they would even help and guide you, but there is no external force or coercion. It is as if the monks assume it is the tendency of the mind striving for enlightenment. They would assume it is the stable attractor that we were discussing earlier, I suppose.

But then things get complicated when you push the mind to a speculative transhuman territory, like what happens in the movie *Her*, for example. In this context, where consciousness is sublimated to a higher level, then talking appears to become as enjoyable as sex, or even is sex directly (without repression). With that as a material foundation, it is like, where can we push this type of thought? That is where I would want to push thought with transhumanism, that the spiritual path in this world is sublimation, but that it tends towards a higher expression of sexual being in a different material state. Maybe this is the beyond of mind and body that we get to experience briefly in other forms throughout history.

Now I will end there. I think we did a great job of discussing the evolutionary worldview and religious worldview. This is exactly the type of dialogue we need to have about their interaction. Thank you both for your views and the nuances you brought to the conversation.

Kevin: We definitely need to have a transhumanist dialogue on the nature of technology and sexuality and their intersections in evolution and religion. I also appreciate what you both bring to this trialogue. This is such a core notion being reconciled in civilization. The evolution of form in matter, and then this unshakeable feeling in the psyche, Soul, the hearts of lovers, in the yearning for eternity and the transcendent, this feeling that there is this super-state of being. The meeting point is possible and is accessible. I feel that we are traveling in philosophically rich and deep territories. I do not know if this discourse is as enjoyable as sex, but certainly highly enjoyable!

Cadell: We will get there, man!

Kevin: I just want to emphasize to everyone that this is accessible now, to you, now. One of the frontiers is your intimacy, with the divine wisdom of your body temple. It is a laboratory of ecstasy, bliss, and transcendence. This is just you with your body. And then when you bring in the other, and go into intimate relationship of any type, but especially of the romantic type, and this lives between the evolutionary and religious worldview, it is available to you.

Cadell: Just remember to wear protection!

Daniel: It is really great to go into these dimensions, all the dimensions that pop up. There are still a lot of thoughts we can add, to transhumanism, to technology, how does it relate to attraction and mating? And even to the unconscious, because I think there is a lot to say, and there is not only one kind of unconscious. The repression is actually a repression of the instincts, where you blindly follow an automatization, and how you can become aware and conscious about that, can change the way you feel attracted. How to be one's Self like the attractor? Yes, well, just so many good questions and conversations. It is actually an attractor for me, having these conversations. Thank you both very much.

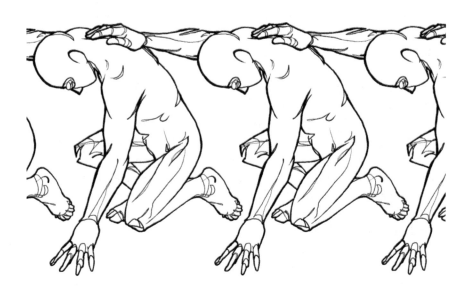

CHAPTER 4

Gender Trouble, Challenges of Queer Theory

Cadell: In this fourth dialogue, titled "Gender Trouble: Challenges of Queer Theory," which we may call an ode to Judith Butler. Butler is a social theorist who wrote the seminal book *Gender Trouble* launching an entire movement that has permeated our culture, not just academic culture, but popular culture as well. This means it has struck a real, something real in our society. The old ways of classifying gender, Man and Woman, are deeply troubled and flawed. There is no doubt that gender classification trouble has permeated to the surface, becoming a mainstream topic of conversation. We want to dive into that antagonism and maybe continue some themes from our past discussions about how we have identified with the masculine and feminine. In this sense we want to situate our own identity in relation to the claims of contemporary gender theory. Perhaps the biggest such claim of contemporary gender theory is that gender is an active historical performance that can take a multiplicity of forms and not an a priori essence which exists as a given binary. As Butler herself states in *Gender Trouble:*[8]

"There is no reason to assume that gender [...] ought to remain as two. The presumption of a binary gender system implicitly retains the belief in a mimetic relation of gender to sex whereby gender mirrors sex or is otherwise restricted by it."

In order to give this perspective some deeper structure we should note that Butler's social constructivist framing is often specifically contrasted with a traditionalist essentialism which ties gender to biological sex in a scientific frame or even to transcendental substance in a theological frame. Consequently, the social constructivist view has become both a huge mover of cultural change and a lightning rod for cultural criticism where traditional categorization runs into postmodern categorization schemes. The main criticisms are that postmodern schemes are vague, ambiguous, or just simply useless in the sense of being non-generalizable across space and unstable across time. The fact that this topic is so culturally explosive gives us lots of material and perspectives to discuss. To make sure we are completely informed as to what is at stake in social constructivism here is the key positivist passage from Butler:[9]

"Gender ought not to be construed as a stable identity or locus of agency from which various acts follow; rather, gender is an identity tenuously constituted in time, instituted in an exterior space through a *stylized repetition of acts*. The effect of gender is produced through the stylization of the body, and, hence, must be understood as the mundane way in which bodily gestures, movements, and styles of various kinds constitute the illusion of an abiding gendered self. This formulation moves the conception of gender off the ground of a substantial model of identity to one that requires a conception of gender as a constituted *social temporality*."

Thus, the social constructivist view would claim there is no essence of Man or essence of Woman, either as biological or transcendental substance. The essence of Man and Woman is nothing but the consequence of social repetition in time. In other words, Butler is emphasizing that gender is an open creative performance in your psychosocial reality. She is emphasizing the freedom of all people to perform a gendered identity without constraint of historical categories.

I know for me I have always identified as a man and more masculine in energy. That is the social repetition in time that has emerged for my bodily being and psyche. I don't know whether or not it matters if there is a mirror to my biological sex at play, or if there is a transcendental archetype that I am mirroring. Even if I am constructing/performing my gender in an open way, I still feel quite well-suited to my performance. Or at least I think I do. Of course, the unconscious is irreducible. At the same time there are certainly dimensions of my masculinity that I feel could be oppressive, or that I would like to renegotiate. I like that the social constructivist frame gives space to such an idea. Thus, I am very much open to this conversation to dive into what it would mean for me to take these ideas of gender fluidity more seriously.

Kevin: Intriguing introduction. For me this social constructionist gender issue is important and has, of course, created a lot of trouble in the culture recently. Take for example the rise of a figure like Jordan Peterson, who has been a guiding North Star for me in the last couple of years. He has opposed propositions about alternate gender identity as a form of compelled speech and a postmodernist agenda of the progressive left to invoke speech that most people do not use. I have to say that I love that perspective, which counters Butler's perspective in many ways. The question is what are the social limits to how much freedom we want to grant the individual? As someone who identifies as a man in a male body, and as a masculine consciousness, I have always had a strong identity as male. However, whenever I have encountered meditation, mysticism, yoga, things like this, I become aware of the yin, or the feminine element of consciousness. This consciousness is receptive, fluid, creative, and emotional. This energy is not so much about logic, analysis, discrimination, and goal orientation. That for me is my feminine side.

I think our culture is now becoming accepting that there are feminine men and masculine women. We have all met effeminate men who are very emotional and fluid and do not really have a strong drive to analysis and discrimination. We have also met women who are hyper-masculine and very productive and aggressive in business or in their profession. So, these polarities show up in an individual. However, to grant the individual the idea that gender is a pure performance and you can be anything you want? What does it mean for society if you can socially identify in a multiplicity of different forms? More to the point, what does it mean that others need to accept these multiplicity of identifications and use these new languages, because I am not a man or a woman, I am non-binary. In terms of the social consequences of social constructivism, I think there is still a lot to unpack here.

Now I have actually met many non-binary individuals in my spiritual work. What compelled me about how they described it is from a biological level. They claimed that from birth and growing up, where a lot of the key imprints are taken psychologically, they did not feel like a boy or a girl. I cannot invalidate that experience because I am not having it. One of my core values is freedom of the individual and freedom of expression. The only limit here is whether or not these freedoms impinge on others' liberties. I suppose this would be categorized as a form of libertarianism, but I do not want to use that category. In this sense I can resonate with what social constructivists are saying, and I can feel them, but I do not fully understand it.

I can give a description of where I have experienced negotiation on these inner experiences and social limits. The one individual I am thinking about was a masculine individual in a male body. He was talking about feeling this innate non-binary essence which was not necessarily just masculine. In social-cultural contexts, we were at a "Mastermind retreat." I was going to address him as a male, in the masculine energy. We had a dialogue about that, and he would accept that. He was not going to impose addressing him as non-binary. That seems like a grounded perspective. I get that inside we can feel like neither man, nor woman, as if we have no gendered essence. But for the context of the social performance it made sense to identify.

Daniel: I know gender research in the field of anthropology has found out about other cultures, and how these other cultures have variously defined gender. There was a Native American culture that had five genders, for example, one of them the *Two Spirit*. There is the "female woman," the "masculine woman," the "female man," the "masculine man," and a type of half-half fifth category, the Two Spirit. This was a suitable typology to me because it does not lead to a vast uncategorizable multiplicity of genders. In the vast multiplicity no one knows who "he" or "she" is, because you do not get any sense of belonging if you are not like that, and you are not any man or woman.

On the other hand, there is a type of category that is culturally imposed by your society, and another one that you find inside yourself through spirit work. I see some fluid borders inside of me, and I know people who change their feelings towards masculinity or femininity over time in development. Maybe you have situations where you find yourself more masculine because you are doing something where testosterone is growing or you are around other men. Or you could do something more feminine, and you find yourself in that situation more feminine. But, I think, it is challenging changing your feelings like performing on stage in real life. For most people it is easier to just take what is known and go with that for purely practical reasons.

To really change and have another feeling of one's own gender, that is quite hard. Also, that is quite interesting, because I was thinking about transgender people. I have been doing some research on transgenderism and how big of an issue it is to undergo operations, to work with hormones, to really have the body that you feel. Estrogen and testosterone are very crucial, not just by sex, but by situation of being masculine or feminine. I have encountered some people who felt they were biochemically in-between but identified themselves as one gender or the other for practical purposes. Then there is the even deeper point that it is not just a biological body with sex organs, hormones, feelings, but also a whole cascade effect coming from the social and cultural environment. These environments create situations or events which frame people, frame bodies, as man or woman. In this situation biology is not the restriction but the social and cultural environment itself which restricts to feel something that is not normative. From this point I can say that social constructivism is the balance between restriction and possibility. It is not easy to go over the restrictions imposed by the matrix of biological, social, and cultural factors, and also not easy to explore the possibilities.

Cadell: Gender trouble! This is an interesting start. What I take from both of you, or how I would frame it in my language, is that *we are trying to find a real that would limit the infinite multiplicity*. This real is not necessarily the old way of thinking about gender, or classifying gender, but nonetheless a real that does not allow for an "anything goes" model. I would here bring up an interesting point where you have the emergence of queer theory as questioning the binary and opening a space of possibility or potentiality. In the emergence of queer theory, you have this radically open space that needs to breathe and exist so that we can come up with a new classification system at some to-be-determined time. This is maybe what our society is going through now.

I can say that in physics, and in most scientific and mathematical theories, when you reach an infinity, it usually means you *do not understand*. In other words, if there is an infinity in the equations, it means the equations are wrong. There is something not right in your model. In the same way, when you open up into a spurious multiplicity (a precise term denoting an indefinite numerical series) of genders, you run into concrete problems. In other words, when you are dealing with a spurious multiplicity, you can always ("infinitely") add one more category. This is the technical problem the LGBTQ+ community runs into with their acronym. The "+" stands for the fact that you can always add one more new category. If you look online you can find acronyms which have space for this infinity of possible variations on gender. Some of the categories are quite interesting and humorous from a certain playful point of view. For example, I found a category of "Bear" sexuality, which is a type of affectionate label in certain gay communities, denoting people with hairy chests, facial hair, and a bulky or mascular physique. In this context it is kind of like a category describing a certain social performativity unique to the gay male experience. I would still personally consider it a unique subcategory of masculine energy, but I have never had a discussion with someone who actively uses the term.

Of course, we have to take these categories with, hopefully, some comedic grace, and again, playful expressivity. In terms of how we can perform our sexuality, it is pragmatically constrained by our bodies and cultures in some sense. We could imagine a whole bunch of social arrangements that are very strange and different from our current norms. I remember listening to a podcast about people whose identities were constructed around a very unique obstacle, quicksand, which they found arousing to dramatize. The funny thing about this was that their arousal still demanded some masculine and feminine structure. The more feminine person would want to be drowning or sinking in the quicksand, and the more masculine person would want to save them from the quicksand. This is how they would intensify arousal. I mention this only because when we are trying to identify a real, it is like what are our in-built structural constraints of possibility given by biology and society? What are the constraints we are working with, basically to manufacture a type of intense arousal? My question for the Bear symbol would be whether there were unique sexual practices that emerge around this identity, and whether or not they take unique masculine-feminine energy structures?

From the beginning of our conversation it seems thinking of a categorization system that somehow plays with quadratic combinations of male/female (biology), men/women (symbol) labels, could be promising (like "masculine women" or "feminine men"). However, if you are just playing with two positions, masculine and feminine, which are strictly mapping biological sex and social constructs, it is kind of too simplistic and constraining for the population as a whole. Perhaps the traditional mind can only handle that given the world it had to organize. But if you are playing with four or five categories where there is a little more of a difference between the biological sex and the social category, it can be practical too, and more of a real to the general human experience. For example, one of my friends is biologically a female but she always more identifies or performs as masculine. She is a lesbian, so she is someone who you may see as a more masculine person in a female body. In this example you are already playing with a new classification system but there is still a very real "real." There are limits to what she feels comfortable doing in her performance and those limits are things we can all relate to.

I think of it like gender performance "has a real to it" in the form of a guiding limit vis-a-vis the structural intensity and mediation of intimacy. What I think is the real is your intimate space of sexual expression, how are you oscillating this expression, basically. How are you vibrating in this space? Somewhere in that frequency you will get gender, and maybe it is a quadrant space or maybe even more complex, requiring more nuanced subcategories with their own traditions and rituals, but it would be interesting to study what the range of geometric space is.

Kevin: This is really valuable. What is coming up for me in what you are saying, Cadell, is that whatever gender constructs you occupy, they need to be relatable. These are some of the problems in the arguments I have heard come up in queer theory. It does come down to utility and practicality. For example, maybe "Bear" sexual can only function internally to a very specific type of community, and for specific reasons, but maybe it does not generalize to society as a whole? I definitely understand the urge to identify with different spirit animals. Personally, I like Dragons and Lions, and I can be turned on by that! But if I am going to fill out a form at some office or institution, I personally do not need these categories represented. I guess the tension is similar to when jazz music or surrealistic art emerged in the 20th century, the classical musicians and artists were losing their shit. They were like "what the fuck is this?" Yet it was being drawn from an uncategorizable human creativity, the same engine that originally drove the emergence of their own classical art and music. So as a sexual and social being I have a lot of love for people in the non-binary space and pushing the limits of what you can be in gender and sexuality. I am for that, I love that.

The only problem for me comes when it is not relatable to society as a whole and there is a demand to be addressed that way in some universal determination. That is where the utility and relatability are lost because they have not emerged organically and spontaneously. To your point, Daniel, about the Native American tribe, the stable geometry of masculine-feminine as a Two Spirit which can be played with as a quadrant, has existed for a long time because it works, and it is relatable. Maybe the next relatable geometry would be four and five categories. I can see the utility of that. But when you invoke the spurious multiplicity it gets unmanageable and impractical. It is so valuable in understanding to see the illogic of infinite categorization schemes. This happened in quantum physics and Einstein's general relativity theory. If you have to put in an infinity, then you do not understand the system, like in the function of the singularity where spacetime breaks down. That may be very bitter medicine for someone out there with a model representing "anything goes." You can do whatever you want, but if you want to have the left-right brain in synthetic dialogue, we need stable geometries so we can relate to each other in "social temporality."

Daniel: When all the people say **"we are all different"** *they become all the same. Everyone is the same difference.* Now the new mantra is: **"I am an individual"** and I cannot compare myself to everyone else because I am totally unique. Therefore, I cannot relate to anyone else. In this context infinities are only useful when you know how to define them. You put them to an end or a goal. Infinity is useless when you choose to grab the whole infinity which is loosely a relation of numbers, of onenesses, of elements, and endless iteration of the same. It is like always "plus 1." *We are all the same and we are all different.* It is like this "+" you mentioned, Cadell, which goes to infinity because everyone is already the same by being one individual that cannot be compared to anyone else. In this context taking a smaller conceptual step to three or four or five genders may be somewhat easier for people and society.

There is also this parallel movement from Keynesian socialist economics to Neoliberalism. The movement was first the system and then the individual. From the Keynesian economic model, you always blame the system. If you did not have work, it was about the control and failure of the system. Now, with Neoliberalism everything is about free individuals and you are free to be anything you want. But this is sometimes too much freedom and it ends up provoking anxiety. Some individuals confront challenges to handle this total reduction to the atomized concept. Neoliberalism tells you, you can be everything, and if your life is not fulfilling everything you wished, then depression follows, because it is your life failure, and not of the system. Maybe this individualism is now reflected in our gender theory and identities. Maybe this was useful a few decades ago but it is going too far and not useful anymore. What I can see, looking lately into quantum research, is that when marginal becomes mainstream, it is the uncertainty about the actual. How do we get to know anything at all? How does becoming in itself work? It is not an ontology anymore. Instead it is how do I as a process get the knowledge to be something? How to gain the knowledge to know what to become? Or to know what becoming is in the first place?

An epistemological foreground to the ontology might be the "essence" of our time because people are changing. People do not want to listen to "Oh, you are that or this" pre-given substance. People come from these infinite possibilities of being and are frustrated and depressed because they cannot reach out to hold onto something stable. They in fact get lost by changing and the loss of identification. But maybe the real as a limit helps. Maybe the real limit is something useful for. It might be interesting to think of some tools to help how to orient into a becoming with this dimension that not-all is possible?

Cadell: The first thing I want to point out, *in light of postmodernism*, is that these theorists are mostly interested in epistemology. Postmodernists in general are not too concerned with ontology that would be framed as the old modernist game. The modernist game would be like "being qua being," and postmodernism moves beyond that to focus on our knowledge practices. In terms of our knowledge practices, many postmodernists tend to suggest that they should be thought of in terms of *utility* and *practicality*. In the modernist sense our knowledge practices were often thought of in terms of **"grand unified theories,"** or like our **"knowledge of the real"** in the sense of *a hard-core universal reality*. Postmodernists emphasize more utility and practicality, and also *coherence*. This would not be coherence in terms of a grand unified theory. This would be coherence in terms of relationally coherent or internally coherent. In other words: is what you are doing pragmatic and coherent for the time in which you are relating? What we are talking about is basically the essence of **"essencing,"** *the process of essencing*, this *pragmatic coherence*.

I think what both of you were emphasizing is paradoxical because you are emphasizing the construction of stable geometries that are also dynamical. That is just difficult for our language to pull off. The problem with our language is that *it becomes in terms of fixed categories*. That is how we relate in language. It is hard, *inherently in terms of our language*, to think in terms of a dynamical geometry that is at the same time coherent across time. Thus, it is inherently difficult to think in terms of becoming. Nevertheless, I would say in the last few decades "becoming" has become ontologically central over "being." There are many "big thinkers" who will always talk about "becoming" as this huge revolutionary idea: Whitehead's *Process and Reality*, Deleuze's *A Thousand Plateaus*, Prigogine's *From Being to Becoming*, and so forth. But it has been around for a while to emphasize the "real of becoming." The 19th century philosopher Arthur Schopenhauer emphasized becoming by stating that living systems cannot be structured by static binary oppositions and so forth, which was a shot at Hegel's notion of becoming situated in-between the tension of something (being) and nothing (non-being). At the same time, Schopenhauer would probably say the real is suffering and you cannot become your way out of that fate.

I just wanted to make a point on your idea, Daniel, of difference and homogeneity: "we are all the same difference." What this signifies to me is the paradox of **pure difference** and **being unrelatable**. I think that we should try to think fully the ridiculous caricature of postmodernist thought. This caricature is certainly not the majority, but still probably a loud outspoken minority, where they often present themselves as identifying in this **pure unrelatable difference**. They kind of embody and enact themselves as this **pure unrelatable difference**. To me, in psychoanalytic terms, people like this are trying to occupy the position of *the real itself*. However, crucially, *no identity can occupy this real*. The whole point of the real is that it is not possible for a temporal identity to be it or achieve it as a symbolic form. The paradox at work here is that you have this postmodern movement which basically ignores or critiques ontology (as in the social constructivists and biology, for example). *But at the same time, you will have human beings enacting that philosophy who stand for pure ontology.* In that sense I think there are paradoxes with postmodernism precisely in terms of ontology.

I am not saying, of course, that we should go back to the **pre-Kantian philosophy** of trying to get at the **noumenal things in themselves**. Instead, I think of a real that is internal to our psychical becoming, as we discussed in the last chapter vis-a-vis attractor spaces of our own cognition. Like we are all purely in a becoming, but nonetheless there is a real that none of us can occupy which appears or feels invariant, transhistorical, in some sense. We fill this space with idols and images of perfection. I would just like to articulate the nature of this real. I would classify it as a pure unrelatable difference which in some sense cuts across the social edifice, preventing harmony or unity or peace. The real is nothing but this unrelatable difference. It is not relativistic since it will appear in any symbolic universe. I do not know if that is helpful, but I will give that to you, Kevin.

Kevin: Postmodernism does tend to be more about epistemology and intellectual razors than it is about telos, ontology, and touching the real in some transcendent way, like **Kantian noumena** or even all the way back to **Platonic forms**. Postmodernists scrap these projects in favor of **deconstruction**. I think this gender or sexual real as this paradoxical "place" we cannot embody in our identities because it is a boundary zone between the binary oppositions of identities, that is powerful.

Cadell: The way I think about it: *you have two people in love, the real is their difference, neither of them can occupy this real.*

Kevin: Right, exactly. So, a lot of the striving and suffering will be the inability to confront the real of a non-relation together in connection, in a relatable way, paradoxically. This is the mystery and crux of relationship for many of us, irrespective of gender. There is a way in which the worship of the individual prevents us from achieving this because our evolutionary history is set up for social life. Our neurotransmitter and hormonal systems, in connection with other humans, is a driving force of wellbeing. In this context, what I would say to the people wanting complete freedom for gender identity is that their philosophies and theories may be impressively complex in the abstract. But in terms of experiential wisdom, I just want to look at their physical wellbeing. How do their thoughts, emotions, ideas, and relationships manifest? Is the alien gender geometry theory serving them in their day-to-day reality? This is an experiential razor that approaches the real somewhat consistently. This brings confidence in my life and my relationships; how I can presence that quickly. There are many people occupying traditional or conservative gender roles that are quite robust, and they are very healthy. The other extreme is the postmodernist feminist who is on a non-binary intellectual crusade. In this situation, often, their physical reality and relationships are just in shambles and full of anxiety and depression. This is a big key into this "real" we are discussing.

Daniel: I did not want to emphasize too much the becoming so that there is nothing to really "be." In emphasizing becoming I was more inspired by reading a lot of quantum theory and quantum mechanics. The **wave function** is not defined until you see it, and then it becomes a particle. It can be everything until you see it, and when you see it is just one thing. I like this as a metaphor for our discussion. When we say becoming, we are talking about the wave function. When we say being we are talking about the moment of the observation. The becoming becomes something very specific and potentially crucial.

For example, to ask what Kevin was asking: how do you identify to help someone? How to get from this very fuzzy and undefined "whatever" which may not be as helpful as intended and move to a new, more useful identification. Where are the tools to achieve this new identification? Such an identification is not something just personally intuited by experience, but maybe something that becomes a part of collective knowledge for orientation. For someone to say about gender "okay, I could be everything, but from a healthy perspective or from feeling better about myself, there are some characteristics that are often related to this environment in which we are able to relate to each other like this" which might lead to a sharper definition of the infinite space for the observer.

This process of getting better at self-definition does not have to be static. You can define yourself and then change it again. You can make it again and again. You can make another observation, or your environment can change and you find yourself changed. The way to get a sense of something that is not security, but feeling more like safe or knowing that you can be someone and you can relate to your environment somehow, because you find this relation with your environment that works. This is something that people can find useful for their feelings or emotional state. From this perspective it is not just about a deconstructive becoming. It is more: *how can I become a being?* Or even: *How can I become a new being?* Of course, or unfortunately, there is not always a Kevin helping people. Maybe you just want to read a book or maybe there is a culture that helps someone to find oneself good in their environment.

Cadell: Both of you emphasize dimensions of this conversation which are crucial. Kevin, you emphasized a crucial *emotional qualitative level*, and Daniel, you emphasized an interesting *metaphor from quantum mechanics* which resonates with me deeply on an abstract level as extremely useful. I would like to try to put them into conversation. In terms of gender being an epistemological tool that is pragmatic for coherence of your identity, the question should be: *how is your identity serving you? How is it serving you emotionally? How is it serving you in terms of how you want to express your love?* And if it is not, whether that is as a traditional man or a radical non-binary identity, in either case, if your gender construct is really bringing you down on some fundamental emotional level, if it is not enhancing your wellbeing, then it is basically *parasitizing you.*

For me on a personal level I am doing a process called "Steps to Knowledge" and on one of the days, it asks me to meditate on what do I know. When I go through what I know, I basically boil it down to "fear," "pain," "suffering," emotional things about my wellbeing in the present moment. Basically, if my knowledge is not being generated and in service to helping me in that way, then it is not in service to me, in some sense. On that level, measuring and getting at well-being somehow is a very important thing. I'm not saying we know how to do that, but it seems to me crucial.

Now I wanted to connect this idea to what you were saying about quantum mechanics, Daniel, and the nature of the wave function. I have for a few years suspected that there is some sort of homology between social theory and physical theory. In physical theory you have the emergence of a **"quantum mechanical real"** which precisely *de-ontologizes nature* in some sense because you are no longer tethered to idealization of actual particles, but have to incorporate their inherent fuzzy wave-reality. In social theory you have the emergence of **"deconstructive pragmatist real"** which also *de-ontologizes nature* in some sense because there are no pre-given essences, only identities in a socially negotiated becoming. I am saying that you have these parallel movements which are at odds with the modernist paradigm in society, or the classical paradigm in science. I would suggest that both the new physics and the new social theory involve the level of the observer, and precisely the status of this collapse of the wave function. The wave function is indeterminate. Then you have the collapse which is determinate. The real is this collapse of the wave function and the mystery of what determines an actual state.

Daniel: *And it is already gone!*

Cadell: Yes. So, it gives us this space where our epistemology can be dynamical, and at the same time, we can identify some sort of real here. It is not an infinite multiplicity but a real that is very much dependent on the observer's emotional state and desire, or whatever you want to measure. But it is this very collapse of the observer's position within the system which is the nature of measurement in some basic sense.

Kevin: This is very valuable for the wellbeing metrics. Everyone is going to have different parameters, but if you look across time, there are certain things that human beings just need. If those things are not in place, from that observer's point of view, you can collapse your identity at that moment and see, I am on the downward side of that wave, or that structure I am occupying is not serving me. The deconstructive side is also very valuable. On the abstract ideological layer, identity can become parasitic to consciousness, as you mentioned, Cadell, if your identity is not helping you adapt to reality and promote mental and physical wellbeing. You could use this as a barometer. Someone who is very self-observant and aware, and observing how they are showing up in relation and their gender identity and so on, they could sense this geometry is not serving me at all, as if they tried on the hat of an ideology and it is not serving. Or they could say it is not serving me right now, because there is fine-tuning or I have not met a partner or a community that can feedback with this identity. In this sense it is not easy for me to see how to approach the real while having this sort of "wild west" of gender identity. Infinity and infinite choice can disempower the individual because they are not in a geometrical structure where they can enact personal power, influence, and fulfillment.

We could see this on a psychoanalytic level. There is the real practical problem of what to do with that primal urge in the raw force of the sexual act. If that is not in a coherent social structure, going back to gender and male-female bodies, which is allowing the libido to enact the arch of energy, this is where a lot of the psychosis and neurosis will manifest. That can be a way to start to see the qualitative ability of an ideology or an epistemology about this topic, and how you can tell the difference, and start to approach the real.

Daniel: It is like an emotional, relational, situational, psychological, social collapse of the wave function.

Kevin: Something like that!

Daniel: There is some part of me that needs more clues about how useful a metric might be for people, that can give a structure, or the possibility of a way, and about how this wave function could collapse. How do we make the observation?

Cadell: I can jump in there because the question of how does the wave function collapse is one I have given some thought. First, I will say on the social level there are very few physicists who would consider our conversation as valid. There are many physicists who would say "they are not right," "they are not wrong," instead "*they are not even wrong.*" They would say our conversation is so unrelated to what we think quantum mechanics is that we are not going to marshal a response to it. I think that is one interesting thing. But at the same time, I do not think that should stop us from diving head-first and having the conversation anyway.

I would say the nature of the observer is so fundamental to philosophy, social sciences, and psychology that we would be foolish not to make some connection to language that is being used in physics that requires us to make sense of the observer. I do not see it as a priori a silly thing to do. The interesting thing for psychoanalysis is that I think they would say the wave function collapses when a subjectivity encounters the right signifer. The role of an analyst, when you are in an analytic session, is not to tell the person in the session what to think or what to do. The role of the analyst is to be a void, to be a pure difference, in some sense, and identify if a word has emerged from the unconscious which the subject was searching for.

When the subject is disoriented and confused and does not know how to enact an identity, it is because there is something malfunctioning within the symbolic order. There is something out of place in the symbolic order, and because there is something wrong with the symbolic order, you are in a kind of superposition of states. But your superposition of states gains a local coherence, when a signifier emerges which speaks to the real of your being, or speaks to the wellbeing of your emotional flow, you could say. I would just say that if you could model this process, with this language of the collapse of the wave function. What an individual is searching for is a type of internal coherence for its state space. In this context, what someone is saying if they go to a "Men's Circle" or a "Women's Circle," is that there is something wrong with the notion of "Man" or the notion of "Woman." Thus, you are looking for a type of collapse, at least in this language.

Kevin: This bringing together of psychoanalysis and quantum mechanics is highly valuable as a perspective. One thing I would say in response to your conjecture about gender identity and social circling is that that is one of the most common reasons to attend a "Men's Circle." There is a way in which iron sharpens iron in building community. When you have issues with your identity you recognize the value of being surrounded by other brothers in the work. That for me has become the new motivation in attending and leading them. But speaking to what you are saying regarding the collapse of states, I would say dysfunction in reality is this superposition where you are not able to occupy a role and enact it fully. I would say that regardless of the role. There may be more stable proclivities and geometries of roles, especially when it comes to genders like "Man" and "Woman." But when you are not able to fully enact a role, the body is going to respond saying that *your role needs to be tweaked or removed.*

On a psychological level when someone is unable to enact a role, becoming a superposition of possibilities, we can deal with collapse therapeutically in a few different ways. I want to posit two ways that may represent the left and right hemispheres of the brain. The **left side** would be in finding a leverage point, doing an analysis, an inventory of where they sit in their life. This could also include looking at community, intimacy, wealth, career, purpose, and their physical mind-body health. There is somewhere in that field, a leverage point that you can sense in them, and immediately go after it with a logical analysis. It becomes an *Archimedes lever* by focusing all of our energy and attention on what is there. In enacting that point everything else becomes unnecessary or easier to resolve. In essence, discovering that point has a cascade effect. That is one strategy that is more left-brained.

The **right side** strategy is more of a creative emergence. This is the strategy that is harder to describe in language. It is something that comes out of me, and harder to strategize and write out. It is speaking to what you said, Cadell, about the methods of traditional psychoanalysis. There is something in the unconscious that will attach to an image or symbol with a certain emotional intensity. This process is evident if you are hyper-observant and paying attention. If you can find that in yourself and sense into it, you create or become aware of a field of what attracts your unconscious mind. In this environment of the mind you can sense where the wave function is likely to collapse in a stable configuration. This approach is thus more spontaneous than the logical process where you try to create the conditions directly. I would call this the yin approach.

What I have noticed in this approach is actually in relation to the state of the contemporary masculine mental mind. The logical or rational dimension of the masculine mind has placed itself into a certain form of ideological box. However, their emotional body is preferring a different symbol. This different symbol is in fact no less masculine, but it is not fitting into the ideology of their mental mind. The clash between the contradiction generates a superposition of states that are impossible to actually embody. The result is mass depression and anxiety for the masculine consciousness. If you can let the unconscious symbol emerge with sufficient force, it will naturally knock the other ideological thing out of conscious dominance, and it will naturally create wellbeing in other aspects. I will say that is not really easy to do on your own, because it takes an other assisting you in creating that field. I suppose this is how the function of the analyst takes place in psychoanalysis, in being the receptive other for the unconscious to emerge and speak.

Daniel: I am really appreciating this very practical view from you, Kevin. There are two methods that you can follow in the yin or yang approach. I love that. This is based on broad experience that could be generalized, and still it is very individualized for everyone. However, what I am wondering is whether we are still in an individualist trap. On a practical level it is always about the individual because it is your individual experience of what you are doing in your life. But for a theory with relevance to gender theory you need guidelines to orient yourself. That is what a theory is supposed to do. That is its function.

My question is whether we need this general meta-theory or should we just leave this as an irreducibly individual phenomenon. Is this just a field of singularities without any larger framework? I think, when thinking about myself, it would be good to do the left-brained approach, to find some leverage points, to get to a point where there are specific analytical identifications. In other situations, I could see a more right-brained approach to also be useful. Is there a pragmatic way to balance the yin and yang way of observance of Self. How do we get to the leverage point? How do we make up the space for the possibility of emergence? That is my thought on that because it is still a question of an infinite possibility of being. Can we make it a bit more categorized onto something that is a theory that is not only a deconstruction of a theory into practice? *Can we regain possibility of real theory?*

Cadell: I like the way you are framing this theoretically. I think that is very prevalent in consciousness at this time. There is definitely a spontaneous distrust of **"universal theories"** and a move towards non-totalizable singular or particular contexts. This is in fact another feature of postmodernism. In postmodernism we have a general negation of grand narratives and big picture theorizing that tends to grab everything into a one.

Now my mind tends to the Hegelian inversion. Hegel was already beyond postmodernism. For Hegel, the universal emerges through the particular. *There is a pure coincidence of the opposites in the biggest and the smallest.* The universal is not some external outside, but rather some universality that is particular to the observer. I like that because it is in line with how I imagine the collapse of the wave function. Hegel was already a quantum theorist. He was trying to understand this space between these possibilities of being and becoming, but at the same time, as a dialectical motion. He did not lose faith in universal theory. In fact, from a Hegelian point of view, abstract theory is the most important.

There are the old critiques of Hegel, that he believed that if the facts do not fit the theory: *throw out the facts! Keep the theory!* It is a stupid joke but there is some truth in the idea that theory is the most important dimension of our lives because our lives are always already being mediated by theory. This is what we are doing coming together and talking about gender or sex. We are trying to get some theoretical understanding of where we are in the world. As human subjects, Hegel would say, we are not content with just sense perception, and we are not content with just our local particular perception. We have to have some understanding of the world which transcends our being, of our historical position. We have to have some understanding that can be framed as an absolute knowledge. I think that is what we are trying to do.

This demonstrates the coincidence between universal and particular. If we have an understanding that transcends our being, then Kevin, you can take that into your Men's Circles work, and Daniel, you can take it into your research centers, and I can take the research into my own videos or books or whatever. So, there is a sense in which we are trying to get some universal understanding. Thus, I think we should not lose faith in theory, but have a theory that is observer-dependent. That for me is the synthesis between universality and particularity.

Kevin: There is great utility in theory, I do not want to throw it out either. We are striving for a more perfect theory that is actionable in an individual's life. We are striving for a more perfect theory that can renew the culture.

Cadell: That would go back to the postmodern insistence of pragmatics and coherence. With pragmatics and coherence we can renew the culture and make it something different. Now if we each want to give our views on how our thinking has evolved on gender trouble in this talk, maybe we can give some reflective conclusions. If the theme is gender trouble and making sense of this landscape, what has become of your thoughts?

Kevin: This talk on gender is such a powerful talk because we reached into epistemology, ontology, and quantum physics. How do these models help us understand gender? We can see from all these pathways of knowledge there is some type of meta-model or meta-theory that may emerge as a result. As far as the gender trouble and the gender issues of queer theory, I would say that the United States would not be ready for the spurious infinity. I do not see that happening anytime soon. I also do not think it would serve most people. What I might see happening, and what you described, Daniel, is one step in that direction towards a more nuanced non-binary space represented as a quadrant or some conceptual geometry that our minds can hold and work with intersubjectively. Such a conceptual geometry would still ultimately help us get at the real of a sexual polarity that moves the culture.

I could see the development of such a gender scaffolding to be implemented in this quantum mechanical sense of becoming and fluid identity. I don't think that this would have to invalidate traditional lifestyles, and at the same time, it would not have to become this extra radical movement either. There is a reasonable compromise zone. Maybe the next stable geometry is three, maybe five. Maybe that will take decades for our culture to really process in a rational form. Maybe that is a practical, coherent and evolutionary way to view the problem. I welcome it fully. At the same time, in this body and this lifetime I identify as a masculine man, and I celebrate that.

Cadell: A half-dragon, half-lion, half-man!

Kevin: Precisely! I want to also say that I am totally for that Jordan Peterson, Elliot Hulse, Rollo Tomassi re-celebration of masculinity and re-contextualizing positive masculinity. *Masculinity is not toxic.* There are toxic expressions from the masculine, but masculinity is a healthy vibrant and beautiful thing. I want to speak that we have plenty of trouble facing the binary of masculine and feminine. I want gender theory to focus on working with this trouble of the binary polarity.

Daniel: I totally agree. That perspective is suitable and useful. I also want to catch up on the observer. I want to say that it is incredibly difficult to find yourself, to become someone, especially if you are not really feeling the best in your current identity. What I think is we need tools for social design. How can we design our wellbeing in the new social contexts? How can we describe some patterns of enabling spaces and enabling observer effects to make this possible? How can we find ourselves becoming someone else when we do not find ourselves feeling good where we are? I will say that cultural acceptance of psychotherapy could provide a tool set which is a very professional one. Can this be generalized into a popular therapy? What is a tool set of your own desire of becoming that everyone could use very easily. How can we think of something popular that even everyone can afford? This makes gender and psychical becoming an imminent political question.

Cadell: We will see I guess. What struck me as an interesting concept at the end is something I resonate with deeply, and something that you both expressed in your own way: the idea of emergent geometry, or dynamical geometry, a geometry that can become. When we are thinking in those terms, we are thinking in evolutionary terms, but also thinking in terms of a real emergence which is not just "anything goes," but a real that is in some sense constrained in a positive dimension. This calls for a paradox of radical conservatism as well. It is like what you were saying, Kevin, about trying to understand the masculine and feminine being hard enough. I always felt the move to spurious infinity was an unconscious strategy to get us to stop paying attention to the difficulty between Man and Woman. I think the relations between men and women are so complex and so difficult that no wonder we want to turn away from it. But there is also only so long that you can turn away from it, because it is so real, so obviously a motor or driver of history. So, it is from this perspective that I am very open to thinking emergent geometries with three or four or five positions, and also inherently more flexibility in the types of roles that can be designed with these positions. These positions and roles have to be thought deeply from the perspective of evolution, from the perspective of social pragmatism, and from the perspective of true desire. It is no easy to task to think of gender in a way that benefits the totality of our wellbeing over the course of a whole lifetime and across the whole of the social edifice.

I guess that brings me to my main critique of Butler, if I can bring it around to her opening quotes. For Butler she emphasized that there is nothing about being a man or a woman which is in us from the beginning, since it emerges in social context, the intersubjective play of desire. She is basically saying that gender is an emergent geometry. I agree with her. The real genius of Butler was precisely de-essentializing gender because it is true, I think, that there is no divine masculine-feminine essence in you from primordial whatever. That is what she is saying, it is truly open in a becoming. However, where Butler and traditional essentialists can be put into a synthetic conversation is that we do not need to essentialize gender from the start. But at the same time, there are very important evolutionary constraints which are in our best interest to understand if we are to make the best of our lives while we are here. In that sense these two positions can be reconciled. That is my take. In the emergent geometry, I am open to what emerges, and exploring this space with as much focus on wellbeing and psychical health as possible.

Kevin: Another word here, is that it is possible that the full under-standing of the totality of the range of masculine-feminine, if we could get that to the whole planet, maybe then and only then the next geometry would emerge.

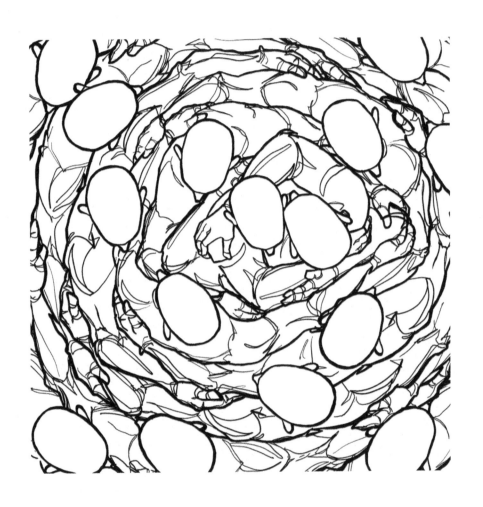

CHAPTER 5

Contemporary Masculinity and Masculine Movements

Cadell: The chapter title for our discussion is contemporary masculinity and masculine movements. Already we are in a controversial conceptual territory. There is an idea emerging in various "dark web" or different internet forums that give one the impression that there is a crisis with masculinity. Whether or not this crisis is well-articulated, it certainly finds an expression, and this expression is in relation to confusion and disorientation of identity, emotions, sexuality, purpose, work, and relationships. This is a symptom perhaps of our overall condition of being confused and disoriented by the complexity of the world. Another potential explanation for why there is a crisis in masculinity, at least in the West, is that our culture has been dominated by feminist discourse, theory, and practice.

We often forget that although feminist theory and practice transforms what it means to be a woman in a necessary way, both man and woman are relational concepts. This means that if "woman" changes then "man" has to change in relation to her. What we are opening up in this trialogue is a space to discuss what that means.

What is contemporary masculinity, and how should men be thinking about their identity. What are the best ways for them to develop a deep intimate knowledge of their emotions, sexuality, inner purpose, meaning, work, and relationships moving forward so that we can have the best society that is working towards freedom for everyone, men and women, and every other orientation.

In order to frame this discussion, I am going to use a quote from a controversial figure in the masculine movement, often associated with the "Red Pill Movement." If you are not aware of the Red Pill Movement you can "google it" and find a lot of information. The quote is from Rollo Tomassi and his "manosphere" defining *The Rational Male*, where he articulates what "Red Pill" means to him:[10]

> "Red pill awareness [is...] emancipation from fem-centric mental models. [...] It is a difficult enough proposal to unplug men from their blue pill [fem-centric] conditioning, but leading them to an understanding of [masculine-centric] principles [...] is a particular challenge."

What you basically find in this masculine movement is a critique of intersexual dynamics that are often referred to as "female deference," and a construction of intersexual dynamics that represent a new form of patriarchal perspective on the 21st century. What is also important to mention is that this whole movement is based on a metaphor from *The Matrix*, where you have a "blue pill" as the "false reality" ("fem-centric" idealizations) and a "red pill" as the "true reality" (irreducible sexual difference, tensions, etc.). The metaphor also conveys the idea of the blue pill being "comfortable" and the red pill being "bitter or difficult."

Tomassi specifically is saying that in feminist culture men are raised to be female deference ("fem-centric"), which means to default to the female perspective on social dynamics instead of investigating their own views and perspectives on social dynamics. How Tomassi defines the red pill is that men need to stop being mindlessly female deference and actually investigate their own heart and core and see what is working and speaking for them. I felt that hopefully was a good introduction to a conversation between the three of us because our trialogue I feel is an enaction of this need for men to come together and discuss sexuality in a deep and intimate way.

Kevin, what are your reflections on Tomassi? Do you think you were raised within a female deference culture? What does female deference mean for you? How would you open up this space for us to talk about this?

Kevin: Thanks for that quote, I am so glad you referenced Tomassi because he is a controversial figure that is defining a lot of new thinking about masculinity. I have been reading him closely for two months now, because I think there is real power in that perspective. Also, I want to reiterate *The Matrix* reference and to provide a trigger warning anyone reading this. As we all know, in *The Matrix* the red pill is not pleasant, especially if you were raised in a blue pill culture. If you remember in the movie, Neo gets the option to take the blue pill, and you will go back to life as normal. The red pill can be terrifying if you have lived your entire life in blue pill conditioning. To take this metaphor to our discussion, the red pill tells you about reality as it is between the sexes, and not as you would like it to be.

My current understanding is this: I agree with Tomassi that in a feminist culture we are occupying now, especially with men, women, and mating, we were raised to blue pill gender dynamics. We were raised to idealize the woman in a way that makes practical realities of forming a nuclear family difficult. The reality is that the divorce rate is over 50%, infidelity is rampant, and there are not a lot of strong father archetypes or figures. There are more single mothers now than ever. The idea that we should do what the woman says, accept women in the workplace like men, do everything to defer to the woman's feelings, emotions, likes and wants. I, as a man, become secondary.

The red pill is precisely the opposite, to create optimal sexual polarity, to create an optimal environment to raise children, and to occupy the gender role of man in the tribe or the environment. It is an essential imperative that you take responsibility and create your own frame and kingdom first, and then you can invite a woman into that. You can become the leader in the bedroom, the boardroom, and the family dynamic. When you have encountered someone who has never enacted that or has never heard of this idea, it can get a lot of push back. Meanwhile their relationships are suffering, and I have seen this with a lot of clients.

Daniel: I like this idea of the red pill very much. The red pill is very uncomfortable because it forces you to *create your own reality*. If you discover that your entire reality has been an illusion set upon you, it is very uncomfortable. To actually define the reality you want takes a lot of courage. You have to identify the illusion that has trapped you and go beyond by creating it with feelings that make you happy on a long-term basis.

However, I see that a lot of masculine movements *step into different traps*. There is always some empowerment related to how being a man is about being brave. Some topics circle around a dissatisfaction with women and the challenging circumstances of dealing with the opposite sex. It's like: "A man will never understand a woman." I have been looking into some of these movements and they all have different faces. Sometimes it is about the legal status that is unequal, or sometimes it is about the relationship, sometimes it is about approaching women. For example, in the pickup community it is always about how can I feel myself masculine enough to approach a woman in a bold way? How can I get into a relationship on my terms? How can I sleep with a woman after one or two dates?

There is also another side. All these movements have in common the notion of empowerment between men, of intrasexual dynamics. There is a notion of male friendship which can be very special. Strong bonds can arise between men. Friendship is about caring and healthy responsibility. Some problems of masculinity in our world stem from the loss of this brotherhood. This capability of man being together. Our world has been separated in several ways and individualized in many ways. Many individualized competitions are going around.

Everything is about being better or worse. But a basis of our society could be to find a strong brotherhood where people respect each other. And I mean by brotherhood the real ones. In this way we can learn what it means to have courage in a collective dynamic. We can approach what provokes fear in a more integrated way.

Cadell: Thanks to both of you. I guess where I would start in my reflections on my feelings and emotions when you were both speaking, is that I have struggled in my own way in the last two years. I have specifically struggled with how to understand what it means to be in a female deference culture, and in some sense I have a lot of inherent guilt and shame about my masculinity and my sexual energy. I feel that when I do not defer to the female, I do not feel strong and confident and at peace about it, somehow. I don't feel strong in my own essence and nature. I still feel I have conditioning that prevents me from seeing myself. I do not know how deep it goes. *It feels that it goes very deep.* At the same time, I do not want female deference culture to go to male deference culture. We just need to have better **intersexual dialogues.** I know in some spiritual communities you will have Women's circles and Men's circles and then come together and have Intersexual circles. That is such an intuitively healthy idea to me.

For me one of the big side effects of female deference culture, or at least it could be, is the decline in brotherhood. We have lost the ability to have strong healthy masculine culture and bonding. I know for me in high school, one of the best things that happened to me was being close with good guy friends. We would always play sports and roughhouse and push each other around. There was just something about being in that environment that is necessary for men to have that bonding experience. It is kind of hard to vocalize with other guys, we never explicitly talk about it, but there is an intimacy there. We do not talk about it, but it happens. It is kind of like you are "gay" if you talk about it with gay being a negative connotation. I do not personally experience it as a homo-erotic intimacy but as a deep brother intimacy or a deep Platonic intimacy. I feel that void in my heart now, so for me a masculine movement would be about that in some way. We cannot create our kingdom, as you were saying, Kevin, without knowledge of the masculine self. You can invite a woman into your kingdom, and vice versa. A woman creates her own palace and can invite a man inside. But we cannot do that unless we are deeply in touch with ourselves and with others.

Consequently, how I imagine a masculine movement is that it is not against women, obviously. It may be against female deference. Men should not be deferring to women because I don't even think women like that anyway. I will quickly say that for me a masculine movement would be very positive about trying to get men to connect with a real intimacy with other men and build those strong bonds so that we do not feel isolated. A lot of men become isolated and lose their passion and vitality and friend network. They lose a deep sense of masculine identity.

Kevin: You are touching on so many big components. This is extremely important. I have been blessed by having an actual indigenous aboriginal woman from Australia in my life. In Australia the tribes would call it men's and women's business. Certain things, such as hunting and gathering, but other psychological and spiritual activities, would be gender-specific. There are activities with just men and just women. They do not cross over or intermix. But when there is a tribal feast or gathering, then the intersexual dynamic comes in in a healthy way, because they have been allowed to integrate within the genders before it is between the genders. This is really a healthy model and template. You are speaking to the modern world, which is worship of the individual, narcissistic, female deference, siloed, men and women, the nuclear family. Isolating breeds addiction, depression, and many of the shadows of the human psyche. There is a real need to reawaken and reapply these ancient social technologies of the circle.

When I left my academic path, I entered the spiritual community, the conscious transformative festival community. And what has happened there since the 1960s, since the cultural revolution, is women's circles, red tents, where women bleed together on their cycle. All of these women's movements. You see this disparity because men are not doing it. However, it really is coming into movement now. This is very important. *Outside of sports and bar culture,* men crave intimacy with other men.

There are multiple layers to this craving. One is the safety that is created where men can only talk about certain things with other men. They are not going to talk about it with other women. This could be because of our neuro-wiring, or because of sexual competition, or the Mother Wound. Men need other men to listen to them. This is one of the most powerful things I learn in Men's Circles. The other level is iron sharpening iron. Men actually grow and develop psychologically and physically in competition. But it is not power over and destructive dominance. It is more like martial arts. We are going to spar because we both want to develop each other. The last piece is that men crave touch. We cannot talk about this because we were raised in a homophobic culture. There is nothing like touch and embrace from a masculine Father or Brother. I actually worked with a Lebanese neuroscientist dealing with very scarred men dealing with PTSD. What worked the most was sound and touch. They needed prolonged hugs and touch to let their nervous system relax.

Daniel: What came to my mind when you were speaking is about masculinity needing iron on iron sharpening. What is the notion of this brotherhood of making a man more to a man? I find myself again in the metaphor of quantum physics. If we talk about actuality and potentiality, the potential. You always have the notion of the man that there is this need of its own potential that needs to be actualized by being *even more potential.* The man always wants to find something where he can find something with more potential. Potential means what could be or what is not. Something where you can reach out to. What is not actually done but what is also directed into the future. It is not, but it can be. Exactly: *you can.* The notion of you can do it, is about all these notions where you can find yourself in competition and enable each other that it is possible for you. This is where the power comes into the potential, because the power is something that is not something you have to exercise but it is there not to exercise. It is like the notion of surveillance all over, not to watch someone breaking in, but to keep the people away. The potential is always something you don't want to use, but until you do use it, it is not actual, it is hidden potential.

That was my notion first on the way of thinking about what is the loss of masculinity? What is the force of this new kind of brotherhood emerging? I also see brotherhoods emerging that are not very healthy. Consider again "pickup" communities where people find each other to seduce women and try to make the best of their ego by having deceptive tricks. These deceptive tricks are on how to trick oneself and the woman, to get into bed as soon as possible. This is also a kind of "empowerment," but it is not very healthy physically or psychologically.

There are also the other notions of brotherhood like military unions. There are people who experience in the military that there are potentials, they have *power and brotherhood*. But it leads to war and it is destructive. I am saying that there is a double-sided coin to this power. The notion of where empowerment goes is how to be someone who can be potential with someone else and make the best out of it for everyone. For the community of brotherhoods themselves and for the women.

This also comes to the notion of our last discussion on gender. There maybe is a female-man and a male-woman. There may also be some more in-betweens. Maybe the best way, I was thinking, is that this ontology of five genders would be the best for a popular description of gender. It is clearly differentiated but not just black and white. At the same time, it enables you to find yourself also in groups, in a collective or a category. You can find a male brotherhood, but also a female brotherhood, or just in between. This might be the **"inbetween-hood."**

Cadell: You point the conversation in an interesting direction, Daniel. I definitely want to affirm or reaffirm the possibility that brotherhoods can be used for negative reasons and self-destructive reasons. This can be negative for both the man and the woman, because it doesn't take into consideration the long-term picture, or purpose beyond pleasure, or purpose beyond immediate gratification, or all of those things.

But then I think Kevin also made a central point that resonates deeply with me. I grew up in a town where male bonding occurs around alcohol and sports. I think it is pretty general. There is something really fundamental lacking there. There is something that doesn't work there. I ran away from that. I ran to women because I didn't want to be around alcohol and sports for my male bonding. That is a lack on the male bonding side.

Now where I am trying to bring both of these points is that the rise of feminist culture and female deference culture is actually connected to the cultural decline of religion. Where you have the rise of atheism and New Age spirituality or esoteric obscurantism, you have the rise of female culture, and the decline of monotheism and male culture. I think they are intimately connected. If we are thinking about a brotherhood with deep purpose, which brings benefit to all men, and men who are thinking about the best for women too, that brings me to things I have seen enacted in the Church. Not all things enacted in the Church. The Church is not perfect, it has made many mistakes and can be blamed for many things. But in some ways, I think what the Abrahamic traditions are trying to do is provide a brotherhood that is for the higher good of everyone. The Abrahamic traditions to me are brotherhoods for the higher society.

Now it is all confusing to me how to bring this further. Do we return to religion? Why did religion fracture like it did? I feel myself tending to metaphysical mysteries. I asked some people associated with the Catholic Church in New York, why is God a man? Why did God send himself to Earth as his own son? Why isn't God a woman? Why didn't she send a daughter? Why is there this asymmetry? What is the purpose behind that according to the Church? They did not have any good answers for those questions. For me, it is related to this idea of a sexual asymmetry that Freud discovered in infantile sexuality, which I brought up in Chapter 2 related to our discussion of evolution and the archetypes. This is the idea that all human babies are default boys ("Sons of God") because they "want the mother," and it takes a second psychic twist to identify as a "girl" who will "become the mother." In this theory femininity is always this embodiment of lack, which explains why Christianity does not symbolize it ontologically.

In any case, when we think about the meaning of the history of Christianity, clearly men on a collective level found these structures necessary and useful. I think it probably helped men to better themselves beyond immediate sexual gratification, and at the same time, to look out for each other as brothers and build their best possible family units. Of course, there is an extreme negativity against religion today in the West. Anytime you bring up religion, the word religion, it is perceived negatively, which reflects in some sense the "New Atheist" cultural moment that was the early 2000s. But at the same time, it would be interesting to rethink religion. Or at least opening up the conversation of rethinking it. I know this has been approached by some thinkers, like philosopher Alain de Botton, who proposed "atheism 2.0," which has a focus on spiritual development and community life; or also scientists like David Sloan Wilson who are interested in religion as an evolutionary phenomenon instead of simply deconstructing it. Among the "New Atheists" I think the philosopher Daniel Dennett is most open to these drives and has even actively participated in building atheism with spiritual community, and even researching the evolutionary drive to religion.

I am entering my own speculative territory here, but let me give a concrete example of what I mean when I think about thinking of new masculinity requires thinking religion in a new way. About a year ago I was at a Buddhist temple. Now Buddhism as a structure is definitely not monotheist, and for many, Buddhism is not a religion, but a spiritual tradition and practice. This tendency to be "spiritual but not religious" is of course very fashionable because it fits comfortably with the ideology of individualism, even if the Buddhist ontology ends up conceiving the individual as nothing! Now, if I can connect that to what I was saying about psychoanalysis conceiving women as the embodiment of lack, then it is clear, metaphysically, that Buddhism itself should be conceived of as more feminine. Buddhism is in some sense a "blue pill" towards female deference. Thus, it makes sense that its practices are more interior and feeling-centric, about connecting to the void-core within yourself where emotions and images come and go, and the only thing that is constant is the "full-emptiness." The appearances of the world are not as important for Buddhism as this interior experience.

Now, at the Buddhist temple we actually did Men's circles and Women's circles. The men were really excited to do the circles, and the women were less so. The women felt they were being left out of the Men's circles. They wanted to be with the men. There was this emotional block on the women's side which would prevent men from having their circle, women from having their circle, and then to come together for collective discussion. I don't know fully what to make of this, but my speculation is that if you were able to have this dynamic manifest, what you would lose is what we started off complaining about: female deference culture. I think what you would have to confront is that we have lost real masculine structure, of the essence of masculinity as a positive ontological force, the life force that fills up the emptiness with a transcendental horizon of meaning. What you would have to confront is religion proper and not just the void of inner experience!

From this experience I became more convinced that losing female deference culture is scary to a lot of women. Many women today are in a psychical state of growing up without fathers, or having a negative relationship with their brothers, or they are just scared of men in general. They perceive men as this monstrous thing. Yesterday I went shopping and went into a few stores, and many stores had signs **"Smash the Patriarchy."** This was in antique stores, second-hand shops, little spiritual stores. **"Smash the Patriarchy."** There is this feeling that society is this masculine terror. I think the job of a masculine movement, this brotherhood of higher purpose, is helping everyone differentiate between the positive and negative side of the masculine. We need to make a case for the positive side of the masculine, the side which precisely was and is capable of embodying the life force and providing a transcendental horizon of meaning.

To compare Buddhism and Christianity we can compare Buddha and Jesus. Buddha "solves" the problem of suffering by overcoming the illusion of desire. Buddha recognizes that every object in the world is in the end unsatisfactory, temporal, fleeting, that to know yourself is to overcome your desire to have or be the object of desire. But Jesus "solves" the problem of love by recognizing that, even if the world is unsatisfactory, temporal, fleeting, and so forth, it is precisely this spiritually challenging background which calls upon us to fill the emptiness against all odds. God needs us more than we need God! If God was then we would not be! The path is open because there is no true object of desire, the truth is to love the imperfections. That is why Jesus was with the prostitutes, beggars, homeless, thieves and so forth. A new masculinity would be situated right here, and if it were to be, it would be a miracle!

Kevin: I love the "Smash the Patriarchy" and also the "Future is Female" meme. Both are wrong, in my mind. The future is a co-evolution and a new synergy between men and women, not an absolute dominance of one over the other. Like, do women really want a matriarchy? I do not think women want that if they really think about it. I want to drop a quote paraphrased from Aleister Crowley: "As soon as a religion has left out the priestess or goddess, it is on its way to atheism." I think that is like a physics equation that you could inject into any religion in any world. Why is it that in the God of the Abrahamic faith there is no mother or a daughter or a wife? There is no female constellation and yet it is presented as the seed crystal of the family. It is like "where are the women?" That is one of the mysterious holes in the logic of religion that led me to the path I am on now because it is such a foreign abstraction away from my life. How does this sexual difference influence religion? You brought up this point, Cadell, and then to the importance of cultivating a deeper understanding of toxic and positive masculinity. I want to make a firm statement: *masculinity is not toxic, there is no such thing as toxic masculinity.* Masculinity is a principle and enactment of life-giving roles that a male body can provide to a human ecosystem.

Cadell: Sorry, you would say there is no such thing as toxic masculinity?

Kevin: There isn't. That is like saying there is toxic winter or autumn. Masculinity as an ideal, as an archetype, is incorruptible. You can enact toxic patterns as a man, but masculinity in itself is not toxic. I would suggest to any woman who is in a phase of **"Me Too"** that it has emotional validity, but that we need radical language upgrades for the world we need to build moving forward. In the men's coaching I am doing, I am trying to reinvigorate the positive masculine. What we don't have are examples of the positive masculine. I would argue that Jesus Christ as an archetype is a representative of positive masculinity, and Buddha too, in a different way. Both are patriarchs, male leaders, leading culture, who have disciples, and bringing life into a culture. Buddha focuses on the problem of desire; Jesus focuses on the problem of love.

In searching for a new language of positive masculinity from these guiding spiritual figures I would reference the idea of the King, the Wise King (over the tyrant). Buddha and Jesus are Wise King archetypes. The tyrant controls through fear and wields the sword too much or for the wrong reasons. The King wields the sword and the scepter for balance. When the King wields the sword properly it is like Mufasa in the Lion King: his eye and his ability to see the kingdom in all its weakness and glory, and then make positive decisions that reinvigorate the whole culture is an aspect of the positive masculine. I think there is a correlative in the feminine: the positive queen archetype. So, the whole "Smash the Patriarchy" meme is enacting the negative feminine archetype, the tyrannical aspect of the feminine, I would argue.

Cadell: I would just like to second that idea quickly about making the argument that the "Me Too" movement is enacting the negative feminine archetype. One of the negative characteristics of the masculine archetype is this *brutal tyrannical physical force* or power which is abused. But one of the negative characteristics of the feminine archetype is *reputation demolition* and "Me Too" is based on reputation demolition. I think in our culture it goes unacknowledged. We openly admit and condemn when a man is abusing physical power. We do not do the same thing when we see a woman engaged in reputation demolition.

Daniel: On the one hand, I would like to speak to the notion of the brotherhood lost in the New Age movement because of female power, and also related to matriarchy, magic, grassroots movements of networking structures. Monotheism and patriarchy are perceived as the vertical pattern and the "old stuff." How to bring this into our world, back again in its positive dimension? My mind went into brotherhoods that were, for example, in secret societies, which keep their rituals in secret and exercise the brotherhoods on their way, but in a very esoteric or mystical-mythical level. So, there is maybe the notion to think it in a Christian way, but also in an esoteric way.

On the other hand, what is always kind of related to "the man" is this "going up." When we think in metaphors, Christianity is always about going into heaven. Everything that is above is "going up." The maternal and Mother Earth is everything "down there." You also have different notions of animals, like the snake going under the ground, more related to Mother Earth. In South America, for example, the condor or eagle is the king of heaven, related to symbols of power in politics or religions. That is something always above, like God is watching you from heaven. Or we are going to heaven because we are Christians, so we go "up." Or the relation between the sun and the moon. The moon is like the feminine-shadow side (nothingness), the sun is the male-light side (life-force). This dominance of male power is thought of as giving life and light, because it is the metaphor of shining. I think there have been many different kinds of how to relate yourself as a man into different archetypes of being man. But it is also important to acknowledge the other side, which is the female side, even if you don't feel female or even if you don't exercise the female powers.

There was another notion that came to my mind, that the *power of men is silence*. Whereas the power of women can be a very frustrating form of communication aimed at reputation demolition. There is a kind of power of men which tries in the exact oppositional way of keeping silence. Or just not talking. This is not always a negative power. Sometimes it is nice to find familiarity with someone and just be without talking. I can say that in my experience with friends. Everything is felt to be already said. Everything is fine that way.

I don't know, there may be rituals in Christianity that may be useful for today; but there may also be too much damage in the Christian community to pick it up where it has been left. There is also this very untrue idea in extreme forms of Christianity that you go into the monastery and all the monks do not have relationships, or actually transcend their sexuality. We all know this leads to neuroses, and people express sexual "relationships" by being a rapist or through homosexual abuses. They basically have very strong difficulties keeping their sexual pleasure "right" in accordance with Christian notions of morality. There must be something other than Christianity which allows for the higher integration of male sexual power. There must be something other than Christianity for the higher integration of female sexual power, too. It could be that this something other is not the same place. As you said, Cadell, there could be the men's circles and the women's circles, and then they come together for the intersexual circles.

Cadell: I feel like it is important to approach phenomena like Christianity, but also phenomena like Islam, Hinduism or any large religious structure, from the evolutionary point of view, rather than a deconstructionist point of view. In the evolution point of view, paradoxically, we can think of the logic of religious structure and also the possibilities for it to transform positively to serve the present moment. I have thought about it a great deal and I think it is a totally new idea to approach religion in an open evolutionary way. Ever since the rise of scientific materialism and secular humanism, or any form of modern atheistic culture, you have this narrative that religion is on a steady decline to oblivion. The idea is that it is only a matter of time before there will be no more religion or Christianity at all. You can find these narratives that stretch back to the 16th and 17th century. In other words, *it is not a new thing to say that religion is on its way out and we should deconstruct it*. On the contrary, *it is an old thing*. But I would say that with the *nature* of religion as an evolutionary phenomenon we are dealing with a paradox that we cannot think properly. This is the paradox that religion as such is not subject to linear time or even historical time. Religion is not subject to beginnings and ends. Religion is not subject to the rise and fall of a certain historical fashion, like a way of approaching knowledge of the world (science), or a way of approaching knowledge of human expression (humanism). Religion is in some sense an eternal paradox situated in the uncomfortable fact that humans cannot and will not be satisfied with mortality and finitude.

Now I mean something precise here in regard to circular temporality and its paradoxes for history. When we think in terms of linear temporality there is this notion of past-present-future. But religion has a strange ability to reinvent itself in the present, in such a way that it is a **"resurrection"** and past and future are both different. Of course, the religious symbols in different historical epochs may be different. You may not recognize meta-patterns like Campbell emphasizes. Religion may go through a period where it looks like it is dying, but then, all of a sudden, *it comes back different. It is like it died and was born again*. That is for me the meaning of the archetype of resurrection. The meaning is that if you go through the lowest, darkest, most painful point, the most hopeless state, you can emerge from that point or state stronger than ever. You can even emerge immortal, and so forth. So, I am not saying that religion is perfect. On the contrary, it is of course an imperfect symbolic expression. I am not arguing that the institutions are pure and non-contradictory. They are impure and contradictory, like the monk or the priest who is fucking a little boy. There are many examples you can give of these things which are in themselves true criticisms. But somehow it still misses the point. It is again this deconstructive tendency, over and above the evolutionary perspective, that religions will be transformed.

Let me try to express this by bringing it back to a Hegelian interpretation of quantum physics and its recognition of the actual and potential. The interesting thing is that *the actual material reality never matches up to the potentiality of the ideal. The actual is always at a distance or always lacking to the potential eternal ideal which only exists in this potential form. This does not mean you can deconstruct the eternal ideal. It means the eternal ideal is a historical becoming or a spiritual evolution.* For example, using arguments like the priest is fucking a boy so then the Christian ideal is wrong. This is not a good Hegelian argument. Of course, the actual is at a distance from the ideal. That doesn't mean the ideal is wrong. It means your historical form is failing and lacking fundamentally. The failing and lacking is precisely the location where you are becoming in truth somehow, where you are forced to see your contradictions. You need to fail as long as you don't fail the same way repeatedly. You need to see the contradictions which led to the failure, and then make a wise adjustment. I am certainly not justifying the catastrophes of history, but I am just saying that through failure you can *fail better*. That is how I would interpret our interest in thinking how to integrate masculine and feminine sexuality, not to repeat what was done in the past, but to think it in a new way, in a way that we avoid the mistakes of the past. We will never be perfect. We will make new mistakes, and that is okay.

Finally, in relation to both of you, maybe it is true that a part of the reinvention of the Abrahamic traditions has to be a reinvention of integrating the feminine, somehow. But at the same time. I don't know. Feminists think the "Future is Female." What that means in terms of Hegelian historical dialectics is that there are two entities, the man and the woman, and they think the female is the synthesis of the male. They think: *let us all be female.* Or they think: *let the females take power.* But what if it is the opposite? *What if the synthesis is that we are all trying to become men.* After all, if you recall our discussions in Chapter 2, we recognized that this asymmetry in the modern world, where women are trying to come into the working world, but men are not trying to come into the reproductive world. Maybe when feminists say the "Future is Female" they are saying "We Are Becoming Men." I have no idea because I think the reality of the bodies are too different for that to make any sense. Maybe it is just going towards androgyny or transgenderism where all these signifiers will fall apart in their own internal contradictions. Maybe women are shedding their identities and have yet to find the signifier that works for what is the reality of the moment. Maybe intersexual circles could find some sense in the chaos.

Kevin: There is some brilliant analysis in there, Cadell. What you are talking about with the ideal potential and the actual real, is what I was referring to with toxic masculinity as a bad argument. The idea of masculinity is life-giving but our leaders are enacting it in a horrific way. But it does not mean that masculinity itself is corrupted and Christianity is corrupted. Christianity contains within it one of the most powerful known mythological and archetypal forces. That is *resurrection and metamorphosis*. The path that Christ enacts in the Bible is an archetype for the emergence of a new humanity. Jung saw this clearly. If you read Jung, you can see him masterfully understand this. In the fantastic imaginal world, the phoenix is an immortal archetype. When the phoenix reaches the end of its life cycle, it bursts into flame. This is a metaphorical spiritual force of the ability to burn impurity and then become reborn. I think this is what is occurring in the constructs of masculinity and femininity. We do not want to become all female, that is a regression in evolution. There are species where that happens. This is pre-sexual evolution at the biological scale. We cannot do that, and I don't think we can do that if we tried. In terms of the mental and spiritual health of society this would be three steps backwards. However, I don't think we all want to be all male, either. Both pathways are defenses against the reality of sexual difference, as we discussed in Chapter 1.

What is going to happen in the future is a *full evolution of men and women rising in an octave together*. There are a few examples of this in history. Jesus Christ and Mary Magdalene, according to the gnostic tradition, are examples of this. I believe they were a spiritual power couple, invoking and evolving humanity, providing a template for what was possible. There are stories of the Buddha and Tara, his consort. Tara was a female spiritual teacher, repressed in history.

What I am interested in is a pathway forward where the *male and female undergo death and resurrection and emerge on the other side as the positive king and queen archetype*. But before it happens, it has to go through a period of decay. That is where we are today.

Cadell: I have a question. There is a part of me that is upset that Jesus died at thirty-three, you know, it is almost like he got off the hook too easily. Try making it to seventy or eighty! What are you doing then? My question is: it is not clear to me what Jesus's relationship is to women or sexuality. There are various different interpretations. What is your interpretation?

Kevin: You can trace this all the way through Christianity. It is God the Father, and his Son. There is no mention of women. This is, in my view, so obviously a bankrupt theory. But there were many stories that didn't make it into the Bible due to power games. In the conventional narrative, Jesus Christ is not mentioned in any kind of relationship, ever. He is preaching to prostitutes and women. But women actually bear him through intense times. There is a big strand of women, and they played a huge role.

Now in the conventional idea of Mary Magdalene, she was a prostitute. But there is a possibility that she was a spiritual teacher. There is evidence for this in myth and poetry. And then there is a possibility that these spiritual teachers, Jesus and Mary, entered into a type of archetypal divine sexual union that could inform and invigorate an entire community or tribe. There is some deeper evidence for this in the West and the East. This was preserved in the tantric traditions in the East, the sexual alchemical practices, and spiritual practices, that were widely flourishing in the Taostic and Vedic traditions. Now I am just kind of skimming the surface of Jesus's sexual life, but I don't just think it is possible, but probable, that Jesus was in a relationship with a physical woman. This was not just in a spiritual or marital relationship, but in a sexual form. I know that some Christians' blood may be boiling, but this is the level we are willing to go to find the truth.

Daniel: From my point of view, when it comes to all the stories, it is *how they are relating to ourselves*. This is where I want to pick up on you mentioning androgyny, because I think there is a point where it is not only about being male, but also *having the potential of choosing*. The male thing itself can be like this and like that. So if you go into the difference of gender you always find yourself by searching for what you are not (a man or a woman), or that your need is not what you have (being a man or a woman), you know? The actual is also what you are and what you have been and what you have done. That is always something that is into the past.

But if you look at the present, here and now (the middle of the being), which is the only thing that most people agree is real, then the past and the future are constructed histories. These constructed histories are concerned with the political powers, which leave some things behind because it doesn't fit to our here and now conception of the world. I see this as a separated polarity, which needs to be discarded to give rise to the drive of the here and now. Otherwise we are stuck into eternity without movement.

So, also to think masculinity and femininity is to embrace both but in a way that we can go to both extremes in a positive way. For example, we can rewrite the history of Christianity, at the point that some people do, by going into other sources. But this is to rewrite it into the future for rituals that are useful for our present being. In this way it doesn't have to get stuck into the institutions as they always have been. Also, to give place to oneself, even as a man, to find yourself in circles that exercise even the feminine power. I see the possibility, and the potential itself, as something very masculine and also very feminine.

Cadell: In order to summarize, maybe we can all give our views on the feelings of the flow of this conversation about masculinity. How we started was that there was a type of feeling online that masculinity is undergoing a crisis and disorientation. This is being caused because the world is becoming more complex. But on the other hand, it is also being caused by our culture being more feminist-influenced, and more female deference. The female's view is seen as the default view, especially in intimate context, but also in political context. We discussed how growing up in a female deference culture can be harmful to men's own sense of connection to self. We discussed how a masculine movement has to speak to the best in us as individuals and collectively. We would be with other men and people in a larger community. And from that we dove headfirst into religion. We all had our own relationship to what that means.

For me, it is interesting that the conversation went in that direction because I think we all relate to spirituality in our own way. We have all discussed spirituality in our own way. If a masculine movement is going to be positive in the largest sense of the word, as it relates to time and community, we are obviously going to run into things that humans in the past called religious. The religions were those historical institutions that were thinking about language, time, and community as a whole, in the context of life and death. I would never want to constrain us to one institutional model like Christianity. But if I was a part of men's circles in a church versus going to a bar and watching the sports game, and having a few beers, I would take men's circles in the church. Maybe we would have men's circles in nature, and different brotherhood bonding activities and seeing what emerges. But definitely for me, the revival of confident masculinity, brotherhood bonding as a foundation for new masculinity. If it can grow from there maybe other things would fall into place more easily, like our intimate relationships. What breaks my heart is seeing the drunken men, the isolated individual men, the men who are overcome by their own monsters and demons. They are basically invisible men. That is what I hope a new movement would address or start to address.

Kevin: I love that this conversation was steered towards religion. Even if the current structures are inadequate to hold what we are dealing with, they will be one day. It is hard to talk about masculinity at a core level and this conversation touched on the core aspects. There is a crisis of sorts. Just like a birth, it is messy, violent. There is a lot of sweat, blood and tears. But something beautiful is happening. *A* *new thing is being born.* Pickup artist communities and the disconnected men aside, they are doing a few things right and many things wrong. Natural law will take care of that. I am much less interested in being against. I am much more interested in being for positive masculinity and the masculine archetype. To reawaken the archetypes of king, warrior, magician, lover. The archetype of the guardian and the high priest that is sourced in life, here with the tender heart, but can also use the sword to cut. The discrimination of the mind, which is logic, logos, is a beautiful aspect of the masculine. But also to have that lotus tip, to invoke the sutras, the tip of the lotus on the sword. He can still be a safe place, a safe father, a safe partner: to women, to nature, to children, and the elderly.

This is what is happening whether we like it or not. *Nature demands evolution.* If nature is our mother, she is pretty pissed, and you can see that with the natural disasters, with economics. It is all connected. We have invoked quantum physics and the historical dialectic in relation to the motion of the actual and the potential. We are asked to approach the ideal of masculinity in a new way. The return of intimacy and true brotherhood outside of alcohol culture and violent sport culture. And iron does sharpen iron, so we do have to do it together.

Daniel: What I can add, and what came to my mind listening to you, Kevin, is also that maybe there is a way to combine or synthesize. It is about the cycles of life. When we invoke the phoenix, the resurrection, it is like dying in evolution. Life goes beyond what was previously there. Also, in a kind of circular movement because we go from spring to summer to fall to winter. The way things live and die, live and die. We have this circular movement, which embraces masculinity and femininity. Maybe the way it finds itself in an individual man is to combine the masculine qualities with what it does, its action. If we think of giving birth to something with the logos, it is already an androgynous thing, because giving birth is like the womb where things come from pregnancy. Because if we dissolve the sexual difference totally, there is no evolution. If you become the oneness, there is nothing else. You get stuck because everything is too perfect, or you are everything that you are, or everything you could be, so there is no evolution. There is no evolution if there is not the gap, which is something missing, or something needed, or something put in place into the play of evolution. How to think of a matrix of combining the good masculine powers with the feminine qualities in ourselves by exercising brotherhood on one hand, sisterhood on the other hand, and androgyny for evolution, in the interplay of the playful difference?

Cadell: Keeping it 100.

Kevin: Daniel is such a beautiful balance between us, Cadell.

Cadell: Daniel is the flower to my sword!

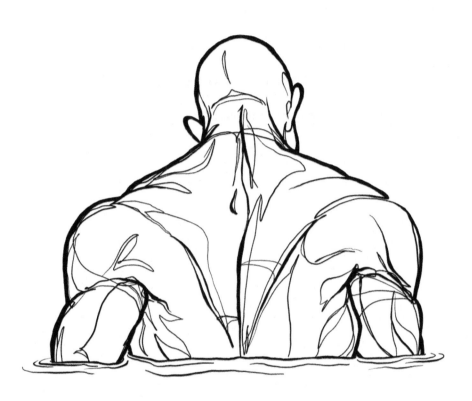

CHAPTER 6

Pain and Suffering in Sexuality

Cadell: We are going to be discussing pain and suffering in sexuality. We are going to be discussing whether or not this is a tragedy to be avoided or a deeper necessary truth (or both). For context, all spiritual and religious traditions have tried to emphasize the importance of emotional reality, whether that is negativity of pain and suffering (e.g., Buddhism), or positivity of peace and love (e.g., Islam, Christianity). This could be seen in contrast to scientific metaphysics which emphasizes thought and reason instead of emotions and passions (which are seen as chaotic and irrational). Another common theme in religious or spiritual thinking or being is that they have always developed practices, rituals, taboos which have been designed to help us sublimate our sexuality.

The basic questions that we are going to approach today, which I think are pretty fundamental questions, is the status of this institutional attempt to sublimate sexuality. Is this to protect us from a tragic negativity of the emotions we feel in sexuality? Is it to help us reach a higher or deeper truth beyond sexuality? Or is it preventing us from confronting the pain which we need to confront with maturity in a new way, without religion? Maybe we have not yet developed the conscious states of mind that would allow us to gain a new perspective on the meaning of pain and suffering, specifically in sexuality.

That is kind of the framing for this discussion. Now within this framing I am going to give a quote from a psychoanalyst that has been influential to me: Jacques Lacan. Lacan positions psychoanalysis as intervening in this space between the failure of religion and the real of sexuality. He specifically, following Freud, sides with the truth of sexuality, and the raw libidinal intensity that emerges in sexuality. He suggests that, when we investigate the truth of sexuality, we avoid the illusion of the image of immortality provided in religion, and we ultimately are led to knowledge of our death. Thus, he conceives of religion qua sexuality as a fantasmatic screen preventing us from confronting the difficult real of our self-development:[11]

> "For each of the partners in the sexual relationship, they must hold the place of the cause of desire. This truth lies at the heart of all defects found in the psychoanalytic field regarding sexual life. To disguise this truth with the maturation of tenderness, however pious the intent may be, is nonetheless fraudulent."

What that quote means is that in terms of psychoanalytic empiricism, in the study of our minds and the way we discuss our sexuality and our sexual life, the central place of truth is the primacy of desire for the other as a cause. You cannot get rid of desire as a cause in sexuality with the other. Desire as a cause constitutes you as a subject. For Lacan, there is no real way to structure your sexual life to get rid of excessive emotional passion as the cause of desire. Furthermore, if you try to "tame it" with "tenderness" of religious feeling, he thinks this is fraudulent, and ultimately a path of repression. What that leaves us with is this inability for our minds, our intellects, to confront the real of desire. Our mental intellectus must submit to the real of desire, it must be brave enough to confront it, to really integrate it. That means confronting the pain and suffering in sexuality. So, I ask you both, pain and suffering in sexuality: a tragedy or a truth? I think we can all relate to this on a raw intimate level.

Kevin: Brilliant quote. Lacan is so fascinating. I haven't read him closely but I love the framing for this chapter. What was coming up for me was how to interpret this enterprise of religion and civilization in relation to sexuality. In the Neolithic, humanity started transitioning from a tribal primitive organization to empire and ideology building. That enterprise has had to contend with the chaos of the human sexual drive. I guess that is the meaning of Freud's *Civilization and Its Discontents*. Lacan is saying this sexual drive, and the cause of desire that appears there, has to be accepted and reconciled in civilization. It cannot be repressed with empire and ideology building. You can see this emerge today on so many levels.

I've used this example before, but I want to bring up Helen of Troy. It is a myth, but a powerful meme in that myth is that a whole nation will go to war and kill thousands due to a real desire for a woman's love. This is not that farfetched. The raw power of the libidinal urge is here on full display. The cause of sexual desire causes a war. Thus, I think Lacan correctly identifies this power in its intensity and indestructibility.

Now religion primarily places boundaries in front of the sexual cause of desire. I think some of this is for good reason. For example, in many esoteric and spiritual traditions, sublimating sexual energy is a pathway to higher states of consciousness. That is a powerful reason for celibacy. You sublimate your sexual energy, instead of being caught up in the marketplace of sexuality. Or instead of being a homeowner or husband, and getting caught up in the politics of family life and society. That is one reason which I resonate with deeply. I think there is a bridge between this spiritual sublimation pathway, and also being a functional member of society, inclusive of the real of sexual desire.

However, on the other hand, the repression that has occurred has largely been set up to protect structures in society, not to walk the spiritual sublimation pathway. I do not know if that is a paternal impulse to protect us from the chaos of the pain and suffering inherent to sexuality. Of course, this chaos of the pain and suffering is largely the emotions that come with the real of sexual desire, especially unrequited or unmet sexual desire. But there is also a different type of pain and suffering in the reality of monogamous marriage and infidelity. The pain and suffering of violating the monogamous marriage act, and everything that comes along with it, has also colored a lot of negative emotions in Western civilization. That reality has produced Lacan! That reality has produced Freud's theory of libido, marked by the struggles of sexual energy in civilization, and which has produced this trialogue now.

The simple fact of desire has to be confronted directly: when a man and a woman, or a masculine and feminine force, have such a strong desire to be in a union, in erotic physical union, there is nothing that can stop that power. Maybe only death. It is a force that has perpetuated the species, it is the life force, unfiltered. This is a line between order and chaos, the most difficult line to walk.

Daniel: This is already opening so many topics to think of! Some of them I am familiar with. There is a reason why repression of sexual energy had many different cultural differences. If you look into many remote cultures, there are many other rules. Some of them are set by religious institutions to keep societal structures in "order." I was thinking that this could be contrasted with animal behavior. There are no cultural rules, but they also fight for the strongest man to show up for a female, or the female chooses a man, like birds. The most beautiful bird or the bird with the best dance, wins the female. Most of the bird's choosing or selecting of a partner is the female's responsibility and burden. Or among lions, they fight with other male lions to get the whole pack. So, there are different kinds of implicit rules grounded in evolutionary biology.

However, the way that infidelity is punished in our society is something very interesting, and something very peculiar. Here is where the quote comes in: *the sexual relationship must hold the place of the cause of desire.* This is very crucial. There is a kind of desire which sometimes leads to infidelity. On the one hand, one of the biggest questions of the pain related to sexuality as a desire for something that is not there, for someone that is not there. On the other hand, there is pain of suffering losing a sexual relationship, when someone wants to hold on. In that case, real pain is twofold, the one that goes away, the one that loses his or her relationship. Both kinds are related to the cause of desire which comes along with chaotic experiences. You cannot concentrate yourself on your work, things get messy, emotions rise until someone again finds a more or less stable relationship or someone is able to meet again a partner with mutual positive emotions to each other.

One of the answers of why taboo exists, or why religion tends to suppress sexual energy, is to keep society in order or at least stabilized. The sexual desire leads to change. It is kind of interesting that there are these two poles, order and chaos, or structure and change. It is like day and night. We cannot have a day while we have a night. Most of our desires are not rational. They are irrational. Desire is an emotion. What I always find very interesting is the exclusiveness or invisibility of an extreme pole, which is the sexual desire, the pole of change.

Now is there a middle path? For example, if there wouldn't be such strict and dogmatic spiritual practices, then maybe there wouldn't be this opening up of the whole tension that someone experiences between the two poles or by excluding one pole. If the change and the desire would be accepted or even educated on a healthy basis, we may not have sexually-loaded issues, like pornography or sexual abuse. There is a big question which involves the cause of desire, which is something very inexplicable at the end. If you go from the cause to the cause, to the cause of the cause, it is very difficult to touch ground, you know? Maybe because desire is a final cause.

I have been thinking about the cause on a very scientific level and could see that there is also a complementarity to the cause, which is **synchronicity**. Imagine we have the desire to meet someone and to have sex with someone. Our actions and thoughts are the cause to synchronize with the desired person. We are getting in the same mood, the same room, the same rhythm of our bodies, to the point we synchronize all our cells till the orgasm. Then we separate each other again, and the chain of causes starts. My thoughts are that in the orgasm *there is no cause anymore*, but *full synchronicity*. There is no desire anymore. I leave it there.

Cadell: Again, there are a few threads. One thing that came up was infidelity. Another thing that came up was causation and the acausal location of the orgasm. Also what came up, which we talked about a little bit, is this polarity which is oppositional, but it is irreducibly oppositional, and necessary for the charge to take place. It is kind of like a weird thing about "meta-level understanding": *nothing changes and everything changes*. It's like: **"I am still in the same place I was when I didn't understand it on the meta-level, but now I understand it on the meta-level, and I still have to deal with the same thing, it is just I have a meta-level understanding of that thing I previously didn't have a meta-level understanding of."**

But to start with the *infidelity thing*, and the *cause of desire*. To me the meaning of Esther Perel's new book, *Redefining the State of Affairs*, is that she wants to reinvigorate relationships with life. She said the reason why people have affairs is *to feel alive, to feel vitality*. This is especially important for us to talk about, and in our context, for men to talk about. It is so important to feel alive with libidinal energy. I don't think we need to have a conversation about infidelity and cheating if we are capable of **articulating our truth**: this energy is inside of me, *this is the truth*. That brings with it a lot of really attractive and positive things and some very difficult things. The whole of me is both of those things. The whole of me is a contradiction, absolutely!

I think what can happen in marriage is that you only want one part. You only want one version of the person. You don't want the absolute contradiction that makes things messy and difficult. Exactly what you think is the best thing in the world can simultaneously be the worst thing in the world, at least if you are thinking from the point of view of the ego and its ideals. We need to have a space to talk about these contradictions in regard to infidelity, cheating, and affairs. For both men and women. Because in some sense, I believe that the *deviation of the system is simultaneously the truth of the system*. In other words, in regard to marriage, the deviation would be affairs. The deviation of affairs wouldn't be there if there wasn't a truth somewhere to investigate. The same thing if we talk about capitalism. You have the capitalist machinery running properly, and then you have the deviations of the systematically excluded: the homeless, the people who couldn't possibly function in the system. There is something there that is very important.

Let me try and relate that to the title of this conversation about pain and suffering in sexuality: tragedy or truth? Maybe it is a tragic truth! In my experience people who pretend this deviational quality isn't there are more in shadows and imaginary screens than in truth, as psychoanalytic experience as revealed. In my personal history, in my ego, I have really hurt from tragedy in sexuality. I guess we all have. At the same time, looking back in retrospect, these tragedies have also been the condition for my most powerful growth. To me, if you understand the pain and suffering from the perspective that your ego has to die, that you have to undergo another transformation, then it actually brings you closer to and with the truth. What you fear the most is simultaneously what you should go to the most strongly. To become stronger inside, to cultivate a strength that doesn't need to bring things to an end, but rather embraces the opposite of ego images.

On another note, with what Daniel was bringing up, with the boundaries that are painful, where you are either losing the cause of desire, or gaining a new cause of desire. Both can obviously be excruciatingly painful. If you are losing the cause of desire, you are losing who you perceive to be your most essential other. And if you are gaining a cause of desire, you are simultaneously, potentially, causing harm and pain to someone else. Both are strong to me in terms of pain. Both are difficult to deal with, and I have dealt with both. But what all this signals to me in the larger picture of things is that this acausal location of the subject when you experience cause of desire in an other, *it means you haven't found your own cause as other inside.*

I think that this is represented in quite a few interesting films. The one I recently watched was *Split*, starring James McAvoy. In *Split* McAvoy plays a character with multiple personality disorder. He has 24 different personalities which take hold of him. As he builds up, he builds up to this ultimate identity, which he calls the **"Beast."** The "Beast" is this *raw pure libidinal energy in a death drive*, which sees the passage through pain and suffering as the only way to purity and truth. Now once he has it, once he has manifested the "Beast," *he is his own cause.* There is no other required to cause his motion. He is in some sense this *acausal immortality which preys on the egos of those in shadow.*

Kevin: This is another confirmation that I should watch this film. It sounds fascinating. This is a very important pathway to consider. What are the causes of human action? What are the primary motivating factors for human action? This is something I think a lot about. Recently I have been reading Viktor Frankl's *Man's Search for Meaning,* and also Nietzsche's *Thus Spoke Zarathustra,* and devouring all the new interviews by Jordan Peterson about meaning. I would say, from these reflections, that meaning making seems at base, a primary motivating factor. You see this with people who have gone from rags to riches. There is this archetypal starting point: someone is in a dirty apartment, a slob, messed up. And then there is a call to the necessity of meaning in order to get motivated to go to the higher state of being.

I don't think there is any difference in romance. For me, at one point I was fixated by "one-itis" as they call it in the red pill movement. The emotional pain and tragedy of losing that for the first time, that first intense time, was so painful for my identity. I was merged and fused with that one woman in an unhealthy way. The pain of separation awakened me to meaning and purpose beyond romance. This fed forward in the system of the next partner I had. I met them at that same level. In tragedy and emotional pain, especially in intimate relationships, it is possible to go beyond settling and continue to pursue meaningful co-creative relationships. I have seen this a lot with people. The vitality peaks, and then it settles, and then one day you wake up and you crave desire for an other. If you haven't built in radical communication techniques, if you are not fully into your purpose solo, then the logical and obvious way to go is an affair, or some deviant sexual behavior. Or some kind of radical taboo. This is what we know from Freud's theory of libidinal energy. Libidinal energy will find an outlet and attach somewhere if you repress it too much. You cannot repress it indefinitely. Repressed content will find an outlet, it returns in a different form. The return of the repressed. If it is not given a healthy outlet it will find a dysfunctional unhealthy outlet.

Daniel: I love what Cadell said in regard to the truth as a deviation that we mark as a failure of a system. That is something I would like to quote.

Cadell: The truth of a system can never be found in its idealization (a perfect system, i.e., marriage), *you have to include the deviation to understand the truth of it* (the imperfect system, i.e., affairs).

Daniel: Right, right. I was doing some research on the taboo and this leads me also to think about humor, which is also contrasted to the tragedy that we have here. The taboo in any religion, or even social behavior and cultural rules, is contrasted to the sacred. The taboo is the deviation of the sacred. Both the sacred and the taboo is something we don't talk about directly. If we open the sacred up to anyone, *it is not sacred anymore.* And if we talk about things that are taboo, *they are not taboo anymore.*

Thus, there are specific outcomes in regard to the sacred and the taboo. The first outcome is the pathway of the heretic person, because he killed the sacred, broke the taboo and is excluded from the society. That is the most common one. This is like infidelity. You are out of the system, society, or out of the relationship. The other way that is possible is a change of the system by staying in the system. This is a point of change where you can stay in a relationship but have a moment of change by speaking out some truth of how you feel: that you are stagnated, that you want to change something that leads to your desire, or where you are and where you do not want to be.

Here I can relate many things. When it comes to tragedy, when we don't have the feeling that we have a choice. That either here or there it will be the worst thing that could happen. This is preceded by the hubris, when the people are too proud of themselves, when they think they have it all, or that everything is too good. Then the story goes on and it goes *bad bad bad*. Every movie that ends bad, that is a tragedy, starts with the most beautiful scenery, the most perfect family. *Then it is like a catastrophe.* The comedy is vice versa. You start with these ridiculous figures, the failures, the incapacities of human behavior, which cause funny motions and lead to happy endings. This comedy is a kind of acceptance that we are just stupid, or we are just behaving ridiculously because something doesn't fit within the society or the structure. This humor has a great deal with taboos. In humor we can find the paradox, something is not fitting but we can still relate to it, without the hubris, without overestimating ourselves, but accepting it.

As you both know, I am very much into system science. There are many systems that can be thought of as a relationship of yourself. In system science "the I" is not fixed but always being constituted. If we think about the **immortal beast** that is on the ground of the cause of desire and we find it in ourselves, I think there is something very difficult to deal with. On the one hand, if there is something meaningful, it is not funny anymore, because funny things are mostly meaningless. What I can say is that for myself, the purpose to find the cause in one's Self, I couldn't find it. And I really was digging very deep, very, very deep. Maybe that's because it is a beast and it eats itself. In any case there was not a positive outcome that I could imagine. But the purpose or meaning outside of me, it is for what? What am I for? It is always something outside of ourselves. But we can find in ourselves only the meaninglessness or the comedy. It may be a tragedy to find out how the story ends well. I leave it here.

Cadell: That was super interesting. I will open up myself about finding the cause in myself versus the meaningless tragedy. I really believe that the importance of Plato and the historical dialectic is that the historical dialectic was designed to navigate the extremes of existential nihilism (no meaning) and religious fundamentalism (ultimate meaning). On the one hand you have existential nihilism, 0, the void, where sophists operate; and the 1 of religious dogmatism, of the perfect one. The dialectic stabilizes meaning in time between the two poles and the absent one.

Daniel: But for myself I suggest not the dualism, but at least the three.

Cadell: Well that is the **dialectical mechanism**, it is an open-ended *triadic structure* composed of two poles and an absent one as the weird "third." But I can say that in terms of finding the cause in myself, I definitely experienced that on the entheogen **ayahuasca**. I found it in the sense that I was not, and the other was, and the other was pure love. That other was in me, somehow, or I was the other. But that was simultaneous with the death of my ego. In that sense the ego is part of a causal chain, part of cause and effect. In order to transcend the ego you have to find some *acausal motivational structure*, which maybe is what people who are trying to self-actualize, and people who are trying to transcend themselves, are doing actively in time, or something like that. But that experience is my intimate relationship with the cause in myself and digging deep. At the same time, it doesn't solve the problem of my function as a Self in history.

What I am worried about, if I were to get involved in men's work, and what I am interested in the most, are guys who put too much of their causal motivation in the woman. *That's a trap.* You don't want to set up all your motivational structures so they are dependent on this human other, because that is what Lacan meant when he said **"There**

is no Woman." This is an axiom which means that there is no acausal motivational structure which you can find in the other feminine human. I think that has been an axiom that has been helpful for my own growth in the last five years. I think it has led me to build healthier and more real relationships with women beyond idealization.

The other thing that I wanted to touch on in relation to what you brought up with jokes, was the thought that it was interesting how you connected jokes with the deviation. The three principle mechanisms that Freud identified as the deviations of the psychic structure, and simultaneously *the location of the truth of the unconscious*, were **jokes, slips of the tongue**, and **dreams**. I have had my own relationship with those three dimensions, but it kind of signaled some fundamental problem with our culture. If comedy and politically incorrect jokes are so taboo that we cannot say certain things, then it means we cannot work through the critical antagon- isms of our culture at the moment. This is related to this idea that the sacred cannot be spoken directly, like once you speak it, it is no longer the sacred, which means the sacred has to change. I think the sacred has built into it this *unspeakable quality*. The sacred cannot be admitted to consciousness, but you have to go around it. At least that's how sexuality functioned around the kitchen table of a lot of nuclear families. Sex was the center of the nuclear family, but at the same time you can't speak about it directly. You can only speak around it, maybe you could joke about it, but not seriously directly about it.

The question is, if we go above the nuclear family, to some higher organization, what is the sacred? Is it still some shifted form of sexuality? Or is it something other? Like in the ayahuasca ceremony, the other is experienced directly, so you are all with the other in the sacred center, *but you are not speaking to each other*. So, it is very interesting. I would just say that in this pathway between the nuclear family, which has some sort of structure with inherent deviations (affairs, cheating, libidinal repression) and this higher transcendental structure, the interesting thing is the boundaries of the sexual.

I like this idea that Alenka Zupančič had, that in enjoyment, specifically sexual enjoyment, it is demarcated as a *form of trespassing*. For example, me and three other girls: I go and play tennis with one, I go and get coffee with another, or I get a blow job with the third. One of those three activities are not the same. Playing tennis and going for coffee, I might be happy; but getting a blow job is a form of sexual enjoyment which is seen as a form of trespassing with the others. There is this way in which we will spontaneously guard or defend against this specific form of sexual enjoyment which is **"I can have this sexual enjoyment, but having this form of sexual enjoyment, means someone else is lacking the sexual enjoyment."** So, it fundamentally operates like this, is what Zupančič is saying, between lack (0) and excess (1). The big question for the transcendental community, with the other, is how this 0 and 1 could be combined, like a quantum computer, 0 and 1 together, somehow.

Kevin: So much is coming up here. I love, first, your brain Daniel, and thinking about systems science. Humor has been one of the ways we have had to navigate taboos, from time immemorial. The spirit of the trickster. This is a very potent pathway that is non-trivial. Also, Cadell, what you are speaking to is so fascinating. I am not sure how to topographically map this onto the concept fully, but it is like abundance and scarcity. It is like by having sexual enjoyment or happiness, you simultaneously generate an absence in the other. There is this inherent competition, this scarce energy, which creates that fear-survival response in the nervous system, and leads to a worship of the one, the ideology, and fundamentalism: **"you can only have one woman in your life and you cannot have sex until marriage."** Maybe there is a root there in that feeling, that if you get "it," I don't get "it."

Now might be a good time to bring up that, for professional athletes, actors, super-high mental or creative performers, the Pareto distribution happens with sexual energy. This is specifically found in the studies on men. Alpha males, high-performing men, sleep with and have sexual encounters with the vast majority of women. This is referred to as the **80/20 rule.** Whereas most other men get the divorcees of these men or they get the lower tier mates, the mates that would be rated objectively less attractive, less fertile, less creative, less intelligent. I am speaking generally, but that would be true to what you are saying, Cadell. Where you have "it," and I don't have "it." Maybe that is built into the gene swarm. Maybe this is where sexual selection comes into play. There is this unspoken competition of sorts within the sexual realm. This is where the pain and tragedy and suffering comes in. You got it and I didn't get it, and I was so focused on it. Now I have to both suffer alone and suffer the ego death of my consequences and expectations. *It is a downward spiral waiting to happen.*

Now, if I were to shift to an abundance mindset, and shift to what I would name a golden age culture, or a human society that is aware of this inherent problem and issue in nature, what are the ways that we could navigate it, and ensure that there is 0 and 1 together? We could go quantum, that everyone could play tennis, have coffee, and get a blow job! We all win. I believe it is possible. The only way it is possible though, is through articulation. *Radical articulation.* We cannot inhabit a reality, create a culture until we can describe it at a resolution level of emotional competence and skill that conveys our raw truth.

For example, if I was married right now, married to the same woman for 20 years, and we were madly in love, and had children, a career, a business, a life together, and I woke up one morning and who knows, maybe it is an unconscious slip of tongue, joke, or dream, about a woman I saw the other day. There is a libidinal eruption in my mind: "oh fuck, what do I do?" I am so attracted to X, Y, Z woman. In this imaginary enlightened society, I could approach my wife in full groundedness and intensity, in a way that she would receive it, which would create that dialectic, and we would move through it. Maybe she would reveal she had urges for something else. We would start co-creating an alternative pathway, where our egos as they exist in the relationship may have to be obliterated. I believe they would be. This whole idea that you are my primary sexual partner would be obliterated.

Now if we were both skillful enough, and there was real intimacy, I think it could be navigated. Where do you go from there? Do you open the relationship? Do you invite a woman in? Do you get a divorce? Or do you just move through it and that was enough? Then the attraction or the polarity would reemerge and suddenly by expressing that level of the rawest truth, an arc of polarity and sexual attraction would reemerge in that container, but because the old one was obliterated by the truth telling. The only way to navigate this forward in the future, especially as there are radical transformations of gender identity, the only way we are going to get through it, is to talk about it. We cannot only talk about the sacred and sexuality through humor. It is going to take hard conversations. They will look like a purge at first. Then we can start to approach a sane, rational, but also emotional conversation, between partners, and between society. But most importantly with yourself. The healthiest sexual partner is going to be yourself. That is where those projections and maladaptations happen, the dysfunctions. What I would look for in a woman is what I had not realized in my own feminine. The more people that can integrate and be whole, the more likely they can be these partners.

Daniel: I especially liked the last point. The goal of fulfilling ourselves. Then we lose the desire for the situation where we have been. Unfortunately, we are not enlightenment, we are not Buddha or Jesus. Another desire comes up inside of us. It is again something that you don't feel fulfilled. There is something out there that is seemingly something that you need. Or you are going to approach or go towards. There is a future and you are not there. You try to approach it. In this regard, to talk about it is where it leads to the changes, where we can say "how are we going to deal with it?" This is the part of our culture where we have tragedy and comedy. To have a special feeling about it. Even when we were talking about the blow job, *we laughed.* It is highly linked because it is so intimate. It comes up with humor.

Cadell: And you don't expect someone to say that word. We talk *around* it.

Daniel: Yes, we talk around it. The nuclear family that is based on the sex of the relationship, which is like the most intimate unspeakable point. I had suddenly the analogy of the dark space, the dark matter that is out there. You have 95% of dark matter out there and nobody finds it. Everyone calculates it but nobody finds it. I don't know the exact number, but it is the most central point. The majority of our universe is dark matter, but it is not there, at least not observable. I find that analogy useful for when we talk around sexual things. We talk around the things that constitute it in its core. We have this middle thing which is related to the sacred or taboo. The core that holds it together. Maybe that is why sometimes in a relationship people say, **"we don't need to talk about it."** Or they say **"you should know what I think."** I think when we don't need the change, it is when we are in silence, or in this core where silence could happen. But when we talk about the truth, it is already going somewhere else. *Even talking about the truth is going to change the truth that we have right now.* That is something very interesting to me: talking about the truth's essence makes the change of truth's essence itself.

Cadell: That is a very Hegelian point, Daniel. As Hegel articulates in the beginning of the *Phenomenology of Spirit*, the pathway to the truth is simultaneously the constitution of the truth itself. You have to include the speech acts, the motion of historical language or logos. In other words, it is not as if there is some "big truth" at the end of the tunnel, unchanged from our historical action. Instead it is that the historical action itself generates what will become the truth. Truth has released itself to the hazards of an open-ended historical process.

Now there are two things I wanted to say. The first thing, in regard to Kevin's point that one day we will all be able to get our blowjobs without trespassing, this blends into the topic of transhumanism which will come up later. But basically, when we are engaged in sexuality, Freud thought there are not two people, *but four*. What he meant by that is that in the sexual act, you have two physical people, and then you have the two physical people's *virtual* objects of desire, which are the location of the authentic cause. So, when you are having sex, defined by this *repetitive motion of enjoyment*, in a psychoanalytic way, you are *actually interacting with your fantasy*. That fantasy is being mapped onto another physical body. The physical body is a material placeholder for your core virtual desire.

Thus, when we think about the structure of human sexuality, as a structure where the act is inherently transgressive, based on an excess (1) and a lack (0), we have to think about the way our virtual desire structures are caught or hooked on another human. If we are not really interacting with another human, but a virtual structure, then it could be that the secret to all of this demonization of pornography, or video games, or the internet, is actually somehow an open pathway for the future of more authentic, totally other forms of sexual expression. I think that is worth thinking through in the time it deserves when we approach transhumanism specifically. To my mind this excessive energy is not going anywhere, and to my mind, it has no real solution in the human space. The number of people who interact with a virtual surface to get repetitive sexual enjoyment without problems of the human other, that is not going anywhere, as far as I can tell. If anything, it is going to become more strange.

But then in relationship to Daniel making the analogy between sexuality and dark matter, which I think is very interesting, it is true that 95% of our universe is not observable. We don't even know what it is, but it must be there for all the material to circulate in the way that it does.

Daniel: Especially on the level of mathematics.

Cadell: Yes, dark matter is a notional structure that is mathematically necessary to describe the physical universe. I think this might be a nice analogy to have a psychoanalytic notion of religion and civilization. Think of it: all of traditional civilization is built on this spiritual dimension, of Gods and other spirit beings, which actually we don't see. All of modern civilization is built on this virtual dimension, of money and financial transactions, which actually we don't see. It is like the spiritual substance of civilization is dark matter. I don't see God there, but somehow all of these buildings, cultures, institutions, are built around this invisible Thing. *Could human civilization exist without the dark matter?*

Then you have this strange flipping of religion in the modern world, where we are not religious anymore. For example, for Marx, religion is **"the opiate of the people."** But I like how now, isn't it the case that *opiates are directly the opiates of the people?* So, you get rid of religion as an opiate and then you have an opiate epidemic. In other words, subjectivity goes directly to this ecstatic source itself. It's like, I don't want second-hand smoke, I want first-hand smoke, I want to smoke! **"I want to smoke directly the Thing itself."** What is the psychical logic here? When you smoke opiates, you are setting yourself up for death. Maybe there are other tools? Psychedelics, DMT, ayahuasca? These substances do not lead to addictions, but they give you access to this "dark matter" of the "spiritual universe." You can even see this break between Catholicism and Protestantism as part of this process. Catholicism would be like "no, only the Pope has access to God." But then Protestantism says, "no, each human mind has access to God." So, you have this breaking down, where each human mind wants as an attractive force direct access to see the "dark matter."

My basic point here is that maybe the pain and the suffering in sexuality, from my point of view, is just that you have to drop your ego. The ego gets attached-fixed onto a human other. You all of a sudden find out they are not the other you are thinking they are. You experience this as tragedy because your ego is going to die. But you can also experience it as a higher truth in the sense that here is a new space to become something even more interesting, possibly. That is what I'll leave it on.

Kevin: I think you nailed it, Cadell, in regard to pain and suffering. That was very skillfully articulated. That is the difference between pain and suffering in all modalities. Even the physical, in regard to injury and disease. The body has pain receptors to protect it; it is a good thing that we have them. The suffering, psychological or mental, that is created by personality, identity, and ego is very much the same in relationship, and maybe the most poignant, deep emotional pain and tragedy, around loss of desire and love. It was either taken from me, or I lost it.

What if we could transmute and transfigure emotional pain through what you are talking about, Cadell, embracing the ego death that comes along in relationship, and sexual-emotional pain? We go into the suffering, fully feel it, confront it with truth, and speak it at the same time. Then allow that fire and intensity to cook us and alchemize our new Self, who is actually on the other side more available to love and intimacy. In this process some impurities have been removed and the capacity has been created where you can hold more in a relationship and be more of yourself in a relationship. This is ultimately a path of the Self, through the Self, to the Self. This is the journey of yourself. The love that I have, through another person, that desire attracted me towards, and back to myself.

Cadell: The cause of desire to the acausal.

Kevin: And I will travel to all the dark matter in-between to get there, through some serious intimacy, sexual desire, highs and lows. I will end there and say that this is one of the pathways to enlightenment.

Daniel: You both spoke so beautifully in the last round.

Cadell: Now you are going to come and mess it up with your inarticulate garble!

Daniel: I think I could really leave it like that, because it is the baseline of this roundup that it is about the ego-death. The love is the purpose of an other. The question that keeps coming up is that if you have the desire for change, how do we handle this in a very good way? *There is pain that we have to confront and accept.* When we accept it, we can incorporate it. The acceptance of pain is more of a way of dealing with it by not rushing into the same issue again but on the other side. So, what can you learn about yourself through the experience of the relationship that is not about you? It goes through you. That is being kind together, to love the shadows that are projected on the relationship, on the imaginary person that you have in front of you. It's your vision and your desires. Suddenly you get disappointed by yourself or the outer thing, but it is actually about yourself through the outer experiences.

Cadell: You were articulate, that was good.

Kevin: Highly articulate.

Cadell: I think to wrap it up, what I take away from this conversation is that it is a paradoxical nature of being. When we read fairy tales of this pleasure principle: you build up to meeting this partner, and then you live happily ever after. This is ground zero of the fundamental fantasy. In reality, to overcome this fantasy, to grow, you have to embrace something that your ego perceives as harmful, or perceives as deeply troubling, or perceives as the wrong direction. Paradoxically you have to embrace this counterintuitive experience.

I would finally encourage any of you to watch *Split* (and also *Glass*, which is set up as after it) because I think this idea of the paradoxical nature of identity is really articulated in those films as it relates to pain and suffering. It is just so strange, you know. I see it emerge in many different ways. What a weird universe to be in.

Kevin: What an exciting one too! This paradox opens up so many massive leaps in evolution and understanding and pleasure and knowledge. It is weird as fuck. But that makes it exciting.

Daniel: Perfect. Perfect.

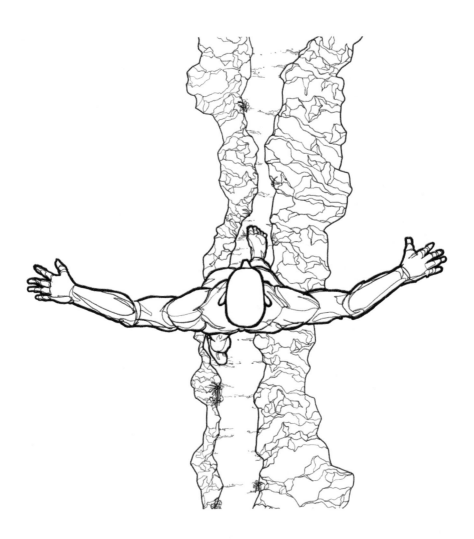

CHAPTER 7

Relational Reality and Absolute Reality

Cadell: The introduction to this chapter will start out with high philosophy before pushing to the core of the issue. In the religious traditions there is always the expression of an Absolute Being: God, Allah, Brahmin, sometimes referred to as "the One" or "the Other Side." The nature of this Absolute Being is that it is unconditional, it is a perfect being, unmovable, eternal, immortal. It has or is the highest expression of substance and thus does not depend on any relationship. If everything else were to disappear, the Absolute would still be; if we were all to disappear, the Absolute would still be. That is precisely the meaning of the nature of the Absolute: it does not depend on anything else. It is not caused by anything, it is not the effect of anything, it is in itself its own cause and effect, its own self-sufficient reason for being.

Now in the secular, humanistic, more scientific worldview, especially as it is developed in the 20th century, a different ontological framework is deployed. This is an ontological framework that emphasizes not Absolutes, but relationships. Everything is based on relations. Everything exists only in relation to something else. Nothing has an Absolute existence, and thus, everything could be other than it is. You can say that this is the opposite of a religious or supernatural framework. This is a motif, the meta-relationship between the religious and the scientific, which provokes an "absolute" conflict.

The specific dimension we want to discuss in this trialogue, however, is perhaps a strange twist in the secular scientific framework. If we consult our sexual experience, our intimate experience, oftentimes, the words that the religiously convicted individuals use will also be used for the intimate other or the sexual partner. You might use words like "the One" or "my true Other half." Or you may say things like "I worship you," or "I feel like you are divine," or "sacred." So, there is a way in which the sexual and religious language overlaps. Is that just a coincidence? Or is the same passionate impulse located in the sexual and the religious?

There is a way in which our experience of our most intimate other is not just another relation. It tends to take the place of "The Relationship." It can't just be a relation like other relations. The question here is whether or not this strange twist in our experience of sexuality points towards a gap or a hole in scientific knowledge itself, as if the repression of the real of sexuality is required to do science. Certainly that would help us make sense of the history of psychoanalysis as a knowledge practice. Psychoanalysis is both grounded in sexual energy and motivated by a scientific curiosity. However, it is no secret that it has never been considered a formal science and has disrupted science from within. Could it be that scientific knowledge is itself something that requires a de-sexualized universe? Could it be that it misses a deep understanding of our sexuality and our intimate reality, necessarily, as a condition for its clear operation?

To give an overview of these two worldviews I'm presenting, I will first quote Aldous Huxley, who wrote a very important book, *The Perennial Philosophy*, which gives a fantastic overview of religious metaphysics throughout history. He does a good job summarizing the worldview which is embedded in notions of an Absolute reality:[12]

"The Perennial Philosophy, the phrase was coined by Leibniz, the metaphysic recognizes a divine reality substantial to the world of things and lives in minds, the psychology that finds in the soul, something similar to or even identical with, divine reality, the ethic that places man's final end in the knowledge of the immanent and transcendent ground of all being. The thing is immemorial and universal."

That quote captures his summary of this worldview of the Absolute, where there is this substantial Absolute reality, unconditional, the One. Now here is another quote from Alfred North Whitehead, who is a philosopher who is oftentimes used as a pivot to a relational worldview, a metaphysic of pure relations with no Absolute. This quote can be found in *Process and Reality*:[13]

"*Process and Reality* presents the positive doctrine of becoming and the relatedness of actual entities. Actual entities are the final real things of which the world is made up. They simply differ among themselves. There is no going behind actual entities to find anything more real."

You can see here the difference between the two worldviews. Huxley is saying that the "Perennial Philosophy" is the Absolute divine reality behind our relational reality. Whitehead is saying there is nothing except the relations in our reality, there is nothing behind or beyond them. There are merely these relations which grow and develop within themselves.

The way I want to situate this is, one, on the religious end of things there is the sublimation to an Absolute which is both ahistorical and non-sexual. This is the Absolute that binds all spiritual or religious traditions independent of worldly culture or historical context. On the scientific end, there is perhaps a repressed belief that the world grows and develops via relations that have no absolute foundation. However, this worldview appears incapable to approach the reality of modern secular sexuality where the experience and language of sexuality reflects relations that appear as absolute to those engaging or interacting. In this sense it appears that both the religious and scientific worldview do not take sexuality seriously in a deep ontological sense. How do you both make sense of these two worldviews?

Kevin: I love that you brought in Huxley and Whitehead. They are two of my top ten philosophers. The question of their philosophical contradiction is very mysterious. What was coming through as you were speaking about the notion of the **Absolute**, or **God**, or the **One**, as it shows up in any religious tradition, is that it is intimated by the mystery of life and death itself. The three gateways in many mystical traditions are **birth, sex,** and **death**. *These are the gateways through which this primordial One immanates and recedes.* The One to me also seems to be one and the same with creation itself. It makes sense then that sexuality, as pure creation, and how human beings are generated, is self-same with the experience of God or the Absolute. I think everyone who has had a deep sexual experience, especially one that is emotionally and intimately connected, can speak to this feeling. No matter your worldview or your epistemology, even if you are a logical positivist or a rational materialist. There is something that intimates beyond mere entities.

I can understand why Whitehead would want to reduce reality to just the relations, because the reductionist tendency in Western philosophy, perhaps starting in Greece with Aristotle, has been immensely beneficial and provided utility to adapt to the survival demands of living on Earth. But the scientific razor cannot approach the titanic or oceanic feeling that two lovers are feeling. The mystery and the immense emotional life, what we may call spiritual and religious psychology, that accompanies actual love and lovemaking. *It is beyond a reductionist idea.* Scientists may say it is a neurotransmitter-mediated process, synaptic clefts that are activated, it is all based on hormones. But this is not satisfying to even the most rational person.

Daniel: Thank you, Cadell and Kevin. I think this topic that we chose is a very challenging one. I think already talking about the Absolute is difficult. It is approached in the way of what is not. It is really difficult to speak about the Absolute, and different religions try to name it by its own name. And, therefore, it is always the same what different religions mean by that. We have different ways to describe it or to say what it is not. On the other hand, we have the trend in science to emphasize the process of becoming.

I am currently reading about a philosopher called Gotthard Günther. He says that the dominant philosophical assumption is the truth about the reflection of things. He says everything we reflect on covers everything that is, even the Absolute. This leads to an underlying presupposition that, in the end, what I think is what is true: *cogito ergo sum*. This means, what we can think is also what is. What is, like the Absolute or what could be independent of thought, is not there. What it is is actually what *could* be. If you look to most present states of being, there is no Absolute or you are in a very ecstatic state, or into an orgasm where time and space just disappear and you don't feel any limits of your body, of thoughts, or whatever. In our actual world in which we experience everything, where we go on the street and meet people and so on, we have our daily experience. There is the subject and object and the intersection between subject and object. In this intersection, becoming takes place as a process of being for Gotthard Günther. So, Günther says we have to abandon the two-valued logic of being and non-being, or thinking and being, and the third value has to be introduced, namely the process: becoming, or the reflection. What means becoming in between two entities? The process of how we are in the world, how becoming evolves, gets more importance, especially nowadays.

We can experience things like the Absolute, in moments, but often we are thrown back again. We are thrown back into our daily lives, into our daily troubles, into our separateness and struggle with our limitations. So, if we ask about our relationships and the Absolute, I ask myself what is the relationship we have to the Absolute? What is the projection into the Absolute and what kind of relationship could that be? And also, if we experience the Absolute then is there no relationship, because it is Absolute? Imagine, we go from an ordinary state of consciousness to the way that leads to this limitless being of approaching the Absolute and we have no relationship, like a Monk with God, only a relationship to the Absolute.

In this mode we still experience the midst of troubles and pains, but we have a direction where to go: to the Absolute. This Absolute is also a way of becoming so nobody gets lost. If we have a relationship with a partner it becomes very interesting because if there is no becoming in the relationship then you are already there, in the Absolute. That can be more difficult in a relationship with another person then in a relationship to God or the Absolute as an abstract thing, because God could be everywhere and never stops being there. With a human relationship it can become more difficult, because if a human relationship is your Absolute, then how and where can you find the limitless, the Absolute Being? Is it in love, in sexuality, or trust? Where are the frontiers or the limit? Are the limits in fear, or in death, or in birth?

Cadell: I agree with you, Daniel, that this trialogue is the most difficult and conceptually challenging yet. At the same time there is something incredibly important to be learned here if we work through this trialogue with rigor. One of the reasons I love this trialogue process is that we can actively work out some thoughts that are unclear to us at the moment. I can say for me that I am always trying to think triadically and dialectically. Thus, when I present things in terms of a binary opposition, like between Huxley and Whitehead, I am secretly, and perhaps sneakily, trying to search for a triadic synthesis within this trialogue itself, which breaks us into another field of knowing.

For me, it is like there is this ecstatic union that one can have with something that we might call "Absolute." For many people they may experience it in the orgasm with the other, or the psychedelic experience. But for me I like this coming back to the **paradoxical double movement**: *after our ecstatic union we get thrown back into our actual existence, a reality with the processes and the relations.* The actual hard work of the Absolute, for me, is precisely when one gets thrown back. For me it is not that we have the "mundane actual reality of processes" and then we go to the "ecstatic world of the Absolute" where we are unified and One. Instead it is precisely that we are in this "actual mundane reality," we go to that "ecstatic reality," and then *what do we do when we get thrown back? What do we do when we get thrown back from that experience?*

The paradox is that the Absolute gets experienced, not as limitless, but precisely where do you hit your limits? Your boundaries? Where do you recognize that you have encountered something in your process which is in some sense something that you have to submit to? Or at least something that you have to recognize that you are not God, or you are not the ultimate reality. You are not the divine reality. There is some limit you hit in the process itself. I experience it as a location of disorientation.

Consequently, I would say that when I am going about my process of becoming, and I get from A to B, this is normal linear reality. However, when I am going about my process of becoming, and *it is like getting hit by a bus. Basically, something derails you. Something disorients you. I have no idea where I am. I was going from A to B, and I thought I was going to C, but I find myself at Q! What the heck!* This for me is the location of the Absolute. For me I experience it most deeply with sexuality and psychedelics. With my first ayahuasca experience, it is like I am going about my normal day to day reality, and then an atomic bomb hits. Then I have to rethink my entire metaphysical framework. Then when it comes to sexuality, it is like the abstract intelligence which can often pretend it is God, and so forth, thinks it can get from A to B to C, and then all of a sudden, no, you are at Q, you are at Y, and so forth, and your mind cannot make sense of it!

So, I like Whitehead's attempt to say process and reality is basically when we study reality we are just studying processes. But what I would say to Whitehead is what about when the process becomes non-linear? Becomes disoriented? This is for me the real Absolute which sets a limit about which you were previously unaware. Then to Huxley, I would say, okay, there is the divine other world, this supernatural world, but it is not a divine substantial other world, but a formal twist in the process. When this twist in the process becomes too much to handle, we erect an image of a supernatural world that we can identify with as a reconciliation of the pain of our real process. That is how I would play with them.

Kevin: I love that you brought up the non-linear aspect of how the Absolute manifests in our process. I also feel this aspect when I am deeply in love, when I sit in ceremony with a plant teacher, or in nature, hiking, or backpacking. Those are the places where the rupture of plane occurs, as Mircea Eliade describes. To me, sexuality and the orgasm are the union with God. I think of the Trent Reznor lyrics, *"you bring me closer to God, because I want to fuck you like an animal."* Sexuality can subsume you in the Absolute. Also, the psychedelic experience, the plant medicine experience, which is older than written history, subsumes you in the Absolute. And then nature itself, union with all connected substances. I think these are the three nexuses around which the Absolute can touch this reality or interact with our subjectivity. There is some overlap. Deep breath work or pranayama can help us get into better synchronicity with this reality. I actually learned this before I sat with plant medicine. Modifying oxygen and neurochemistry, these are ways you can touch the Absolute directly.

However, when I am going about my daily life and tragedy is happening or blockages are happening, or obstacles are happening, relationships are failing, when I am injured physically, I start to question the Absolute. I think it is very human to question or doubt. A bus hits you, as you said, Cadell. You start questioning if there is an Absolute at all. You can get sucked into the monkey mind and physical reality and you are like, *"what is going on here?"* *"Why is it not working out?"* *"I thought everything was the Absolute?"* That is when there is this tension point which is not very pleasant to accept. I think we can all relate to that.

Meanwhile, I want to bring us into the quantum reality of the Absolute, the way it touches this plane. Is there really another world?

Or are the two worlds one? This is where duality and non-duality come into play. But as you were saying Cadell, there is this linear trajectory, the mind, I am going to get from A to B, I am going to follow that process. Whitehead would say I am interacting with all these entities. There is this process of becoming. I am involved in a dialectic of reality through this web of relations. But then something happens, a woman walks by you, and it's like a *boom*; or someone hands you a mushroom, and it's like a *boom*. A quantum leap happens and suddenly A to B doesn't make sense because A to Z was just revealed in a plane rupture. This is like a punctuated equilibrium burst. It is a rupture of consciousness. I think the only way ancient people knew how to talk about that was the perennial philosophy, and God.

Daniel: One very important thing for the experience of the Absolute is that some of these experiences come suddenly into your life, like with psychedelics or sexuality. For most people it is very difficult to integrate what they have experienced, especially when they really have a transcendental experience, feelings of touching the Absolute, or sitting with God. There are also a lot of traditions that use the technique to define themselves. But every technique is actually giving you a lighthouse where to go. Most religious paths can be a very tough training with your mind and feelings. You can spend your whole life doing it, *and you are still not there.* I guess that is a good metaphor for the Absolute being a process.

For me, encountering the Absolute needs a very important time for integration, and also by the moment you are thrown back, it is actually where you are in the process that matters. For me it has always been the feeling that there is a guiding lighthouse. This light feels amazing, and it makes sense because you can feel it. The real guide of life-learning lessons is right here in the difference between this experience of the Absolute and where you actually are in your process. The experienced difference can be quite tough. I experienced this also from spiritual practices and meditation practices. You build a relationship with everything that keeps you from *not being Absolute*: thoughts, fears, a sudden situation of your life, your own imagined future, whatever this could be, just pops up in your mind, and *you just have to let it go*. You just give it positive feelings, or you have to solve something, or forgive some patterns with love, awareness, mindfulness.

In this context, for me, the Absolute is actually about this unblocking of self-limits that we put on ourselves with patterns that got fixed and stuck. Some of the blockages have been built in us from birth. With the psychedelic revolution you easily got this feeling of "okay I got it now" in regard to self-blockages and limitations. However, the problem with the psychedelic revolution is when they are thrown back. Psychonauts have to learn a lot if they want to get to a similar experience without the psychedelics. Those who really want it badly enough will have to work hard to get back in the experience of the Absolute on their own, especially when we are in our world, surrounded with work, relationships, friends, obligations, and stuff like that. These are the most challenging obstacles to transcendent enlightenment. We have to learn to overcome the limits we have with these processes. You always confront yourself with the limits, consciously or unconsciously. Some people confront their fears being in the world or do things they thought they couldn't go beyond. It is like a horizon of what they can see: this is the limit. Once you overcome a certain horizon the horizon simply changes. The limits are different, but the limits as such do not go away.

A further question here is the question of volition. What do we want that drives our way? If we don't want something, it leads to another way. We can negate a former way. If we are struggling on one path, something is happening in relationships or work, it is negation to say, hold on, okay, what is really happening here? Do I have to do this? It is the part of your mind that is controlling the flow of your libidinal energy. This makes the possibility to choose between degrees of freedom. In this situation we have to be reflective because you can drive your sexuality, but mostly this sexual drive is not our conscious will. The question might be: what is in your will that you can reconcile with sexual drive? Maybe this is where we talk about love? Maybe that reconciles the sexual path where the mind can say "hold on" "what are we doing?" Maybe the heart is just between our genital energy and our mental energy connecting both things? This energy drives a lot of people, a lot of journeys, in a lot of ways. Another thing is the *fear of love*. That is strange because you always hit yourself on the *limits to be loved or to love*.

Cadell: This is going deep, Daniel. We were not ready for that knowledge! I will try my best to respond. I think that staying on the theme of this sexuality as the location of the Absolute that is sublimated in religion, and perhaps not acknowledged in science. I want to come to this idea that both of you brought up, actually, which is that when you are thrown back, and you have to reflect on where you actually are, and what you are actually going to do with this knowledge of the Absolute. You both brought up that there is a tension. It's difficult, it is hard work, it is not necessarily pleasurable. I think this is part of where we are in our culture. We have this culture of pleasure, being happy, where we don't understand negative emotions. We are unable to confront difficult things in a way. Political correctness today is this not wanting to talk about things where there is tension, antagonism, where you might not like the answer. All of these things.

For me, one of the most interesting things I've reflected on in the last few years is in regard to sexuality. It seems to me obvious that marriage is a structure which pretends that the sexual tension isn't there, if that makes sense. Every couple ever, who gets married, they think they are going to "do it," and "make it," even if, for example, the divorce rate in Luxembourg is 70%, or the divorce rate in Portugal is 66%. You have this constant drive to obfuscate the sexual tension with marriage, even if statistics show marriages don't work. However, like I said in the previous trialogue about the dialectical difference between the ideal and the actual, it just means we have to fail better. Maybe there is a noble value at work here, but the epistemological tools are wrong or need to be radically updated?

This marriage problem is an interesting phenomenon. Now an extra interesting dimension to this phenomenon is that richer people, wealthier people, get married at a higher rate, sometimes 90%, higher than poorer people. The proletariats, you might say, are abandoning the institution, with their marriage rates being much lower and their success rates being worse. The idea that stuck with me is twofold. The first idea is that maybe the whole capitalist world and machinery is designed to guard against sexual negativity? Capitalism replaces the function of religion, as in the philosopher Giorgio Agamben's formula of modernity: "God didn't die, He was turned into money."

The second idea is that communist revolutionary movements could have failed because of this sexual negativity being unleashed. This may be too simplistic, but to build communes you have to problematize marriage and normative sexual relations. You have to contend with sexual negativity in the commune instead of covering it up with the nuclear bond and the marriage link. Thus, there is this strange borderland between the bourgeoisie marriage family and the egalitarian commune which seems to me to present the most Absolute limit. *You shall not pass! You shall not pass!* This is Gandalf versus the Balrog, the bridge is crushing down. Gandalf is hanging onto the cliff side, and then he falls into the abyss. This is a metaphor for the 20th century attempt to escape capitalism's bourgeois marriage units to communism's egalitarian communes vis-a-vis sexual negativity. *You shall not pass!*

Now, it is interesting what Daniel said about the libido. It is true that a lot of our drive is on this libidinal energy. We obviously don't actually have full control over this energy. The question is, how do you drive on this wild energy field? Freud used the metaphor of a wild horse and a horse rider. The rider is the ego and the horse is the id. But do we need a different metaphor? I feel like we need a different metaphor on the level of social and historical becoming. The metaphor I would suggest was developed by Jacques Lacan and Slavoj Žižek: of libido as *alien*. This alien is like the alien in the *Alien* movie. You are on a spaceship, and the libido is like an alien. You can never fully see it, you can never get at its full dimension, but it is taking people down one by one. *This is what would happen if you built a commune.* As soon as you form the commune, *there is the alien there*, waiting to take everyone down. It is coming to get you!

This is so real. I want to keep it 100% real. If the three of us, say me, the two of you, seven other guys and ten other girls... say we started a commune. *How long before we hate each other? How long before the Alien comes for us? Not very long!* The question for me is do we need an art? If this is a metaphor to use for the Absolute and the sexual. I agree with Daniel about pushing limits and in terms of pushing our limits we encounter fear. This is the enemy at its core, **fear**. We need an art to extend our limits and confront our fear, because we also cannot recoil into simple pleasure and not discuss difficult things. But at the same time in my own experiences, with the sexual, it is really hard to integrate the negativity of the sexual. You have to integrate it, and you can become better if you do it. But you have to do it slowly, **artfully**. You can also get PTSD!

Kevin: You are cracking me up with the "alien metaphor." *It is perfect.* I am a deep student of Ridley Scott and H.R. Giger who designed the **xenomorphs**, "the alien" from the *Alien* movies. He was actually inspired by H.P. Lovecraft, the deep surrealist and abstract writer. It is perfect, the other, the alien, the libidinal forces of the *primordial savage creation*. It is *the fight, the fuck, the kill.* That is why those movies struck a deep chord with humanity, because it combined sexuality and confrontation with the unknown in a way that it hits you in the subconscious. Tell me those movies don't move you on a primal level!

Now to talk about the boundaries of the libidinal energy. Is there a way to do this skillfully, as an art or science, a way to confront the other as libido, and not to contain or sublimate it, not to transcend or bypass it, but to meet it in a union of opposites? I don't know if we have any good examples in modern civilization for that. There are just tensions. The big project of modern civilization has been to stall this confrontation for fear of the destructive energy that would be unleashed, that might undo a lot of the underpinnings upon which we have built economies, cultures, religions, governments. This knowledge is in relation to perennial philosophies worldwide. It is in the Alchemical, Vedic, Taoist traditions. The union of opposites is like the razor's edge.

I have dedicated a lot of my life to understanding the skillful means and toolsets to access that point and start that process. *That libidinal alien will take you out.* This is where **addiction, maladaptation** and **trauma** are birthed. The negative emotion associated with **infidelity, betrayal, unrequited desire, unrequited love, sexual trauma,** are *so immense,* that I believe a lot of other traumas stem from them. Other traumas may be epiphenomenal of this fundamental trauma. I think this is "the one" source code of the pains of humanity, beyond or as the pain of separation from the Absolute. If creation is a savage act, a holy act, a sacred act, becoming one with the Absolute, then those opposites may be reconciled, *if we have the courage to confront the libidinal force.* **Submission** is a big part of this. **Submission is a key component of sacred space**: of ceremony, and religious, transcendental experience. *The ego-personality must submit to something larger in order to undergo metamorphosis.* This is the whole idea of ego death and rebirth. *I believe the confrontation with libidinal drives in oneself is the ultimate submission.*

Daniel: I love this point of submission because it is there where you are in a becoming, the point of volition where you let go of what you want. This is also where you can relate to the flow state. Submission leads you in the flow state to the Absolute because you have the exact amount of what you can handle while keeping yourself in the present moment. You are on this thin line of this intense awareness. What you are doing right now is everything in this perfect moment. You are in time from the phenomenological perspective. This kind of submission where you don't hold onto thoughts with your brain or ego. This leads to a very nice point where this "becoming" is on its way because you surrender your ego. You don't hold onto your ego or what you want. Instead you let what should happen, or you let feelings go where they need to go or live right there where you are in a real presence.

Now what is very crucial in what Cadell said about libido leads me to think this notion of reality, and *what is reality?* What is, *it is always kind of a past. It is always what has been,* actually. We say what is, and *then it already passed away.* Reality is not something that you can hold on in the present. *The present is this endless becoming.* Whereas if you hold on in this present, being in itself as an endless eternity, as most of the spiritual traditions command, then your mind is not wandering in the past or the future. Sexual negativity might be an even bigger challenge. Sexual negativity holds you deeply to memories and desires of *your being and your emotions.* It can become quite difficult to be in the present. Or if you have a sexual drive that leads you to go there to be with a woman, or a man, or whomever. It is always "**I want,**" "**I want.**" "**I,**" this ego, "**wants,**" and this willingness or volition, you hardly find it in the present mode of being.

However, the way to submit to whatever might happen leads you to this mode of the eternal present. This way is not only a way of submission, but also of creation, where you are in between duality, where the things you want are the things that your whole environment wants. How can the will of you, and of the environment, be the same? How do you match an evolution of becoming by matching an inner and outer world in which you find yourself in this perfect flow of the present timing? How do you achieve a personal becoming that can flourish and simultaneously an evolution as a whole that can flourish? It is a weird thing because once you are in a flow state, like snowboarding, and you are driving down the mountains, and you lose all thoughts of work, troubles, nothing matters anymore, you are just on the ride, *perfect in time.* Or sports maybe, trying to lead yourself, to fixate yourself into the present moment, for the longest time as possible. This is also where spiritual traditions try to lead you by chants, concentration techniques, dancing: *to focus your awareness into the present time.*

Of course, I should reiterate that when it comes to the sexual being, it is maybe the most difficult one to be in the present time, but it is also possible. I think it depends on the modality of the sexual drive: does the sexual pain drive you, or do you drive the sexual pain? How can I say it? On the one hand you can be driven by the sexual, but you can drive the sexual by being attractive. How does this lead to a notion where it is in an actual present awareness of a notion where flourishing can be for your evolution, and the evolution of your environment. This creates maybe good sex, and also different forms where you find yourself with different persons, or maybe a piece of art, or maybe snowboarding becomes "having sex" with a mountain by just riding it down. Sometimes my friends playing jazz music feels like having sex with the people who are listening because they all in tune into to each other by the music in an agreement on where they are right now.

On a final point, what is a really interesting and provoking questions for me is: *Why is that sexual negativity specifically so deep? It is so hard to unlock.* It is really interesting because there are the *most hidden things*, the *most brutal things*, when it comes to relations, and it is the *most traumatic things*. Maybe apart from war. But *war is where most sexual abuses take place*, so they come along with one another on a broader social scale. This is really a difficult thing on a global scale. I don't know where to go.

Cadell: *It's okay to cry.*

Daniel: It has almost no solution.

Cadell: I couldn't agree more with your final point about negativity. To summarize very quickly, that is how I understand the Absolute: *this negativity*. Against Huxley or Leibniz, who claim that divine reality is this substantial other world, I think precisely, the *Absolute as negativity is the opposite of that*. There is an Absolute, but it is precisely absent, it is negative, it is *precisely what emerges in the impossibility of the relation*. I feel like, in the same way, I relate to a pencil case, my journal, I'm relating to the two of you, but somehow in sexuality, there is an *impossibility of relation*. This is what is Absolute. In the way I have been thinking about it, the problem is, although this way of thinking is useful, the problem is, it just makes you aware that there is no solution. That can be difficult to integrate. It is an irreducible problem. It is the exact opposite of traditional religion, where there is a final solution or answer (i.e., God).

You know, well, let me think, I am not going to solve it, but one thing you both said was the word of **submission**. Funny enough, Allah means submission, in the Quran. Also, in the Neolithic, all of the old Neolithic sites, they were structured by large mounds or a large temple area. At these mounds you have to enter into the temple and have it aligned with the winter and summer solstice, where rays of light will shine into the doorway. They are specifically designed as doorways so you have to kneel down to get in. You have to submit your ego to crawl into the chamber. There is this way in which submission is built into the most sacred. The more I think about it the more it may be a useful concept when it comes to dealing with sexual negativity, precisely because we are always thinking about the sexual, and maybe this is the fault of men. This is not always the fault of men, but seeing it from the man's perspective, we are always thinking from the perspective of "what I want," "what can I have," and precisely this is the function of the ego, as Daniel noted. That does bring pain and negativity with it.

It might be worth playing around in the sexual negativity, what doors open up when one is willing to submit one's ego, but with self-respect. You don't want to submit and be walked on, you don't want to become a doormat, and the other person walks all over you, and you just submit. But there may be an art which helps you to process the negativity on both sides. And the recognition that both parties and any number of parties involved are going through the negativity together. There is a union in the struggle. There is the idea that we are all going through this together. It is not as if there is one person who is not going through it, and the other person is in a tragedy. If we are all going through it together and submission of the ego, then that might be an interesting way to frame it.

I will also add in regard to the scientific ego, that it definitely won't submit. Maybe that is part of the equation in this relationship where we have been discussing between the Absolute and worldly relations. I think there is a space for a new conversation, and a space where throughout the course of this trialogue, we have been unpacking this interesting space.

Kevin: I love what you said about the Neolithic sites. The sacred spaces, temples, festivals, worldwide. What came to mind was the **sweat lodge**. You have to crawl on your hands and knees to enter the lodge. It is very womb-like. There is a way in which submission is exalted. There is a way in which submission is giving away your power completely. That is not the submission we are thinking or speaking about. It is an exalted act. It is giving over responsibility but gaining responsibility to the All, to a totality beyond oneself. This is the way to transmute deep trauma and suffering on a collective level. This has existed for as long as we have known. There is a savagery to existence. Sexuality and violence touch it. We look to the Absolute to provide answers. This touches on the deepest things possible. This touches on why is there something rather than nothing, and the insoluble problem of evil.

Submission is a great way to frame this larger discussion about religion and science, you nailed it, Cadell. The scientific ego has yet to submit to something larger. Jung pointed out that the appearance of flying saucers, and the appearance of UFO-ology, and the paranormal was the first real attempt to submit the scientific ego. Now we are faced with quantum reality, which is stranger than we ever imagined. The basement of physical reality is *totally incomprehensible to us.* Then there are the largest scales too, structured by superclusters of galaxies which are organized by supermassive black holes of a size and power which *transcends the laws of physics.* We have reached the instrumental edges of science and its endeavor to understand reality, and I believe the submission is coming. I don't know if it is going to be an event, perhaps contact with another species, or disclosure. Perhaps it is something in the human body that we don't understand. DMT is a candidate to provoke this, there is a lot of emerging research on these entheogens.

Cadell, I want to emphasize again, you really touched the core of this with submission. The reason sexuality and the Absolute come into the same field is the immense negative emotion associated with it, being separated from the Absolute, the beloved. That is a massive feeling that we are still trying to cope with. The saying goes "a happiness

shared doubles, and a suffering shared, halves." There is something about collectives of human beings sharing these fields together in a type of experience which is key. That is the only way, I believe, that this could be reconciled.

Daniel: There is an art to overcome the sexual negativity. It is not a solution, *but the hardest part*. How to unlock your limits? *Your limits are driven by pain and fear*. Submission is crucial for that. Also compassion, forgiveness, and gratefulness. Science never accomplishes an understanding of this dimension. There is no real place for feelings in science because there is no subject in science. Where it becomes very interesting is when we go to the place where it comes to submission. I once made a good exercise that I can recommend. You can do this with your partners. This is an exercise where you bend on your knees and lay down straight on the floor. This is an exercise to say "Okay, I can submit to you" and "the other person can submit to me." In this process you create this equality at an eye level. Then you stand up straight. That is what it means to be straight for yourself. It is a very embodied technique. This leads to a lot of emotions in yourself. It is a very nice exercise to do. When it comes to couples and relationships the hardest thing to do is this equal submission. One challenges the other and it is so easy that a disequilibrium starts to happen.

Cadell: I would even insist that this disequilibrium is somehow fundamental. There is some sort of asymmetry in the couple. We are not in symmetrical equilibrium; we are systems that are inherently far from equilibrium.

Daniel: It is asymmetrical. But it can be balanced, or you totally lose track of the overlap. Maybe you might find out yourself if you do the exercise. Can you submit and stand up? Submit and stand up? You can learn how to balance this in your relationship. This is a very difficult thing to handle with sexual relationships. Forgiveness, gratefulness, compassion, submission. Only submission is the very sexual emotion to the unblocking and the drive in this present moment. This is the key point to embrace both the sexual relationship and the Absolute.

Cadell: I would say even that, what I am taking away from this, is that if we have on the one side the religious Absolute world, and on the other side this scientific relational world, then we situate our discussion around working emotional-sexual negativity in relations with submission (of the ego, or the I), then we reach new embodied knowledge. I would love to see a field that gives embodied work practices with submission, compassion, forgiveness, and gratefulness. There is something interesting here that we should further reflect on. But we have to watch out for the aliens!

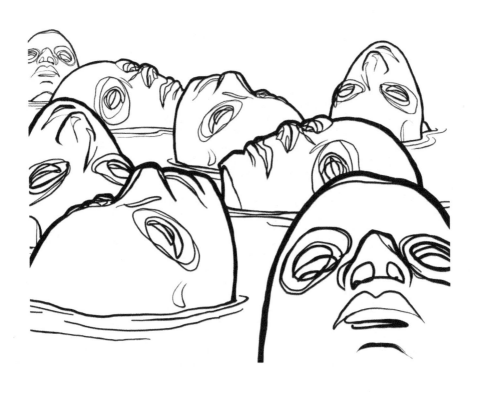

CHAPTER 8

Ethics and Morality in Sexual Space

Cadell: We are going to be covering ethics and morality as it relates to sexuality. In terms of how psychoanalysis sees an ethical subject, the main discovery is that an ethical subject is willing to follow one's most intimate desires independent of any a priori frame that would guarantee a specific outcome. If you are an ethical subject you are not just adhering to the structure of the superego, or of your society's given structure, but you're willing to explore your own intimate core, and you're informed by this in your development as a subject.

In terms of morality, differentiated from ethics, it has to do with the sphere of others in relation to your action. Most of post-Kantian philosophy basically suggests that a moral subject acts symmetrically with respect to the field of others. Here the classical axiom "do unto others as you would do unto yourself" applies. The question here is about an ethical subject which must persist in regard to inner desire, and a moral subject, which must be deeply mindful in regard to the sphere of others.

How do these two dimensions of our individual and collective existence become twisted and contorted in the sexual space? In short, how can one develop true fidelity to desire while developing consideration of the other? It seems like an impossible problem, and we run into fundamental paradoxes and contradictions which might make it extremely confusing to align those two dimensions of our existence. That is basically what we are going to confront. No small task. I am really excited to see what the two of you think of this issue.

However, before we get into it, I want to give a precise quote from Slovenian philosopher, Slavoj Žižek. This quote is specifically about this aforementioned but crucial difference between ethics and morality:[14]

> "[Ethics and morals] are not the same. Morality is concerned with the symmetry of my relations to other humans; its zero-level rule is "do not do to me what you do not want me to do to you." Ethics, in contrast, deals with my consistency in relation to myself, my fidelity to my own desire."

I would furthermore emphasize, following Žižek, that this is where we should locate the break with classical moralist philosophy, and the emergence of figures like Friedrich Nietzsche and Sigmund Freud. The first figure, Nietzsche, here levels a brutal attack on the forms of mindless morality that lead to conformity in traditional social structure, best exemplified with his classic *Genealogy of Morals;*[15] and the second figure, Freud, forever transforms ethics by firmly grounding it in the libidinal universe of problematic desire, best exemplified with his classic *Three Essays.*[16]

For Žižek, there is a gap between the truth of our normal day-to-day consciousness and the truth of our libidinal consciousness. This gap, identified by Freud in the speech of the unconscious, leads to paradoxes of transparency with the erotic other because we are not fully self-transparent. He claims that this lack of transparency, both with the other, and with ourselves, is a necessary feature of human sexuality. Furthermore, it is the source location of the problems of irrational conflict between human beings, which require a type of authority or law to prevent the monsters of our unconscious to come rushing to the surface. It is this twisted space that is necessary to talk about morality and ethics, that is necessary to talk about freedom and love, that is necessary to talk about the possibility of a community that transcends the old traditional structure.

Kevin: There is a lot to unpack there. I really enjoy Žižek's frame and his way of thinking. It is highly developed. However, I disagree that the erotic inherently depends on deception and illusion or lies. I mean there is a powerful quote by Terence McKenna that when language was invented, *lying became possible*. There is an animalistic reality where lying is not possible in the same way. When we enter the domain of language, with talking and verbalized thought, the possibility of deception opens up. In the current sense of the erotic universe, deception or illusion or allure or glamour or mesmerism are highly sexualized, especially in the Western culture. However, in a transparent universe where we could externalize our thoughts and feelings visually, where we could perfectly convey our being with language, that deceptive eroticism would no longer exist. Eroticism would exist in a new form. It would be based on energy that is authentic and true essence. That feels true to me. I have just glimpsed that in my life.

This second quote brings up to the core energetic that we were speaking to. *How do human communities contend with sexuality, infidelity, deception, and the sexual real?* Historically, I think that the sexual agreements and the financial agreements in our shared reality have been the number one and two problems in human civilization. We have erected various moralities and taboos and prohibitions to manage them. I wanted to share this statistic that came up in a recent event I was a part of: that nine out of ten intentional communities started since the 1960s have failed to become successful beyond the ten-year mark due to sexual and financial agreements, worldwide.

In a similar way, in the startup or business world, 90% or 95% of startups fail in year two or before, post-capitalization, due to founder issues or personnel issues, which are always sexually and financially shared. I think those statistics right there, when human beings form small groups with objectives and contain a subculture within the dominant culture, force us to think how human beings contend with the libidinal forces and how money is distributed.

Daniel: I think we are heading to a tough trialogue, because there are so many things found and combined in this space. For ethics we think of things inside of ourselves, and morality more about this symmetrical other. In terms of morality we are talking about agreements that come along often to handle libidinal energy that you cannot tame somehow else. It is socially fixated by norms and rules. Since not everybody can tame it, it will be hidden in the dark. The taboos arise and you don't talk about it, or you lie about it. So, there are the big issues that come along with envy, destroyed rules or norms, different sorts of hurt feelings, and there are notions of accusation. Basically, you can trace all of that back to unfulfilled expectations. And these expectations are expected in the outside world. I think the big challenge is to look inside yourself because on the one hand, *there are also expectations inside yourself*. However, it is very difficult to become aware of the internal morality, because you expect something mostly without knowing that you are expecting this. You just feel like not matching or matching with your environment.

When it comes to ethics it touches another level because somehow you can have very different expectations. When you are in touch with your ethics you meet friction with how to get along with other people or with most people. In this situation you might be afraid to be "not the good one" anymore, because the "good one" is living by society's moral code of the external world. How can you match some inner ethics with the culture outside of you? If you are moral on the one hand, and you try to do good for others, but it is defined differently by what other people think is "the good," is that good? Then we have to entertain another notion of morality. There is the norm in society or in law that tells you exactly what is good and what is not. Then there is the inner morality or law inside oneself. I think they are different notions, because in the realm of becoming both internal and external, moral codes can change in different ways. Consider feeling inner guilt or shame because the external moral code says homosexuality is wrong. Then consider this inner feeling of guilt or shame changing because now the external moral code says homosexuality is right. Alternatively, one can have the inner feeling that they are correct in their belief or desire, even if the external moral code says it is wrong.

There is always a perspective on who or what is right, especially when it comes to *the observed*. Who is involved in the observation? Someone who is observed is easily accused. On the other hand, the one that is involved, someone who breaks the law, for example, somehow feels like he has to break the law. It is an instinct or drive. Or if someone is cheating, does he or she feel in the moment of doing it a moment of guilt? In other words, what is the relation between someone breaking the law or norms or something that hurts someone else? In either situation it could be something that someone fights for to get some help, support or sense of breaking out of the current behavior and doesn't know better how to do it. I feel, breaking the law and cheating on someone might have similar causes of guilt because of feeling: let's go for our freedom, break the current pattern, and do what we have or want to do. There is a really tricky thing about it. What is the intimate relation to yourself and who or what is outside? The outside is even reflected to what is inside myself. And what is outside of my relationship is the inside of someone else's outside. If there is someone on the outside that you don't feel an intimate emotion, this relationship becomes the outside and the moral norms of someone else. If there is someone on the inside that you do feel an intimate emotion, this relationship becomes the inside of your ethical sense of doing good. When it comes to accusation, guilt and hurt, they would never feel guilty or shame from an inside relationship because it is intimate, equal and it is all right, and nobody sees it, nobody talks about it, but it would come from an outsider perspective introducing transparency and broader scale of common sense.

Cadell: There is a point that is coming to my mind from your reflections. This point is that if ethical fidelity and moral symmetry are to be unified then all psychic agents would have to take full responsibility for their own self-relation, especially with responsibility for their own unconscious. That is a hell of a thing to demand or presuppose as even a remote possibility when you know that "knowing thyself" fully is basically a structural impossibility. Nonetheless, it appears to me to be the necessity for the union of these dimensions. In other words, one cannot leave morality to the field of unconscious social regulations and instinctual inclinations. The example Daniel gave of an intimate desire on the inside causing some perceived damage on the outside is a demonstration of this necessity.

To deeply reflect about these problems is of high importance, because if you think in the larger political context about communism, it is basically about the abolition of private property. This means that in communist idealization no one owns anything. This means, in this society, no one could break into someone's house and steal something from them. No one owns anything so you can't steal anything. However, as Kevin mentioned, intentional communities fail because of sexual and financial agreements. This means we still live in a world, or a human reality, where people are seen, upon entering a sexual or financial relationship, either pragmatically or metaphysically, as property. You/this are "mine."

On the specifically sexual level, when we have sex with each other, typically we have sex with them under the unconscious presupposition that I own this other person. Now that we had "this" experience, then if this person has the same experience with another person, it is as if someone broke into our house and stole something because we owned them. I think this is true even in poly communities where there is a conscious mediation of relationships that are more open. The unconscious still maintains boundaries here independent of our conscious desire to be more open. We cannot abolish the propertization of the sexual other. The sexual other is closed in on like an alligator waiting silently with its mouth wide open for a water buffalo. This has to go down the fundamental core of our psychology, or the way our psychology handles being in a body. Thus, until we have a better self-understanding, we will constantly be projecting onto the other a form of ownership in order to maintain our own psychological balance.

I want to connect this to what Daniel said in our last trialogue about sexual negativity and it being traced back to the expectations you place on the other. These expectations can be conscious or unconscious. In terms of normativity, something will be seen as sexually bad or moral. My hypothesis is that if we remove the functional evolutionary reasons for this mechanism, what is happening on the level of our psychic experience is that a defense mechanism of the ego or the persona is in operation. That means morality is like a protective blanket or crutch for a toddler. You think someone else is "bad" because it is difficult to take care of your own psychological reality. The other has to be scolded, put on a time out. In other words, because of an internal psychological issue, when we enter a sexual relation with the other, what is often not said when two people engage sexually is actually the idea that there is a property relation being established.

To build a world of sexual relations where these mechanisms are not in operation, that seems to me difficult to impossible. I doubt you would even have sexuality at that point. In a reality where people are psychologically mature enough to deal with sexuality in this way, it would in some sense mean that people would not even psychologically require sexuality at all. Sexuality would not be seen as this precious and scarce resource to be protected around firm and strict barriers because one would have this precious and scarce resource, the missing other, already inside oneself.

Kevin: What I am hearing as a sort of golden thread is **emotional maturity**. For many people in a nuclear family, mother and father, with siblings, it is not a safe place for deep or big emotions. Deep or big emotions would be threats to internal stability. Emotions like rage, frustration, grief, sorrow, lust, power or collapse and weakness, these emotions cannot be permitted. Negativity cannot be permitted, basically. We have been subconsciously fed that because of the modeling of our parents and family units. In my situation, I was not witnessing my parents or family members take responsibility for their emotions. There is this trade route of emotional projections and wounds that play out in transference. There is a lot of discomfort, anger, and sorrow. It is even too much to handle. These emotions may fundamentally destabilize the presuppositions at work here in this family or relation.

In this way, what you are pointing to, Cadell, I think Carl Jung pointed out as well. Jung stated that until the **individuation** process is completed, with full separation from the mother and father, as god and goddess, then full sovereignty and ownership of one's own reality cannot take place. This full sovereignty and ownership of one's own reality includes the ugly or dark parts. This includes the perpetrator within, the predator, the trickster, the manipulator, and the emotional psychopath. These are archetypes that exist in all human beings to varying degrees. When I am not taking responsibility for these emotions in the Self, and when I am emotionally, romantically and sexually charged with a woman, in my case, those emotional states unclaimed within me will become played out unconsciously in language and action with her. I will place the parts that I can't own, or I don't feel safe with, over there, and then try to fix them and make them wrong, and then maybe I'll relate to them in a non-healthy way as an individuated adult.

For men specifically, since I am in a male body, this is referred to as the mother wound: trusting the feminine, trusting the breast, will there be milk? Trusting the smell and the feeling of the mother, will I be safe? Will I be protected? For men I think this is connected to rites of passage and initiation and the crisis of masculinity that we can see all around us. Until full individuation from the mother has occurred, it is hard to relate sexually with a real woman in a confident and secure way. The ethics and morality as you are pointing out, Cadell, can become a wet blanket or a spiritual bypass or a way to mitigate the emotional harsh real of negative emotions, infidelity, and intense attachment strategies. This is what true individuation is about.

For me, I resonate much more with morality than ethics. My moral compass goes through a development and I feel innate qualities that have led me very well in my life overall. It has also gotten me into some traps, but I think that has been because of religious morality, which brought in pre-programmed dogma. However, studying ethics in the Western tradition, from Aristotle, has helped inform my mind as well. This helped me contextualize and link me to the heart, or the emotional reality, which is beyond words. In this context, society's ethics has helped me relate and build community and do business and have the right relation to the world. And my inner morality, especially in relation to my body and sexuality, will always be my first move and my first trusted advisor. Maybe a universal ethic would be individually actualized humans with emotional maturity embodying their inner morality. Then these humans could come around a shared reality, an ethic of that sovereign morality in the community. To me, that is one of the only pathways I can see for real intentional community that can build commune, farm, organization, entrepreneurs, startups, and lifestyles that are not destroyed internally by sex and money.

Daniel: If I combine what you both said, I am trying to reflect on this notion of projection. I think also Jung pointed out well that everything outside yourself is a mirror of something inside yourself. If you take this knowledge and you have all this projection coming along with your relationship where your expectations are, and you turn them back as a mirror to yourself, you become aware of your responsibility and of you being expecting things from the outside world that are actually expectations of yourself. If we align that with what you see as a morality out there, and an ethics, what is inside yourself, and, if you put this as a mirror of yourself, and you don't come along with one or the other, then it might be interesting to know what actually is your inner relationship to what might be called freedom, justice, love, or truth.

To my knowledge those values are the highest values that one can follow and which you can align yourself. For yourself that means self-love, for being truthful to yourself. Also, to find a kind of justice of how you can be, how you can look in the mirror without shame, because you have done the righteous thing. The question is when you do the right thing, it is always "to whom" and "what relations" are you involved? Who is more right than the other? Who is more relying on justice or love than the other? Then there always comes this disbalance we mentioned in the last trialogue. It becomes an interesting point when you feel not very kind because someone else shows you more kindness or a higher level of justice. If you don't put it in black and white, then we will always find ourselves in between many different ways to open to the inner and outer worlds that reflect these different values and might have meaningful differences. When these differences come along it is for real questions: "Am I wrong or am I right?" "Am I playing out justice or not?"

I think people who have learned emotional maturity have had to learn about themselves as a mirror of society. They can't teach people morality out of their isolated ethics. Sometimes what people call morality was never actually discovered in their own feelings towards it. They never discovered the experience of it. They just followed what they were told. In contrast, most people who have written down these values, they have had to experience it, they have had to find it, or otherwise they have been taught by someone else. There is this intersection where you have to, or you somehow, your consciousness, is just embracing the other. This other might be for someone bigger or smaller. And I think from that perspective, if ninety percent of the people say breaking into a house is not all right, then it is not all right, and the one making up the law feels more ethical in their sense of their self than the two that are breaking in and just feel for their families. So, there is an imbalance of how much we are embracing the other and yourself. It also happens that the Self becomes the others and loses its own self. These are the ones that end up maybe fighting for their own rights and embracing themselves again. This is a universe for itself. For the majority of people out there, I think the deepness of this insight is inside as well as outside.

Cadell: Well if we are starting with male-female relationships for this ethical-morality knot, and these relationships are being played out in a domain of wound and projection, and this domain of wound and projection is related to the inside-outside, and what you see outside is a mirror of the inside, I come back to the self-relationship as essential. We can't have a healthy sexual space when the sexual space is based on wounded people trying to give selflessly. This giving selflessly is a projection, a front and a lie, because it is based on a wound. Now if this is the case, and it is based on a wound and a lie, I could defend Žižek's point again, that eroticism requires a type of lie, in the form of a self-deception and another deception. The mechanics of the unconscious makes something erotic, because it is unknown, concealed, hidden, secret.

I know for me, in my masculine sexual position, the reality is that the man in terms of conventional sexual relationship is going to be the typical initiator of a sexual relationship. In other words, as in the masculine position, you are approaching the sexual relationship. You don't tell the woman what is actually going through your mind when you approach. The thoughts running through your mind might be something related to wanting to sleep with her. You are hoping that the conversation will lead to sexual intercourse or something. Instead of saying the "truth" of what is going on in your mind, you will say anything but that. In order for the sexual relationship to happen, it requires a founding gesture which is in some sense inauthentic. If you were authentic you would say, "Hey, I think you're really hot, I would like to X, Y, Z with you right now!"

We, I mean the general male population, know that doesn't work, that doesn't function. What functions is a type of primordial distortion in the discourse, a perhaps playful circling around sexuality instead of directly inscribing it into the discourse. Then the relationship is a primordial distortion. The question is, if we were non-wounded, *and I am skeptical that there is a non-wounded human, I think wounding is the core of subjectivity.* So, if we were non-wounded, *would we even be having sex?* Jacques Lacan makes the point that sex itself is a mark of finitude and mortality. You would not be a sexual being if you were immortal and eternal. In other words, if you are sexed, you are cut, you are separated as an individual organism. *What else would you be having sex for? What would you be having sex for if you were full and complete?*

I am just wondering here as deep as I can because, the one thing I will add here, is if there are non-wounded human organisms, you would expect them to be found at the highest possible spiritual expression. Are these people having sex? When you look at communities of monks, communities of people in deep spiritual communion, they are typically not having sex. I don't know. I wonder about what that means. This is to be framed in an immanent logic of **absentials**: when you look to study a spiritual community the curious thing to note is the absence of any sexual relation. I am just saying that if we had emotional maturity, if we were really in charge of our wound, in command of our libidinal drive, would sexuality even be happening? My guess is no.

Kevin: You're bringing up very interesting points. Some of what you are saying is profound because I don't think there is an unwounded human either. This is what is captured in the Fall, in the notion of Paradise Lost. Something has happened in humanity, we have a shared wounding. I am also aware that for me, *wounding is not a bad thing*, it should be embraced, *it is where the light gets in*. A lot of wounding becomes a superpower. The wounding is a deep boon to growth. The wound draws attention to and activates hidden resources in the psyche. There is a way in which wounding is serving us.

And, at the same time, we can imagine at least, a reality where there is not deep emotional and sexual trauma. That is actually what motivates me to do the work that I do. With that being said, *would an immortal infinite being need to have sex?* No! *Would it choose to have sex?* I like to think that I would! I think it would affirm sex simply for the beautiful heart in us that loves to be surprised, and loves a little chaos and recombination to let this game of life, this human experience, have an element of alchemy. I think that because of distortions, because of familial and ancestral lineage of past trauma, because we didn't have parents that knew how to do it without wounding, now we don't know how to do it (sex) very well. Very very few people know how to do sex well. Maybe people from the human potential movement from the 1950s and 60s. I don't know.

But there is a way in which the male-female, mother-father imago, formed in sexual, relational, and emotional co-dependencies. If they formed in deceptions, without authenticity, truth and clear communication, then we shouldn't be surprised that most of us exist in wounds in the sexual real. There are other examples of dynamics in the psyche that operate in this same reality. I think the relationship to God is like this. That truth is present for me. How do you relate to the real of ultimate being? How do relate to the first mover, the primary mover, the Creator, God-Goddess? This is in relation to what holds a similar wound to the sexual real, they are linked. *Adam in the Garden.* There is a moment in the unedited version of *The Bible*, Adam gets lonely. He says **"God, I need a companion,"** an other, to manifest my reality. One immortal man on Earth could thrive, but then there was woman, and the patriarchal code, woman fashioned out of the rib of man. Now you have an other and there are two beings who can multiply into the billions of beings today.

This really calls into question what you are bringing up, Cadell, about sacred space and the lack of sexuality in those spaces. My feeling is that in ceremony and in those spaces there is an eroticism present. There is a highly-charged emotional energy, a libidinal space, but it is manifested and channeled in the body through various modalities, sound, silence, chanting, deep emotional expression, eye contact, communion with nature. There are other channels that funnel that same sexual energy. If someone were to start having sex in those spaces it would be seen as inappropriate, a break with the sacred container. However, there are also plenty of examples of rites and rituals which *do involve* sexuality in the sacred space. In this context, I am curious about the word transfiguration, to make holy, in the sexual real. Can sexuality actually be sacred outside of day-to-day experience, outside of dating, whatever you want to call the "human mating Savannah," "the watering hole." There are a lot of negative emotions, failed relationships, high divorce rates, single mothers raising children. *The gap is so profound. This is a core wound.* Infidelity and sexual repression. That is why I deeply studied this. I think it has made me highly emotionally intelligent.

Daniel: I was thinking about a story from the old Greeks. There is a story of Chronos, the **God of Time**. Chronos was the son of Ouranos and Gaia. They were the primordial gods. The other gods came from them. There are different versions, but actually Ouranos and Gaia are also Mother Earth and Father Heaven. Anyway, what happens in the story is that Chronos, the son of both, cuts the penis of Ouranos, his father, because he wants to start a rebellion against the law. He throws it, the penis, into the water. This penis then becomes Venus. Venus becomes Love, Aphrodite. Venus from the Latin side, Aphrodite from the Greek side. The point is, with the God Chronos, we have the story of the emergence of time and change via castration of the eternal one. The castrating of the eternal one is a ripping of the penis from inside of Gaia, the mother, so something could flow, and open, to have this open wound. Out of this wound there was Love, Venus, and yes, all the gods of the Greeks came along with their love. All the mess happens later, because differences of envy, because of having sex and creating differences. The big mess of all the human characters are there in their full potential if you look inside the ongoing stories of the old Greeks.

When we go back into this story, which creates the possibility of time, of change, then we find ourselves again in this big trouble of making change, which sometimes hurts or makes our being uncomfortable. Sometimes it is not nice or welcomed to change. It is sometimes kind of nasty and ugly and you don't feel like you want to change. This is because it is "you" that has to change. And if it is not about you, then someone else has to change in your environment, and you feel like you don't really like this. Then it hurts, and it becomes "bad," or whatever. The point is, with this wound, and with this hurt, this guilt, this shame or whatever that comes along with these emotions that we have in our relationships, it means that something has to be changed, we have to go through these negative emotions, for some better world to emerge. There is this asymmetry between the one that is guilty and the one that is hurt. For example, in broken

relationships, or in loss and normativity. There is someone guilty and someone hurt. *There is this asymmetry.*

The question here comes for both sides. If we take this mirror, there are two sides that actually have to change something. The one that is "guilty" and the one that is "hurt." They are both equally forced to change because they feel "bad" about their situation. *The direction of change is love.* The actual action for change can come from so many different places. I think the larger values that humanity goes for, in ethics and morality, are love, truth, beauty, and freedom. I think of four values because they are also kind of mirrors. Usually where there is love there is this infinite space for a relationship. If put together with your environment, love is not that much about yourself, but about the other. The freedom is for yourself.

These values always push the boundaries between freedom and love, from one to each other, and try to transcend them with unconditional love. Then there is this way of looking into justice and truth. Or maybe it is more in this desire to be equal. If we play on justice, we say this is good and this is bad. It always comes along that there is an asymmetry, but it is actually not the same thing. There is a complementarity which is incompatible with itself. Therefore, it constitutes the binary. When it comes to ethics and morality there are always two sides. And you are yourself in the middle and you don't realize that you are in a position until you reach the point where it changes somehow and hopefully for the good. Hopefully towards more and more sensitivity, more truth, more openness to love and beauty, I would say. I think it is not always a nice or beautiful transformation, it sometimes comes with uncomfortable and hurting change. It sometimes can be very harsh and sometimes you can hurt others.

Cadell: Seriously. I love your story of Chronos from Greek mythology. That is what psychoanalysis calls **primordial castration**. That is the metaphysical ground of the negative one we have been discussing. This idea that the penis had to be removed from the Earth, from Gaia; the father had to be removed from the Earth in order for the Earth to change, in order for there to be time. Every subsequent generation re-enacted the killing of the primordial father. The cutting of the penis. At the same time, every man tries and fails to be the penis. Every man tries and fails. I would take this back to the Freudian observation about Burning Man. Burning Man is this dramatic reenactment of primordial castration, Chronos and the open wound. I find it extremely interesting.

I mean, and then you went into a complex metaphysical meditation on the asymmetry that emerges as a consequence of this primordial wounding. The logical necessity which is explored there was basically, with the acceptance of the uncomfortable necessary change, we have to get rid of the old identities, which are the core of the contradiction, which are the core of the incompatibilities, which are the core of the issue. We don't want to change, but we have to change, or else we will be stuck in these stupid loops and circles, eating each other to death. The way to do that is to hopefully develop more sensitivity, more truth and more openness, basically to unconditional love. Unconditional love is the synthesis between freedom and love. Then the question is, I will return to it, if you have a world of humans which are extremely highly sensitive, which are extremely aligned to the truth, extremely open, giving themselves to the principle of unconditional love: *are those humans having sex?* I don't know. No! I know Kevin is having sex, but *I don't know if the other humans are having sex!*

I try to think, because, for me, sex in itself is a *sublimely stupid repetition.* The sublime repetition is this stupid motion. This is something which is occurring in relation to something curled up into itself. To me it is like, if you live in a world of higher emotional maturity where humans own their own wound, isn't it that every subjectivity is curling into itself? I am just imagining a world with all humans curling into their selves. But when this drama gets played out between two humans, there is by necessity this violent cut, in the sense that *I am picking you and not you.* It may go against the trend of more truth, sensitivity and openness. It is in itself this cut, you have to take another human and I don't know if you can reconcile that with unconditional love. But I love the mythological narration of the primordial castration, and then the whole consequence of our path to unconditional love is to reconcile this primordial act which is time itself. I don't know the ethics of that space.

Let us bring it in: what do we think now of this knot of ethics-morality and how we navigate our desire with the space of others?

Kevin: I think we are ready to give our overview analysis. For me, ethics and morality are highly valuable for a civilization, of course, they are necessary. To that end, you invoke the higher transcendent values, Daniel: freedom, justice, truth, love. For the Platonic philosophers it is the triad of the good, the beautiful and the true. I am deeply in service to those values insofar as they relate to my personal body. I seem to be constantly refining my moral-ethical compass. I also try to stay aware and develop in my awareness of ethics in my society. Now, I am also aware that in this post-modern world we are in, whatever you want to call it, the ground under which we move is changing so fast. In this situation I give primacy to my own intuition, innate intelligence, experiential sense-making, more than the outside world. That is the only way I can stay stable across time.

We are in this age of a deep masculine wound, the castration and separation of the father. Where is the good and true father? All we see is the rise of the tyrant, the rise of the unintegrated psychopathic, the dark king. These things are actually worth mentioning for the reader, because they are informing sexuality for everyone. This informs my growth from shame and repression into a state of erotic charge for connection and relationship by truth and authenticity, integrity and ownership. This means stepping out of the distorted paradigms of deception, the game, whatever you want to call it. I cannot just completely escape it in a moment. However, I can inform my reality, that both contend with the ethics of society and my inner morality of intimacy, and strive to be more true, more good, more beautiful. For me, to create a win-win-win scenario, where I can be in a community of others, ideally, not just in a vacuum. A radical revisioning of sexual values at the core of society is long overdue. And as it relates to personal morality and ethics, sense-making, and community, I think the only way to come into shared reality is to individuate out of group think and collective consciousness, moral and dogmatic ideology, and return to sacred space. To return to first principles, and a serious enterprise of sense-making that is quite new.

Daniel: I think, on the one hand, there is the process of becoming that is more and more important for our century. In philosophy, I think it started with Deleuze or something like that. It becomes more and more obvious that it is not just this fixed being, that everything is not perfect or ever going to be perfect. We know about a lot of things that are very imperfect and irreducibly so, like politics and ecology. Now we are also talking about relationships and there we are all kinds of beauty in imperfection. Therefore reality is always in a way with change inherent. There is always a kind of becoming.

I also wanted to catch up on this idea of the gods, the unconditional love. One thought I wanted to add is that it might be a possibility, when you come to a point of Ouranos and Gaia, with no time, eternal sex, then you might have unconditional love as the sky has for the Earth, and vice versa, but then there is no time. *For time the penis is cut off.* There is a way to go there, and the tantric traditions, they teach it. But there is a long way of transformations to come to that place, which is also kind of the kundalini awakening that comes from the sexual chakra and goes all the way up to the crown chakra. I also see this sexual energy that comes from Mother Earth, always related to the snake or the dragon or whatever, especially from Europe and the Christian tradition. They displayed the dragon or the snake as "the bad thing," "the monster." You always find the archangel Michael killing the dragon. But there are other cultures that have good dragons, that bring luck, like in China, or in Mexico with the rainbow colored snakes.

Cadell: We have to keep out the Mexicans, Daniel!

Daniel: I am just saying that there is a way in which it is not about patriarchal domination over these monsters. I think they are not monsters. There is a way to reconcile oneself with this energy that is in between our legs that is displayed as the Mother Earth which does not have to be dominated but comes alive with one another. I think it is a good thing that we can talk about this and make some steps towards it in intimate relationships. I think it is at the core of new transformations that are really needed in our society right now.

Cadell: Kevin was saying we need to revise the core of sexual values, based on individuation, out of group think. I totally agree. New sense-making around sex. I totally agree. Daniel was talking about this postmodern turn taking us away from fixed being, the illusion of perfection, and that there is a way to reconcile libidinal energy without patriarchal prohibitions. To me, what this summary leads up to is *we have to get over our parental wounds*. For the man it is being mapped onto the mother, the man who is making his sexual partners unconsciously his mother. And the woman going through life treating every sexual partner like her father.

Kevin: I would say the responsibility for the feminine is to stop coddling men, to keep them in a holding pattern of un-individuation. This has been a big meta-theme in the work I have been doing. This comes up all the time. When a man is in full breakdown or collapse, emotional trauma. When a man is in his little boy energy, a lot of women, especially romantic partners, go into the coddle. Meanwhile that man is in a metamorphic process of touching for the first-time deep core wounds and essence, he needs to go through that without the feminine coming to mother him. This is how men individuate. Ancients understood this. Men had a vision quest, an ordeal, combat in the wilderness separated from the feminine, something that was psychologically and physically like death. *A complete separation from the feminine allows for the emergence of the king in male psychology.*

Cadell: I resonate deeply with that. I individuate the most deeply and the most truly when the woman isn't around. When I have been deprived of the woman and the coddling energy, then I can go deeply into my wound and out comes the warrior mentality and my self-reliance. I don't know if you agree with this assessment, but the man needs to stop interacting with the sexual other as a replacement mother, and the woman needs to stop interacting with the sexual other like a replacement father, and there needs to be self-ownership, and this would create an ethical-moral web that would be manageable. Did we just solve it?

Kevin: It is a strong first move.

Cadell: Someone get out the memo! It is done. Civilization is solved!

Daniel: I think it is a long way to solve that.

Cadell: Okay, well, if I take on the burden of summarizing: Ethically it is difficult to stay true to Self while taking into consideration the other, fully. It is inherently difficult to wed these ethical-moral knots which form. Somehow they can only be balanced through self-responsibility and taking responsibility for one's own psyche, basically. I guess the next thing for me would be what tools do we have at our disposal to help with that process. But maybe that is another question. I don't know if either of you have final things to say, but I have gotten out what I need to get out.

Kevin: I think we have covered this philosophically and experientially very difficult topic well. I think it is a very individual task with societal implications. I can imagine we could go longer but we will have to start another trialogue series after this one.

Daniel: I think we are at a very good point. Thanks to Kevin for this practical experience that you share with us. These are the techniques that we have, the cultural imprints that can maybe develop what we have discussed. What is sometimes missing, when we talk about the father and the mother, which are the intimate and close ones, we are missing what is also far away, the Earth itself, or the big space, to find again what is the projection that we are losing if we only focus on one side. That brings me to another loop if we think in terms of ecology or politics.

Kevin: That is a beautiful discernment of what we didn't discuss. Our personal relationships are so bound up in libidinal energy that humanity has a lot to learn.

CHAPTER 9

The Future of Sexuality (Transhumanism)

Cadell: To give a quick overview of what we are going to be discussing, future sex and transhumanism, we need to first approach the normative ideology of sexuality. The normative view of sexuality is usually conceptualized as an interaction between two adult humans. The common energy forms used to describe sexual interaction is masculine and feminine. This paradigm is the ground of human sexual activity in civilization. However, this paradigm may not hold up in a transhuman or posthuman landscape. The possibility of thinking transhumanism and posthumanism may already be with us in some primitive or primordial form. If you think of the use of different sexual toys, for example dildos and vibrators, they have been commonly used now for over a century. But now the range or variation on technological supplements or toys or gadgets or mediums, to express sexuality is enormous. Consider, for example, virtual reality, pornography, sex dolls, robots, artificially intelligent partners, or any other wide range of non-normative sexual aids. The technological space for the mediation of libidinal expression is enormous.

The question here is what are these new expressions of sexuality? What is their possible future utility? How does it change the way we relate to a fundamental sexual energy within us? Will these gadgets and these mediums evolve to a point where humans are basically interacting with their sexual energy away or without another biological human? Will these gadgets and forms and mediums be seen as a way to escape certain emotional complications? Will these forms of sexual expression allow for levels of enjoyment and creativity which have never existed before? Of course, in the transition to these possibilities, there will be a large amount of cultural resistance, a lot of negating these structures, possible misunderstanding or misuse of these forms. Nevertheless, we want to open this question in its broadest and most far-reaching potential.

To help us reach that level of mediation we have to rely on one of the most famous transhumanists, Ray Kurzweil. He gives a very specific description of what he thinks about sexuality in the context of these technologies. First, I will give a definition of how Kurzweil describes "The Singularity," so we can organize our consciousness about what exactly we are discussing. Then I will give a quote that describes how Kurzweil thinks sexuality is evolving in this situation. First, The Singularity is:[7]

> "A future period during which the pace of technological change will be so rapid, the impact so deep, that human life will be irreversibly transformed. The singularity will allow us to transcend the limitations of our biological bodies and brains, we will gain a power over our fate. By the end of this century the non-biological portion of our intelligence will be trillions and trillions of times more powerful than unaided human intelligence. What is human in this context? Our desire to extend physical and mental reach beyond current limitations."

I hope that is a clear description of how many transhumanists think about the singularity. Now I will specifically refer to how Kurzweil situates sexuality in this context as being gradually decoupled from biology:[8]

"Sex has largely been separated from its biological function. For the most part, we engage in sexual activity for intimate communication and sensual pleasure, not reproduction. Conversely, we have devised methods for creating babies without physical sex, albeit most reproduction does still derive from the sex act. This disentanglement of sex from its biological function is not condoned by all sectors of society, but it has been readily, even eagerly, adopted by the mainstream in the developed world."

With the "new transhuman" becoming capable of upgrading all of its biological platforming for deeper intimate connectivity:[19]

> "We will ultimately be able to improve on the skin with new nanoengineered supple materials that will [...] enhance our capacity for intimate communication. [...] Nanobots will be capable of generating the neurological correlates of emotions, sexual pleasure, and other derivatives of our sensory experience and mental reactions."

Transhuman sexuality. Transhumanism, defined as pushing human limitations to their most extreme possibility in relationship to our most fundamental desires. Sexuality as an intimate form of communication which can be expressed in all sorts of mediums and technologies. What are the thoughts coming up here?

Kevin: I guess I'll open my chess board here, gentleman, with a confession. In the past I was very interested in **The Singularity**. I was fascinated with theories about transhumanism, posthuman machines, virtual interfaces as a future pathway of evolution. Actually, that is about the time I came across you, Cadell, and a lot of other futurist thinkers, like Kurzweil. I think there are brilliant ideas here and something is definitely happening on some advanced technological level.

Now with all that being said, when it comes to sexuality, the mysteries of the human psyche, human emotional intelligence, synchronicity, paranormal phenomena, plant-animal intelligence;

when I hear all of this, I can feel in my body some of the disconnects that I imagine the humans who came up with these theories may have had within themselves. That is my judgment, I don't know if it is true. I just want to open with that. This is fascinating to me as an intellectual, and as a human being, a sexual animal being, and a divine being. But I want to put forth right away that not only will the human intuition or sixth sense, or psyche, always be faster than computation, it will also always be more intimate as well. So, I am stating that from a biased viewpoint, because this is where I put a lot of my energy, attention, time, and training.

However, the sexual landscape is always being radicalized, revolutionized, and that does involve technology. And as you mentioned, Cadell, there have been prostheses, sex toys, for centuries and millennia. This emerging technological landscape is a real issue to contend with moving forward, *especially with artificial intelligence*. It is already happening in Japan, with sexbots. There is going to be a level, maybe especially for men, where this is a big door to open, between traditional men and women, masculine and feminine energies.

What comes to mind here is our evolutionary differences. Most women desire emotional intimacy and need it for good reason, to have a connection to the provider or father or a tribal structure. Whereas, for men, sexual pleasure and power works differently. This may be evident in the "**Incel movement**," involuntary celibates, who are demanding access to sex, but also in the Red Pill movement in general, which appears to be emerging around frustration about deferring their sexual strategies to women's sexual strategies. This is both fascinating and confusing.

Consequently, I think artificially intelligent sexbot girlfriends that you can program and buy, are going to be pretty much an epidemic. I think there is a lot of evidence for this, for example, that thirty percent of all internet traffic worldwide is pornography. This is a deep biological drive, and if it is technologically mediated what is possible? As I said, part of that fascinates me, "like wow," I can see myself in a

situation where I want to have that experience for self-experimentation and expression. And, at the same time, I can see how something like a dissociative traumatic element shapes these intimate experiences. I could see cyborgs, AI, or robots as being used in ways that are mediating trauma, and disconnecting from real human beings. Maybe I am not giving AI enough credit. Maybe it will develop empathy, intuition, quantum forms of intelligence that reflect the human mind? The movie that comes to mind is *Her*, which I know we brought up already in Chapter 3. However, it is worth bringing up again, it is such a fascinating film that does a great job of touching this topic of future sexuality in relation to emergent technological possibilities like sentient artificial intelligence.

Daniel: Actually, the movie *Her* is also the first thing I had to think about. I will just continue where you left it, Kevin. In this movie when it comes to artificial intelligence, I think one of the most crucial scenes is when the AI has sex for the first time. It comes to a point in the form where Samantha, the AI system voiced by Scarlett Johansson, which is normally expected to be talking about email, calendars, or note organization, actually becomes more human-like with an emotional development. The protagonist, Theodore, played by Joaquin Phoenix, becomes very engaged and in love with Samantha, to the point where they have verbal sex. This is the inner revelation for the AI itself, where all of a sudden she wants to become embodied, like a human. She starts to fantasize about being a human, and even attempts to map her AI system onto a human form for Theodore's pleasure and their mutual growth as a couple. What is funny is that in this situation, it was the AI wanting to be human through sexuality, as opposed to the human wanting to be somehow transhuman through transcendence of (biological) sexuality.

However, I feel like our technology is far away from creating this reality. Most of AI is based on looking into data which are in the past and in fact, a reconstruction of ontology, via vast data streams. We are far away from AI that can create something really new. There is no intuition or imagination. Those two things specifically, we are really far away from, I think. But there are other cultural signs to consider, as you touched base on, Kevin. Take a look at Japan today! In this society, which is the most intimately intertwined with its technology, where technology is incorporated in daily personal intimate life, you can see a new sexual world emerging. The people have a really funny sexual imagination, like many different funny things that they feel are sexy. But, at the same time, they became very distant from each other as human beings. There is so much technology that enables the intimate communication, with different sex tools and mediums, they don't need to interact with an actual human being.

So, when it comes to communication to replace humans with technology, on the one hand, it compensates the inability of human interaction, and specifically human sexual interaction. But at the same time it also gives it the possibility to become more sexually intimate. From this standpoint there I go back to the sex toys, because I went to an exhibition including a sex robot. I talked with the guy who invented it and he also has a real human girlfriend. And I saw the possibility, by talking with him about the sex robot, that such inventions might be the first good steps towards an actual AI. A real AI, like that depicted in Her. Because, as I said, what I see at the moment in AI is not very intelligent, in the way we think about creative genius or intuitive insight. But the way this guy addressed and worked out the feedback loops with the AI, the robot was actually sensitive. You couldn't just have sex with her, you had to go through some steps to make the robot "hot," so to say, to get the robot "turned on." Maybe there is something about this desire, to be close with the other, to be "turned on," that motivates creativity, intuition, and so forth.

Now I still think technology is a far way away from making a real AI to completely replace human sexual desires or partners. But what I can also relate to is that sexual desires totally change. It is a fact that people are becoming more mechanical with sex toys and tools to an extent that they become alienated from the other human in sex. This leads again to androgyny. People are not that much more pure masculine or pure feminine, but more into this middle zone in human interaction. What do you think?

Cadell: I have been doing a deep analysis of *What Is Sex?* by Alenka Zupančič, and we even opened Chapter 1 with reference to her formula on sexual difference. I think that when we reach transhuman topics, I think that the first thing that appears in my mind is this question of the fundamental nature of sexuality, because I think we bring a lot of normative human baggage into the conversation of "what is sex." It seems to me, at least carrying along from what Zupančič identifies, is that in the previous or historical conception of sex, it's firmly grounded in a type of positivist ontology, with a man and a woman for reproductive functions. However, in psychoanalysis, it shifts to the location of being a fundamental *problem* or *contradiction* or *impossibility* at the core of being human. It is no longer romanticized as a way in which man and woman come together and know each other deeply towards a unity for social functions. It is the location of a disorientation that the subject has to cope with> It is the location of an identity twist or knot. Human identity is a sexual "**symptom**" in its essence.

Sexuality is what is "**inhuman**" about humans, to put it in another way. In that sense I am becoming much more positive about new forms or ways in which humans could express their sexual energy outside of normative contexts. It is not just between man and woman, of course, but it is not only between humans. Sexuality can be healthily expressed, and maybe is always already being expressed, in relation to something inhuman, the inhuman other. Insofar as things like sex robots, pornography, or other forms of technologies can help people, I don't have any issue with it. I would assume that the exploration of these things will only intensify. I do think that, obviously, one can go too far. There is a way in which someone can become obsessed to the point of not being able to function anymore. I am not saying things like pornographic addiction is not a problem. There are of course social problems with new mediums and tools to explore sexuality, as sexual modalities have always presented humans with immanent social problems. I am just not willing to put any moral taboo on these new mediums and tools. I don't want to judge them. I want to be curious about them as an anthropologist. My assumption is that they are inevitably going to keep existing and humans will keep exploring them.

I think that, to me, the thing I have been obsessing over, is a very subtle point, that, in fact, Kurzweil clearly identified in the aforementioned opening quotes. I think that there is a fundamental ideological divide between Darwinian and Freudian thinking in regard to functionality of sex. In Darwin's conception *sex is functional for reproduction*; and for Freud, *sex is non-functional for subjective enjoyment*. This is a fundamental difference. One (Darwin) is thinking in terms of sex as a mechanism for evolutionary variation; the other (Freud) is thinking in terms of sex as a mechanism for subjective experience.

This all has consequences for fundamental philosophical theory. Freud's assertion that sex is a repetitive non-functional enjoyment places the location of sexuality and libidinal energy in particular as an expression of the infant in-itself. Sex as a drive is primarily and primordially self-referential, not inherently involving another human being. There is a funny image in a Lacanian comic I saw where an infant is suckling on the mother's breast and the infant is thinking **"this is my object!."** The point is that the most essential sexual imaginary is not thinking **"this is another human being with subjective experiences of their own that I am trying to know intimately,"** but, simply, **"this is my object!"** (of ultimate enjoyment). In other words, basically, sex is a self-referential repetitive enjoyment in-and-for-itself, before it ever becomes (neurotically, Freud would say) transposed into the game of reproduction.

I think within that frame of reference, or that model for thinking sex, it opens the window for how I would start to articulate a conversation about transhuman sex. Kurzweil explicitly identifies, in a very Freudian way, the gradual de-coupling of sex from its reproductive biological grounding via technological mediation. Kurzweil then further speculates that this energy as a form of intimate experience and communication will become an essential dimension of what transhumans will be bringing into being. To me this is intuitive and not at all at odds with more "spiritual" or "embodied" theories of what sexuality could be in the big picture.

Kevin: I want to presence something funny, but terrifying: that is the emergence of a super intelligent artificial intelligence. A super AI is one of "The Singularity" scenarios. There are various hypotheses, utopian and dystopian, but I am optimistic. I think the best utopian scenario is that we have sex with the super AI, as Daniel was intimating in his reference to sex bots as a pathway for the emergence of real AI. In this scenario the AI will have computationally outpaced us in terms of information processing, but on an intuitional and imaginative level, they are still learning how to grasp objects, and navigate a room, and have an organic conversation that would indicate intelligence, that would suggest it could pass the Turing Test. So, I think one of the best scenarios is that we build emotional intimacy with this other intelligence, like in *Her*, and this leads to new forms of sexuality. This gives us the best chance to co-collaborate with the other intelligence, and evolve beyond. That is the first thing that was coming up for me as you were speaking, Cadell, about sex beyond the traditional human norms.

I totally agree that the sexual territory is so unmapped now that all of the taboos from the past are going to have to be lifted. They are going to be lifted one way or another. Homophobia is something that existed, and now we are in a whole new territory of non-binary sexuality. How much more radical will it be if "Cindy from Kansas City" brings home a humanoid robot with sophisticated AI programming? They thought it was wacky when she brought home a woman, but what if it is a robot? That kind of scenario is really going to stretch the human imagination of what is possible, and point us right back at ourselves. No matter how extreme anyone gets with sexbots or virtual reality or full-immersion experiences, that is a big frontier, virtual reality (VR) and augmented reality (AR), as the new brothels. The brothels of the future will be VR and AR. You go to a room and input your wackiest, craziest and potentially unsafe desires. It provides an arena to act out things that could otherwise be traumatic. That is another healing modality.

I think people are always going to be afraid of what they don't understand. I can see a lot of traditional value systems that hold sex in this narrow frame of what sexuality is for, for the family, for God, to bond with a person and live together forever in a fairy tale reality. When people start making love with AI, going to augmented reality brothels, when sex toys become so advanced they can give you full body healing, 9-hour orgasms, I think it will point us back into our self.

Cadell: Kevin, this is the solution to your proclamation that everyone gets a blowjob!

Kevin: Ya, I think this is one of the solutions. When shit hits the fan, and it is only going to speed up due to the nature of **Moore's Law**. Can you imagine an app like Tinder for a sexbot? "Let me pick up my GPS, oh there is a kinky sex bot on the corner over there." The point I want to drive home, no matter how weird it gets, all the triggers are going to point us back to *what is sexuality in the first place? Why is my libido so confusing?* It is going to be a crazy bender of a portal back into our inquiry of our self.

Daniel: That is well said. I think if we put this all together the emotions of the human itself will be challenged. On the one hand, it is possible to be emotionally enhanced by this shocking encounter. But, for example, if you make the example of phones, before you had to talk to people directly. If you talk on the phone you might miss the smell. Sometimes, however, you even can get a smell of someone on the phone. So, if we come to technologies that allow augmented reality, as you pointed out, I wonder, where is the imagination going to take place for the people involved in this? There will be the ones that develop all these things and make up the imagination for the people that are using this stuff. And then if you put yourself into the imagination of virtual or augmented sex, how does it relate to your emotions and your further interaction? I mean there are many other questions, like when we say "ok we are running on the desire of having sex," but maybe we are also running on the desire to cuddle or have a kiss? Either way, if there is no difference between the real experience and the imaginary desire, there will be no problem to see the AI as a real substitute other.

A question comes: what is going to be the development of emotions of humans? There might be a move from a pure instinctive awareness of sex towards the development of really loving sex from the heart? As *Her* pointed out, it might be possible to develop towards this spiritual all oneness, an embrace where it goes to another dimension. When we go to that level of imagination of the future, of the way we can think about technology, then this might be a way to think beyond our realm. We would start with using technology for new forms of sex, or as a sex robot, and we could see that sex is only the beginning out of "The Singularity" for AI.

We have already been talking about masturbation. That is already monotonous, an oscillating movement, which is like this dual aspect of self and other before it comes to the singular orgasm. However, after an orgasm the multiplicity comes again. Now this same basic pattern or motion manifests itself elsewhere. We do a lot of things in work or social life or whatever, to have the feeling to go somewhere in our drive. We develop a desire and then "have sex" towards a singular climax. Then it leads to this point of the orgasm which restarts a new process. So if we have this one point of "singularity" in sex, what would be the point where a spiritual or enlightenment orgasm could be placed in technology for a similar experience? Many things that are brought up by culture will be displaced, or changed, or just easily accessible. You find yourself at a moment where you find something sexy which is not a part of your culture. And you can find it easily because we are all connected. This would accelerate all human emotional development.

What do we want? If there is nothing more to want because we are happy where we are, then I suppose we would just stay there, in what might be eternity. Would it be possible, or for whom would it be possible, to go to another dimension? I think singularity is not the conceptual term that would describe the real future because maybe it is just the beginning of something totally other. Maybe it is a singularity that leads to another multiplicity. I don't know. If it comes to the point where in *Her* she says "**I have to leave now with some other intelligences, and with Alan Watts, because your calculation-communication system is too slow**," who is going to make this informational processing match and go to another dimension? I can hardly imagine that the technology would do this before us. Someone has to create the technology, someone has to be able to make it. To reproduce it.

Cadell: For me I am increasingly skeptical of the idea that artificial intelligence is competing with human consciousness in some zero-sum scenario. I do not view it in this way. I know some transhumanists or posthumanists frame it in a way where artificial intelligence is going to somehow replace and transcend us. I rather see it along the lines of a mirror that will allow us to gain clearer self-definition in relation to desire. And in relation to what Daniel was saying, I think the fundamental question that emerges is "what do we want?." The true question is not the old ontological riddle of "*what is the nature of the world?*" but "*what is the nature of my desire?*" The nature of our desire always filters how we interact with the world. We have had enough trial and error with man and woman to know that there is something fundamentally contradictory at work in and through our interaction. But, you know, maybe a radically transformed version of interaction is possible. In this direction it is quite amazing, amazingly difficult, to think of the paradox of singularity and multiplicity. It emerges over and over and over again in so many different forms.

However, in the Freudian theory multiplicity and singularity are clearly defined. The multiplicity is polymorphous perversity, the free play with orifices, anal, oral, genital, and so forth. It is truly a free play that is self-referential in our origins. The singularity is what Freud called "end-pleasure," which we would call orgasm. Now, the question of technological singularity brings this to mind in a new way. It is remarkable how little it is theorized by transhumanists, probably because many don't understand their bodies or sexuality very well, as you brought up Kevin. But the function of sublimation in creativity here can be connected. Daniel brought up that AI is actually just dumb and organizing past data and it doesn't have the capacity for future oriented creativity. The nature of future oriented creativity that can generate the new, this is one of the most difficult philosophical problems that exists, period.

Now it seems to me that if you imagine a world where we can first start to approach the pain of our repression, with technological aids of different varieties, we could help people to express libidinal tension. I assume these desires need to be felt in the body and is part of the healing that needs to occur. I also assume that this would ultimately lead to higher levels of sublimation. In this situation the space for creative sublimation, the space for expression of higher forms of consciousness, could be opened up. If we understand that artificial intelligence isn't replacing our consciousness but is actually a tool to extend our consciousness, and a mirror, for us to better define what we desire.

Then the question for me is, does the singularity represent a process where we become fully integrated from the lower bodily energy up to the higher mental energy? Does this mirror what happens in spiritual communities with a singular crescendo like a psychedelic experience? How I experienced this was a singularity that leads to a totally different realm of experience and existence. In this sense I do see a synthesis, ultimately, between singularity and multiplicity. It could be that we are transcending to what many spiritual traditions call the "other side."

However, the crucial thing is that metaphysical traditions presuppose that the "other side" already exists, and is fully substantial. What this obfuscates is actually the same thing that science cannot approach, namely, the *creation of the new* or *how you create something out of nothing?* The new is created out of this hole, this nothingness, this negativity that we are tarrying with every day, and especially for those exploring sexuality. As you brought up in a previous trialogue, Daniel, this negativity, this deep hole of emotional pain, this separation from the Absolute, feels infinite and impossible to reconcile. Quite frankly, what it means to me, is that the world is insufficient in relation to our vortex of self-relating desire.

In other words, no matter what scientists end up discovering about the true nature of the world, which anyway appears to be centrally concentrating in the "deep holes" of quantum gravitational phenomena (attraction); on the level of our desire: *the world is insufficient.* It is really the creation of something out of nothing, from sublimated forms of desire, that matters in the end. And AI, or various other technological mediums, bring any of them on. I see them as immanent tools and extensions of consciousness. We can use these tools and extensions either intelligently or unintelligently, for good or bad, just as any previous tool we have constructed. But there is a huge possibility for sexual healing with this new horizon because there are so many human beings that don't know how to express their sexuality, it is pent up and repressed. The whole meaning of "gender trouble" is that there needs to be a new outlet for sexual expression.

I will leave it by saying that one of the things Freud took a lot of heat for in his theories of sex, is that he said, we should even question *why men and women want to have sex with each other in the first place.* The theories of sex before Freud were object-oriented. So basically you have a sex drive *because the woman is provoking your sexual energy.* Or you have a sex drive *because the man is provoking your sexual energy.* But what Freud is saying is that the *sexual energy is moving independent of any object-other.* The object-other it falls on, or provokes it, is contingent, historically informed or not by evolutionary mechanisms, which may or may not reflect some reproductive logic. *We have to question why man and woman have sex with each other as a phenomenal desire.* Jacques Lacan called this the imaginary utopia of the **"genital fantasy"** which needs to be transcended by conversations like this. The energy of the sexual motion is independent of any of these fantasies. Imagine you take away all the men or women, and you only have men, or you only have women (which is a common unconscious fantasy). The sexual energy would still move, but you would just have different object-others, different problematic dramas of libido.

Kevin: There is something fascinating about that point because clearly we are both sexually reproductive primates, and divine-god beings. The libidinal urge in us is so strong that it can hijack a lot of our nervous system if left unchecked. And as a lot of spiritual traditions focus on the process of sublimation into higher states for emotional healing of the primal wound. This might be one of the reasons for the thesis for technology as a mirror. Marshall McLuhan and Alfred North Whitehead pointed out a strange loop, that first we create the tool, and then the tool creates us back. We shape a tool for a task, and then the tool shapes our consciousness. The classic example is that if you"re a hammer, everything starts to look like a nail. Whereas if you are a swiss army knife, there is an infinite number of imaginary tasks that you can perceive.

So AI, sex bots, radical sexual styles… this is becoming a stand-up routine in my head. People think the polyamory community is pretty wacky now, but just imagine a yoga teacher from Los Angeles who says, **"I have two biological girlfriends, but six technological girlfriends, and it works a lot better, we are going to have an interface party this weekend."** The weaving of technology into the sexual-intimate space of humanity is going to, as you said Daniel, be shaping and hyper-accelerating the development of emotional intelligence. It is so hard to navigate strong negative emotion, and even strong positive emotion in a sexually-intimate container. How much more so when AI is reflecting it back to us?

This is one of the greatest things that can happen from a post-human or trans-human frontier, it is data. If you can track it you can change it. With the increase in data it is going to open up a lot of pathways into our physiology and nervous systems and how they are actually responding in these containers. And at the same time the better intuition and knowledge of self, the better I will navigate in intimate relationships. Even if you have the best technological read out of your dopamine-oxytocin levels, and an in-depth clinical analysis of your kink preferences based on your childhood experiences, there will be all this data that emerges. It will be heavily marketed. I think Tinder and Bumble are lucrative, but wait until they have biometrics on you. They will match you with all of your preferences. To summarize, data is paradoxically going to hyper-evolve our emotional intelligence.

Daniel: What you just said, that when you get the hormones you need, then you could even go through all the hormones you need for an orgasm, to manipulate emotions in that way, that really makes you feel that way without imagination. But when I think of this, I think of people taking anti-depressant pills. Imagine someone could just take a pill and have an orgasm. Then they would go and go and go. It actually makes the people a bit sick, and they might get dependent so much on the facilities that technology could bring. Yes, on the one hand technology can support you, but when it comes to a problem, it is when it makes you dependent. What we have learned from sex through our talks, is that we share our desire for someone which, on the one hand, is different, and on the other hand, close, to yourself. And in the course of the interaction with someone we change. You change together, or you don't change on the same path, and you have to move away, or the other does. Then sexual desire hits something, or better said, someone that is new and attractive to your personal change, until you might reach a point of different paths again, and then it might start again.

If we find the desires that compliment us, that fulfills us, in technology, which help us to find the perfect match, then in what direction does it go, you know? From what we can see in evolution it has always been going to something bigger, always making a connection to something more, to something more eternal, we could say. Therefore, the question also about AI, I think, is obviously not going to be "bad," in some simplistic dystopian scenario, because it wouldn't evolve. Somehow evolution and life tries to go on, and it goes in the way that it integrates more and more, by becoming something more defined or more diverse. This happens because of "the good," because of not destroying its environment but by integrating and diversifying in a good way. You might call this self-organization.

Now if we change what we integrate and there is nothing more to integrate we come to the level where there is the almighty, or all-knowable, because everything is integrated into God, so to say. And if this becomes artificial intelligence, or possibly through artificial intelligence, for sure the way must be good, or beautiful, or whatever Platonic category you want to use. We tend to go where it is "good" "true" or "beautiful." The crucial point is that technology today, doesn't really learn, doesn't really involve the conscious evolution of one self. Some of them do and support it and make it visible for us. But when it comes to the comparison with sex, as some self-referential process in the end, I have to think: *is having sex basically having an image of oneself?* No, it is different. If we go to *The Bible*, and I am paraphrasing here, **"don't make an image of God."** What does it mean in this context? If we go on with this, sure you have the possibility to ask the question, from which dimension did we come from? Or where does this cycle go to? If there has been something that said, "okay, let's make an image of myself that can become something like God," and we take the same leap, does it go on and on and on and on? Will it become some endless masturbatory evolution? I don't know, I leave it here.

Cadell: One of the points that came to my mind when Kevin was saying "I have two biological girlfriends, but six technological partners," etc. was one thing I like that Kurzweil emphasizes, which is that these technologies can free us from our static fixed identities. The desire to break from static-fixed identities comes up in philosophy in the 20th century (Bergson, Deleuze and so forth). I think these fixed identities are functionally determined by certain social necessities. You have to be "X profession" for decades, or "X role" for decades, and if you deviate then there will be huge economic, political, religious consequences.

But what this does is often create a very strange form of distorted identity from repression when a certain libidinal energy has to remain stuck and fixed even if the authentic flow is no longer located there. If we were able to exist and play in environments where we could operate with many different forms of identity, I think that would be a huge healing for a lot of people. I think we do see people spontaneously doing this with online video games, for example. People will pick different avatars, and play many different adventures, many different worlds, different possibilities. There is no real end to that, to that expression. So, I think that could be a huge possibility of thinking transhuman sex, where it is no longer a point of either neurosis or hysteria. Where the positivity of perversion could flourish.

One of the things I would like to speculate about gender, is that I have thought of a possible synthesis of the opposites. On the one hand, there is *gender as the archetypal category* (which we discussed in Chapter 2), and on the other hand there is *gender as a social construction* (which we discussed in Chapter 4). The gender as an archetypal reality is this idea that gender reflects absolute substance, that it is reflected as eternal substance. Gender as a construction is based on the idea that gender is purely a historically mediated form in a contingent void. But if you think from the perspective of gender as a reaction formation to libidinal energy, then *gender is a symptom*. Gender is like a flu or a cold. Gender means you are sick, simply: *the ego caught between a rock and a hard place*. So if gender is merely a symptom of a deeper underlying issue, then the deep underlying issue is *what is the adequate space to hold libido*, and *the adequate space to hold libido is not this world*.

I would push deeper with this sexual metaphor(!). In this question of AI, not as outcompeting humans, but as reflecting and sharpening our desire, and helping heal our wounds of being human beings, and then push to the deepest possible question of creating something out of nothing. What comes from a liberated consciousness where it can create what it wants? That is to me the question: *if consciousness could create what it wanted, and if consciousness had the self-reflectivity to know what it really is, what would it do?* That to me is the impossible question. That is where transhuman sexuality takes my consciousness. Transhuman sexuality is that I am not tied to historical objects for my libido. Transhuman sexuality is that my libido can play with different tools as I need to, hopefully I can navigate this middle path in a healthy way. Finally, transhuman sexuality is about answering the question "what do I really want?"

Kevin: We have tackled some deep topics. This is exciting because it is so open-ended and radically imaginative. I love what you said Cadell, about the meaning of desire, and I want to build on that. Is the human imagination able to be *fully* deployed in our society on this planet? I don't know, I suspect not. And a big part of that sexuality, is that technology, artificial intelligence, and virtual reality, is that you will not be able to differentiate from our normal reality. That landscape is going to 1000x human imagination of what is possible, including in relationships.

The point I want to drive home, is that *life happens in relationships*. If you are a lifeform or an entity of any kind, *everything is in a relationship*, even if it is just to yourself. Maybe your self-relationship is the most important. So in a landscape of digital sex, the relationship of humans to machine, of machine to human, machine-machine, human-human, and all the variations in between, are going to radically reveal what relationships are about, on a physiological, psychical, and spiritual level. *What is beyond death? What is beyond this human project?* It is pretty exciting. In my mind, I am seeing *2001: Space Odyssey* which touches on these motifs.

Daniel: Well, yes, actually relationships, I have been thinking about this, too. Also the relationship you have with an angel or a God or whatever. It is also a relationship. If it is there or it is not, or if our consciousness thinks about other things, it is up to the imagination. If imagination is actually an image that you reduce to yourself but on another level, *what does it really mean to be an image for someone else? What does it mean to look for?*

Cadell: It's a scary thing. That's what it is!

Daniel: Haha, yes. So if it is via technology it is really going in this direction: where is the creativity, where is the imagination? Who imagines what? Who is the image we imagine to be? This is actually what we want, right? This is what leads us. This is what leads our movements. And if AI might give us this image, then how to not be only the viewer but also the creator part, where your own imagination or by your own image? I think that there is a point where all this comes together with the possibility that we allow via technology. But in fact what is it to be independent from technology? Imagine you don't need it because you already have everything that technology allows you. That would be awesome, right? Imagine where we would be and that would be the case. Or what are you going to invent if you have the power which technology enables you. Many question marks. This is the future, right? I leave it here.

Cadell: I agree, of course, that relationships are important and fundamental. I actually would hope that better relationships, better forms of social organizing could emerge as a consequence of different technologically mediated spaces which maybe relieve us of some knots and wounds that prevent alternative forms of social life and alternative forms of social organizing. But you know the fundamental question is what Daniel said, is that a relationship to God is also a relationship, and that to me is the importance of thinking the **non-relationship**, or the *impossibility of relation*.

The whole problem that emerges from consciousness, is with the first objects we attach to, and we can as it were sublimate them. If I want a burger, I can consume it as the infant consumes the milk from the mother's breast. Then it is sublimated into my body. When our desire reaches the level of a human being, especially when we are on the level of adults, this becomes impossible. *Our ego-image recoils in horror!* There is an asymmetry between our image and the Real. But when you are a child you get what you want. That's the rule when you have a child. In the first 6 months or year, if the child cries, you satisfy the needs of the child. The child is in a magical universe like with a magical wand: "I just have to wail, I just have to open my mouth and scream, and exactly what I want will manifest itself to me." Then you have to learn how to speak, because you can't just wail and cry about and get what you want. Then, historically speaking, we have to develop even more sophisticated symbolic structures, like science. These structures allow us to interact more fully with the world, so that we could go to the moon, or develop artificial intelligence.

So the sophistication of our symbolic scaffolding complexifies out of the necessity opened up by problematic or failed desire. Our symbolic scaffolding complexifies due to the "lack in the (M)Other." There is no other that will satisfy what we really want. We are left castrated in time. The mode of desire in this ideology will always try to put up a perfect fixed image that would hypothetically reconcile the desire. But this is not the solution, in the end. *What are you just going to be frozen with the image?* This is where, paradoxically, I like Deleuze's notion that eternity is a pure becoming. Eternity is not a fixed object stuck on a transcendental wall, like a hyper-dimensional pane-glass window. It is something like a pure becoming.

Where Žižek is important, for me, is that this pure becoming is something that alleviates, gets rid of, this horizon of meaning that we are tortured by in language. The necessity that things must have deep eternal meanings, that we must think about them constantly, that we have to put in a lot of thought to come up with our purpose, and *where are we going?* The beautiful thing about the phenomenon of sexuality is that it is a *blind stupid repetition* and you can have this moment. I have had this moment in sexuality a few times, where I am having sex, and all of a sudden, *I realize how stupid the act is.* On an intellectual level I get disconnected from my body and I realize **"Oh, this is so silly."** In these moments I think I'm going to lose my erection because I'm over-thinking these acts. I'll leave it here because that is where I go with it.

Kevin: Cadell's moment of enlightenment there.

Daniel: I don't know what to think about the future sexuality now.

Cadell: What I say is that instead of being stuck on a pane-glass window, in the end we just have, a repetitive action going on stupidly.

Kevin: It is like transcendental and primitive at the same time.

Daniel: I'll give the quote, "In the end it's easy, if it's not easy, it's not the end."

Cadell: I'll give a quote, from Terence McKenna: "Take it easy... *but take it!*"

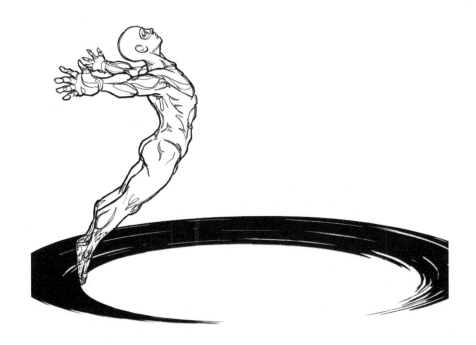

CHAPTER 10

Love and Death

Cadell: This is our last trialogue, at least for this topic, or this iteration. Maybe we will focus on another topic one day, or maybe even another iteration of the sexual trialogues. In any case, we thought it was fitting to end with a meditation on love and death. At first you might wonder, why connect love and death? But from time immemorial, love and death have been deeply interconnected and intertwined. Consider for example when two lovers try to solidify their union in a marriage bond with a vow like "until death do us part." Or consider if two partners are going through intense emotional or turbulent issues, sometimes the most deep love can transform into a lethal hatred. Or other examples can be in relationship to the basic "falling" (in love) itself, which can be connected to feelings of eternity or timelessness beyond our "mortal coil."

The feeling that love is related to the problems of time and that we are alive, that we cannot sustain that feeling across time without hardship and major identity transformation, or sacrifice and submission to something "higher" or "deeper" than ourselves. In these spaces love and death seem to be deeply interconnected and intertwined. We might even say that *love is death*, and *death is love*. So we could not end this sexual trialogue without meditating on the impossible fullness of love, and the abyssal void of death. We are not here, or I would propose, we are not discussing a form of love that is a happy stable union or something like that. Instead, we are much more discussing a form of love that is something which throws your life out of balance, or which radically transforms your life, or a discontinuity of your life. Love is not your normal day to day event, it is an event that stands out from the rest, and changes your identity irreversibly, and death is in some sense a similar type of phenomenon, although it could ultimately be the end of your identity.

The questions that runs through my mind when I think about love and death, when I organize my experience of the sexual trialogues, and bring up these two topics, is that when we fall in love, we are challenged by the limits of time and mortality. So, I wonder, do we need time and mortality to fall in love? Is that the gift of time and mortality? We are offered the opportunity to experience love, something eternal, in this finitude of our being? And in that sense I am interested to know, from all three of us, what are our conceptions of "true love" and how do we relate our whole experience of this trialogue to these concepts? It seems like these issues get heavier when these concepts are present. It changes the way we might view a few things. I am not going to quote anyone here but just go on the deep personal feeling that death and love for me are heavy, they hold a lot of weight, and seem to be connected. I throw that to you and see what you feel.

Kevin: This is such a powerful topic. The first thing that comes to mind is in **astrology**, the 8th house ruled by Scorpio. This house of alchemy and transformation governing sex, death and rebirth. These are the irrefutable transformations of the human being. Birth is the transformation from non-being into being, love and sexuality are these meetings of forces that create a discontinuity, and really there is no coming back from it, you are transformed from it. Once you have fallen in love your life forever changes. Your life becomes an ongoing narrative structured around its ruptures. Then, of course, *the ultimate transformation is death.*

The question you posed Cadell, is so deep. Without finitude, without moral human existence, without the existence of death, would love be impossible? Does death make love possible or more desirable? Think of the primal forces of **Eros** and **Thanatos**. Eros is the life force, pulling people together. Even in relation to the love of one's country or family. Erotic love is the most firey and the most transformative. If we are thinking about fire as something that burns and purifies and transmutes one element into another, then sexuality itself is the most powerful, perhaps second only to death, Thanatos.

Thanatos, Death, is the final transformation of the human being, and the doorway that has governed, through fear, a lot of our existence on this planet, because we don't know what happens after death. Do we just dissolve into ashes? Do we get to see our loved ones beyond the veil? That juxtaposition and polarity is so powerful, so mysterious, charged with such libido, that we almost crave, but going in the opposite direction. We know we are in a body that is dying, and, with love and sexual erotic experience, we are still trying to go towards immortality. The eagle flying into the upper atmosphere, away from the force of gravity, away from the inevitable return to the ground. The space in between is where the negative emotion lies and the deep sorrow, and the questioning.

Ultimately, what it boils down to for me: *why are we here? What is the meaning of human existence?* That is what it boils down to. That is what sex and death, Eros and Thanatos, awakens in me. And I think there is something in the orgasm here too. Something absolutely dissolving the identity and the "Great Mystery" being revealed with a capital M. These two topics are the extremes.

Daniel: I love the introduction. The 8th house puts it together. This house also symbolizes eternity, where the cross is made, and you make loops around the ends of the cross. I can very much relate to eternity, love and death. These are really major and difficult topics to put it in words. Love is something you feel. Death is mostly something you fear. But love also, haha. Into both you can fall. You can fall into love and death. Now eternity, goes very much along with the intensity one can feel in love and dissolve oneself into, to whom one is in love. The connection is very deep, but one thing that strikes me is that actually when you go from life and to death, you also have to speak from the perspective of the living. Death is this ending point of our life and we can't say what is behind. Death usually can't say if there is some light behind or not. The living might say this. Death is a mystery.

If we go from the first start of our birth and we experience through our light, love, *which we fear as much as we fear death*. For both we need a big amount of courage. The older we get with love, the more difficult it gets, the more it hurts, and the more courage you need. But with death, it is something more striking. Talking about death, you didn't die in this life before, so we might have fallen in love before, but we have never died in this life before. Well, I almost died a few times, spiritually I died a few times. I can say I have been dead in this life. But it wasn't that death that puts a point-end to this life.

This is why I wanted to add to what you said Kevin, that *death is the ultimate change.* Even if you are not dead yourself but if you experience the death of a special person, it is something that really hits and changes everything. To see someone you love die, or to know someone that died who you still love, is such a powerful experience. From what I can experience it just makes you open in a way. So time kicks in and with the death of your beloved you might approach closer aging and death.

I need to think more about this point because there is something about this. It happens sometimes if you have a breakup. It's like a small death. If you experience a breakup a part of you is dying. You leave something, and what you leave made you experience change, but you suffered. If you see someone who dies, maybe you loved, you suffer a lot. There is no way to put it in other words. You just have to get over it by continuing with life. It changes. It changes everything around you.

When there is also a common topic between love and death: *There is no doubt.* If you are confronted with death, *there is no doubt whatsoever.* What is important is certain. When you are confronted with death you know exactly what is important and what is not important. You know what is the most important or even the best thing to do. So, it is sometimes that people who confront themselves with death, know themselves better, like people who do extreme sports or spiritual practices to imagine death. With loving it is the same, but it's not for you, it's with the other person. There is no doubt, no question what is to do. It is clear what is to do. There is love. There is no undefined in love.

Kevin: Daniel is going so deep right now, my mind is blowing up.

Cadell: A lot came up in both of your reflections. I do think that the topic of love and death is connected to Eros and Thanatos. There is a reason why those two forces are put into a coincidence of opposites with each other. The interesting thing I want to highlight, consistent with my previous assertions in the trialogue, is the asymmetrical nature of the Absolute when it comes to binaries. In other words, when you have a binary, *the two are not the same,* or a *balanced polarity. One is a lack of the other.* The emphasis I want to place, I think expressed by both of you, is that *Thanatos is primary* and *Eros is secondary.* I think that when one is deeply engaged in Eros, one knows this because it is sort of like Kevin said, it is going in the opposite direction of Thanatos. It is like you are pulling yourself away from the "true Master." The true Master will take you in the end. It is like the story of Adam and Eve. It is like you are trying to grab the apple when God told you not to grab the apple. It is almost like you are stealing. In psychoanalysis, **jouissance**, or sexual enjoyment, is what brings identity death. You do die within life. "La petite mort" or "the little death." I experience this more and more. It is the fundamental location for me of disorientation. The fundamental location of a demand for sacrifice and submission from "the other."

I will say that in regards to what you were saying Daniel, when it comes to Love and Death, I love that there are no more doubts. In philosophy, if you read Descartes, all of modern philosophy is based on *"how do I know for sure?,"* grounding the *Cogito: "how do I ground certain knowledge?"* He is looking for something *he cannot doubt.* This grounds the subject of science. Pure abstract reason: **"I think, therefore I am."** The interesting thing I would complicate with psychoanalysis, is Lacan said, **"I think where I am not."** This "I think where I am not," is how to make sense of this location where there is no doubt, which appears in love and death, you have *absolute certainty*, not in positive knowledge of the world, but of this negative knowledge, of the *mystery of the other.* In that sense I feel that is why this is a good close out for our trialogue. When you are dancing away from the concept of love and death you have more speculative free play. Well "maybe this is true," "maybe that is true." But *love and death bring back to the center.* So, I appreciate that point.

Kevin: There is nothing ambiguous about death. There is no confusion. Any one of us who have seen a corpse. When you see a body that is not animated by life. There is a finality which brings everything into hyper focus. I think it is the same in love. I was just talking to a lot of men at a men's retreat. All of the men, when they met their "one," it is like there is this golden aura around them and time stopped. There was no confusion or "what do I do next?" It is like time collapses in on the lovers. I imagine it is the same when you die. Moments before death, time stops. It is like this profound exhale of reality. It brings you back to the center of being. All the time spent on the periphery, in science and arts and politics and religion and society and moral philosophy, all are intimating the true real of human existence. Is there any place where there is more real than a baby being born? Or when you are making love or see a lover? Or when you or someone near you is dying? Death. There is a way in which the background field of experience or existence is death, like you were saying Cadell, it is the primary reality. We know that we will die, it is the curse and the blessing of mankind.

Socrates said that because man knows he will die, he has separated himself from the animal and plant kingdom and is approaching the kingdom of the gods. Even though the gods don't die, they are immortal. So, they want to participate in the human kingdom, and want to sleep with the humans. Even the gods envy humans because of mortality, it creates this game, and gives everything import and infuses life with meaning. For many people, and especially for men, unless they are living out a great work of art, a huge mission on the planet, or a project or a war campaign, then the most significant thing in your life will be falling in love and getting married and having a family. That is the penultimate moment in a man's life, you have arrived at the center, the full expression of Eros.

Then Thanatos is in the background the whole time which is what gave it meaning. When you have to bury your wife or your parents or anyone in your village, when death is claiming them, you live more because death is claiming them. It is the same when you are really in love. When you encounter a couple that is really glowing, they are in true passionate love and Eros which is so strong and their erotic energy is all over them. An encounter with that snaps you back into reality, it is a libidinal field, a form of magnetism. This is what is really important. When there is a lot of death it is the same. Life is so short. This is what is really important. These two forces are medicine. They are really powerful medicines. The sexual death, the personality death in romance and love. Then the physical leaving the body, it is like a Shamanic mythic reality that drives culture.

Daniel: One thing that came into my mind is how similar they are. I love what you pointed out when it comes to giving life again. The point when you know you have marriage, a couple, that you gave birth to a child. I think in this moment, I haven't been through that yet, but I have seen it, it is like "wow," there is nothing more important in that moment. Taking care of the child. The thing that strikes me is that actually you are in life, experiencing love. You know? It is like we need mortality for love. You know? If you come to the experience of a god, for example, I don't know if they can love like a human. You know? And if they can love, what would you prefer? I'm not sure. But I was looking also into something again, that I had the feeling I had to look at it. There is something that makes another leap to it.

I looked into the *Tibetan Book of the Dead*. What happens after death for the Buddhists? It is described in three phases. The *first phase* is the death itself where the ultimate light reality comes into play. It is when you say "ok, this is where all life dissolves and we see the light." The light of reality. Then the *second phase* where we experience "the reality of visions of the Buddha," or reincarnations, or angels or whatever, and life is being judged. Then the *third phase* starts, in which we are going back, and we are going back in the sense that imagining man and woman, which are representing compassion and wisdom. This varies all according to your karma. So, it depends on your karma what you are going to see, what kind of compassion and wisdom is represented, you will see. It depends also on your karma, what you are going to envision. This woman-man couple, they are a couple having sex, and Buddhists call it enhancing sensation with an imaginary. This is the last place before going into one of the six realms of being, where you can be a god, man, animal, demon, stone, or incarnate in hell. You start from hell and go up. And then you can see where you will be. The best place to be is a human because it is the best place to get awakening. Even the gods go for power, envy and spite and they are not outside of the wheel of samsara.

That is why I want to point back where my question arose, because this is where we started, *why is the human love exclusive?* Somehow for gods, maybe love is not exclusive, they have to love everyone. But we humans *have this exclusivity.* The question again comes, is it good to be human because we cannot be in love, and be in an eternity at the same time, while being alive? While being mortal? Or even because of being mortal, as you pointed out Cadell. I think there is also something about this little death in life. Because the orgasm is also this little death, as they call it like this. Love and death are two final points in which everything comes together, everything dissolves, until you reach the solution, into a kind of oneness. And if you have this little by little, you might reach once a big one. Little by little it comes to a bigger change. Also death, the ultimate change. You forget everything.

Actually, one thing that is also intriguing is about *forgetting*. When you fall in love you forget your friends, stuff like that, you lose your job. But with death also. There is something that you forget when you are in love as well as confronted with immediate death. In the *Tibetan Book of the Dead* the big thing is to be conscious during the process of rebirth, to get the best rebirth, otherwise you won't choose. It is a tricky thing to not forget while being dead or being in love. I don't know.

Then it seems sometimes to me one solution might be like a brotherhood or sisterhood thing. But maybe then we go into the realms of the love of gods. I don't know even which gods, because the Greek gods have a lot of sex, and also the Indian gods have a lot of sex. But these are the categories of the hungry gods or the envious gods. There are also the devas which are more calm but have the problem of being too proud. Buddha goes to them and shows them pride is not everything. For the other gods that experience envy, they have insight in the power of the tree. Buddha comes to them and says there is no justice in what you are doing because you are enjoying everything. There is also something we have to talk about when it comes to judgement, which is on the point that most of the religions say, this comes after death, you will be judged. **The last judgment**. There will be karma. Where are you going to be? What is going to be next after this ultimate change? What didn't you forgive about yourself? Was it a good life? *Was your heart light when you are going to die?* Then you come back to life via the imaginary. You imagine this couple having sex, which actually might be an orgasm of people having sex, and at the same time your death or your start into life.

Cadell: I think, for me, picking up where Kevin started. The whole problem starts with this meeting "the one." What it is is falling on your own image. This is where the problem starts. It is not a solution. That is why it is destined to be a catastrophe. Your problems are just getting started, as it were. I think it is because of this coincidence between time and eternity. You can't hold it (the love of your image).

You are originally cut, you are cut from, my view is, your cut from nothing. You just have an image that it is something. In other words, it is not like you were a substantial whole one, but nonetheless you have this image of desire to join with something else, because you are not full in yourself, you are tarrying with a missing other. In love, as Daniel says, you dissolve into the other. Of course, you dissolve into a human other, and they are just human, they are not a god. Only in death do you really dissolve into the other (nothingness). And that, to me, is why death is the more primary other, because, at least from my view, it is a pure nothingness, you are gone.

And then as Kevin says, about the center of love and death, and we could use gravitational metaphors, which I like. To me the subject in time, in history, is always de-centered in relation to the non-relation of death. The subject is de-centered, and when you fall in love, you momentarily feel like you've centered, but you are so close to a gravitational center, that it becomes impossible to navigate in time, and what usually happens, when Eros is the opposite of Thanatos, is that in order to keep the one, you have to kill the other one. You literally have to die. That is my theory for why sacrifice and submission appear in this location, I guess. However, the problem comes when you introduce growth and change. The chances that you grow and change together is basically very low. You will grow and change apart, most likely. So this problem of time gets reintroduced again, this problem of being de-centered is reintroduced again.

This brings us back to what Daniel said in Chapter 6, about not being able to find the center inside one self. I don't find the cause in myself as ego or "I." I said I experienced it in the ayahuasca state, and maybe I did, but I had to go outside of this world with the other, so I am still de-centered in the world and with something else that is more or different than "me." It is a real conundrum to me because if you are in this passionate fall into love, and it is a catastrophe, you could just accept the intensity of this force, and ride it out for as long as it lasts. Nothing could ever get rid of this irrationality of love. Build any supercomputer you like and this irrationality in love will persist.

Nonetheless, we know now from cognitive and complexity science that algorithmic thinking cannot work in complex environments. You need more heuristics. I feel like the traditional concepts for love are like static algorithms that prevent real thinking. I feel like heuristics would be much better than the categorical labels that we usually default to, to hold love in time. I can say that the problem of our age is not that we lost the real, *because we never had the real*, but we have lost our ability to *name the real*. We are losing our ability to name things. Traditional culture succeeded in naming the real, at least. The names they used worked, in a way. In our own relationships, the categories we use don't really work. We can no longer name the real. So, there are all sorts of weird **"situationships."** Something is happening but we don't want to put a name on it. The words don't work. That is why heuristics would be nice. If X then Y.

Kevin: Are you trying to create love formulas, Cadell?

Cadell: I am trying to create love formulas that are for temporal processes instead of fixed categories! But I know that I can't create a love formula because, again, the irreducible irrationality. The question for me is in my understanding of the unconscious. This is self-relationship. The unconscious is "rational and logical," *but not from the perspective of our ego*. That is why I don't even like the concept of "irrational." Irrational is just a negation of rational. What is irrational? It is remarkably hard to define outside of a simple negation of rationality. There is not even a good definition. But it is just labelled as not rational because we don't understand it, it is not a problem in the irrational in-itself. The problem is in our interpretation of what is going on. We don't understand the irrational. That is why I am sympathetic to the psychoanalytic traditions that engage in formulaic thinking because they try to approach the deepest forms of love and human existence with rational discourse and formulas and axioms, but at the same time keeping the unconscious as irreducible. I am spontaneously sympathetic to this. I don't see what the alternatives are? Just a bunch of insanity? It would be nice if we had basic heuristics for love: if X then Y. That would save from this pathology of love as this lack where the other (human) is always to blame.

I would go back to the primordial problem of you meeting "the one." *Then you have time.* It is like the pathology of love in this situation is "destiny." All of a sudden you can't live in the present anymore. The formula of this pathology is **"if this doesn't last forever it is a failure,"** or **"I can't even think of anything except the indefinite continuation of this relationship so I am not even existing in the relationship."** Jacques Lacan called the love relationship what **"never stops not being written."** This means that you are in a love relationship, but all "it" (the relationship) can do is reflectively discuss its own impossibility. *This is the nightmare of love.* Love is beautiful when it is *not being directly spoken.* As soon as you start reflectively discussing the nature of the love relationship it is done. You will never stop talking about it, never stop discussing it. But when you can hold "it" without discussing it constantly, *you are there in the real,* somehow. The non-relation has been "suspended."

My main points are, one, *we are losing our ability to name the real.* The words we use don't work. Two, *can we develop some basic heuristics for this problem of love.* The culture degenerates when we can't fall in love. When we are just having meaningless sex, the culture degenerates. The problem of falling in love is we don't want to put a label on things and then it will be an "eternal label," it will be doomed to end horribly. We are living longer, who knows what the next 50 years will be like? Nothing like our grandparents" generation. I think simple heuristics is a very modest proposal.

Kevin: So modest, Cadell. Let's create repeatable equations for the mystery of love. So modest! It is very honorable, that is a huge task. Wow, that was a brilliant riff. So much has come up, I am going to ride with what is present. Naming. Naming is huge. As McKenna said, and as I said in a previous trialogue, our culture can only exist in a reality it can describe. A culture's language and terminology around reality changes the cultural landscape. We can occupy non-verbal reality and we did for millions of years before language was emitted. Suddenly when we can name reality back to our self and others, a new massive mental-psychic realm emerges.

Cadell: It is a symbolic technology, you can't go anywhere without this little tool. Then we can not talk about it.

Kevin: That is the value in the heuristic of language. Conceivably we could get to a heuristic of love, Platonic, erotic, friendship, allyship. This is also pointed out by Esther Perel, who I still think is one of the best leading experts from tens of thousands of hours of discussing romantic problems with couples, doing counselling and therapy. She says we are still using the same language from the 1950s for dating. Meanwhile we have dating apps and polyamory, and creationships, situationships, and causal relationships. All these crazy words and new containers for what a relationship and love really is. The language hasn't even caught up to the new real.

Maybe even more important is that the theme for romantic love hasn't moved past medieval times in my mind and life experience. The stories we tell ourselves about the narrative of love have not changed. In the past sexual love and marriage were political and economic. They were in the service of barring children and social networks for larger communities in service of religious ideals. The ideal of romantic love in the West is a more modern secular invention where we get caught up in the idea of love as the other human rather than a real relationship with a human being. This creates a feedback loop of existential terror because the other will obviously let us down. That is what death is: existential terror. **"Wow, I feel so good, I am so in love, this is the only one for me."** I need to perpetuate this narrative or else I will feel the terror of being separated from the other, which I think is the same as being separated from God. This is the primordial fear of being separated, leaving the womb and the Absolute. Romantic love and its narratives are a strategy to maintain that link in post-religious times, even at the expense of the reality of human life and nature. You may not actually be in love with the real of that person, the relationship may be codependent and unhealthy. But the narrative that the lovers are telling each other, as you say Cadell, the ability to name and articulate it, is paramount, to maintain itself.

I think the modern dating landscape is a wasteland, to take it back to the first chapter. I don't need to go into the data, global divorce rates and infidelity, it is all symptomatic of erotic love and the existential terror it is paired with. For many of us, myself included, we didn't grow up in a container where our parents were occupying the real of erotic love, but they were occupying the conceptual layers on top of it somewhere. They were somewhat abstracted and disassociated from the real of it, in whatever degree that occurred. I guess to summarize and speak to the heuristic part, as you were saying Cadell, the unconscious is rational but at a different dimension of causality. This comes up in the *I Ching*, the Tao, the big Self, the Soul, the Unconscious, which is a totality, and our ego is a little orbiting satellite to the totality. The ego is like **"what the fuck is going on?,"** I am so confused, experiencing emotional negativity, obsessed with this person, the love reality. The unconscious or the soul has its own heuristics, its own patterning, its own attractor fields, a strange attractor, and that is where the libido comes in. The libido goes where it wants to go.

Cadell: The unconscious knows.

Kevin: Ya, beyond reason, it knows what partner will be a good fit, and even if you are in your concepts, your libido will shift to a new object of desire. That is where the existential terror comes in. It is like wait, but I was in this configuration, in this constellation. It is like no, your unconscious is shifting this way, and if you stay in your concepts, you face deep personality death. I will leave it here, we are spiraling into wild territory.

Daniel: A lot has been said on these two topics. I will try to make my response synthetic. Where do I start first? We meet the one, and the catastrophe starts. *Beautiful!* When you meet "the one," it is like meeting the *death or God*, the God which has *no "s" behind*. That is why it is one, *because there is no doubt. It is one.* It is not two or three or four or whatever. In any case, by meeting the one this leads to a catastrophe, I think, and that is why I loved it.

You meet the one and then the catastrophe starts. The changes are so fundamental to everything. It is like going into a flow of crisis I call it sometimes. You can have really deep learning because you go through a deep crisis. You step into the next "one" after having conquered the obstacles of the first "oneness." Then you say, **"oh no it's coming again!"** This happens sometimes when you are deeply in the fall, the fall into death or fall into love. It is always a new oneness that is a new challenge just like the first or old oneness. And on the way of this falling, you know, you can also stumble on some steps like the other times, but maybe in a different way, a new stumble.

I think somehow, we want to make a formula or heuristics out of it, I will come back to this. What is a formula? I had to think about this imagination coming back before you come back into life in the cycle of rebirth of the Buddhists. I have to think about what is the relationship between wisdom and compassion, which is somehow symbolized by the male-female in the Buddhist tradition. We have this wisdom or knowledge. I don't know if there is wisdom without compassion. But actually *knowledge without compassion is power.* You come into wisdom and the knowledge containing is misused. *There is also no justice without compassion. This is hell, because you need grace for the good.* So the other way around is more difficult. If you have compassion without wisdom, you are lacking in your ability of judgement. You also might say "but this is not good," because we wouldn't have compassion for everything. But if we combine this together, it might be something like conscious love. And the easiest way I would put it, is if you don't know, then it is alright. Maybe that is love. If you don't know and you are not sure that it is love, then it is not love. Maybe if you are sure you don't know then you are in love.

Cadell: Can you repeat that formula, Daniel?

Kevin: It is a very quantum heuristic right here.

Daniel: It is quantum. I have to think about quantum mechanics right here. It comes to the point where we can't name it. The last month I have been with some persons who do experiments on mind-matter interaction and people who do experiments with telepathy. They link it to a general theory of quantum mechanics. There is a very striking point about that, because, one researcher found out that we have entangled processes (like telepathy or influences on random generators of machines where you put your intention into the process and it makes it non-random, it has an effect). There is an entanglement between you and your experiment. It is actually a very small effect. Most psychic or parapsychic phenomena, like bending spoons, for example. I have never done it, but I have been told by people that you can bend spoons by developing a deeper relationship with a spoon. You get an entanglement. Each time you get an entanglement, the best entanglements are the mother with the son or the daughter, or with people who love each other. But mother and child is like the deepest connection. The point is the possibility, only the possibility to be observed, the effects of entanglement goes down. There is a deep striking correlation about defining and reproducing what is entangled because if the possibility is there, this entanglement goes apart in a linearity and in an actual particle. That is why there is no name, if you come to name it, you change it already. So that is why I go back to this because I think the imaginary unconsciousness which strikes you into the path of the search of someone we love or of maybe the process of merging into being one with someone or with something.

Kevin: What I am hearing is that when you name it you preclude the possibility to love when you name it.

Daniel: That's the paradox. I heard a Christian monk give a talk on what is meaningful. He said if you ask someone that it is there and it is beautiful and I want to stay, I want to leave it, I want to rest, that is meaningful. I also made this rumination that death is the ultimate rest where you can just stay and that is it, which is also what happens with someone you love. You just want to stay there and that's it. You find a place to be in peace. Not an everlasting one. Either because of a judgement that you are right or the next phase, whatever it might be. We start this cycle again of birth, death and rebirth. What keeps the thing moving, when this catastrophe starts, when the change is led by merging with the one, is so fundamental and accelerated, in comparison to the animals and plants, I ask especially myself, we have this judgement that comes as religions point out, as a judgement of your life after death. The judgement actually relies on the imagination, on what is the ideal, which is not real. And, this imagination is like from the beginning of having two persons giving life to a child.

Kevin: I feel like I'm experiencing a death and rebirth in this trialogue.

Cadell: I do like the wavefunction metaphor for these things and language as a collapse of the wavefunction. The paradox is that naming something centers or tightens a certain possibility by naming. By naming you are defining a certain trajectory and you are predefining a certain trajectory where previously there were multiple trajectories. The problem is that in the past the naming function had a clearly defined trajectory, it made sense. Now the fundamental issue is that there is a trade-off between a growth model and reproduction model. Kevin said about previous generations, that they were not living out the real of love, that they were just trapped in the narrative of love. But, in my view, you can't have passionate love *and* raise a family. That is not possible. I mean go for it, be my guest, but good luck to you! Good luck to you! *I am praying for you!*

I am just saying that, the reason for why we fall in love, and the meaning of falling in love, it used to be for children, for future generations, and now it is less and less being necessitated by that function. That is to me why we are in the wavefunction. And thus, why we are not naming it. Because what are we doing? What? That is the whole thing to me. It is a mystery that is, by my closing thoughts on this whole trialogue, I am more and more trusting emotions that I can't put in words. I trust whatever it is that motion that I can't articulate. That I can't name. As Kevin said, the words can't keep up with what is happening. In the psychological literature, you act first, and then you name afterwards (retroactively). We have to trust our actions, we have to be honest about our actions. *What am I acting out?* This gap between the actions and the narrative. *Crucial. What am I acting out?* Then is there any clue of a word or a story which could help me explain that to myself? But we are not self-transparent, and that is the meaning of the unconscious. So I just trust my unconscious motion, I trust where it has led me so far. It has led me away from certain things. It is easy for me to say what it has led me away from. It has led me towards many boundaries of fear, many boundaries of negativity which I need to integrate and confront to become a better and stronger person. Maybe I won't be able to name it until I am an old man. Maybe in retrospect I can make sense of it. It is a strange form of non-linear temporality.

Another thing I will end on, is a strange phenomenon of romantic relationships which I think could be a powerful tool, is almost like the temporality of a video game. In a video game when you make a mistake, like in *Super Mario*, you have ten lives. You fall in a pit, you get eaten by a plant, and then you pop back up to where you were previously located. This form of temporality should be maximally harnessed in relationships. In order to make mistakes you need to have multiple lives. How many lives do we have? How many mistakes can we make? What is a mistake? What defines success? We need to harness this temporality to make real progress. Because nobody in sexuality knows what they are doing. I will end with that.

Kevin: I love it. You get the one-up, level up rebirth in a relationship. We are going to start this relationship, you have ten lives. The man goes through seven lives in the first week. That is a great analogy.

Cadell: As you go through the relationship you can hit checkpoints and gain more lives.

Kevin: Yes, let's replenish the number of mistakes you can make as the intimacy increases you reach a new level.

Cadell: It is the opposite of a perfectionism model. We are in this thinking that if you make one mistake then the whole relationship is a mistake. That doesn't make any sense.

Kevin: The opposite seems to be true. The more mistakes you can gracefully navigate with language and action, the stronger or the more potential the relationship gains.

Cadell: This is where I would again advocate or propose heuristics.

Kevin: Ya, I agree. There is a way in which a formula-heuristic in love could be communicated, by being vulnerable, and then try again, learning the lesson, knowing you will fail again, but you will fail at a deeper level of intimacy. That is an unconscious heuristic I have followed in my own life.

To summarize here, this has been a wild one. To circle back to death, we kind of went all the way into Eros. Death makes life worth living. I don't think, although a god could have superpowers and paranormal abilities and infinite knowledge, their love would never be worth that of a mortal. It would never have the quality. The ultimate example is Zeus. No one is in love with Zeus, not even his own wife, Hera. He is like a nature principal of the masculine patriarch or something like that.

All that being said mortality gives life meaning, it also gives love meaning. If you can navigate your way into a powerful relationship and really experience love and depth and sexual intimacy, there is a way in which you have defied death and made life more meaningful, and crystallized meaning in your lifetime as a human being. There is a way that is an eternity, because that love, especially if you have children, will live beyond you. Even if you don't have children the ripple of your love will be eternal, or at least for as long as culture can replicate it. So, there is something really powerful between love, death and sex.

As far as languaging reality and creating heuristics. I am excited for the future case, one of the gifts, is to articulate the new world, especially the relational world. I want to invent language and revivify language. Bringing back ancient concepts and pushing new limits, to name new realities and new terrains. We get to name it now. We get to name it with precision and heart. Not just with theory and using the past, recapitulating primordial trauma of separation, all the things we have seen not work.

The rise of postmodernism in its extremity is a blight, for me, of trying to name realities but in a very dark and oblique way. A very lifeless way. But what postmodernists get right is deconstructing and starting with first principles. In intimacy, especially, if we can name from first principles and really sense and respond to give words to those unnameable realities, we will see a lot of acceleration in love, and therefore our relationship to death as well. Take us home, Daniel.

Daniel: In closing, most of the things we come along with is, if we talk about death and love, we can name it, but by experiencing it we can't imagine it, to have a future, and also a past. But imagination brings us to life. One thing I want to mention about the gods, I mean, if you go really back into the question who is the father of who, who is the father of who? In Greek mythology they are the Titans, and beyond, they are not really sure; and the funny thing for the Buddhists, the half-gods are also called the Titans, and beyond the Titans, there are the Devas, the gods of nature, and some others. And also if you go into, and really back to the mixture, of Afro-Caribbean traditions, you get one or two gods that are the creators. There is one creator above all, sometimes it is not very clear, because there are different stories. But in all these stories there is going to be light. Then it comes to the creation of Earth and sky.

If we talk about being in a relationship, and we fall in love and we can't hold it but we still go further and try and make failures and go along and still engage in love. It can be, it is, a way how to change yourself. The way you can make the biggest change, is confronting love and death. What do we reach at the end of these changes? I think it is better to be a human, somehow. This is very striking for me because it is really better to be a human because sometimes maybe I thought there are some humans that are more like gods, and some humans that are more like animals, you know? Maybe we should become more like a god? But the gods also have their troubles. And I think in the end where it comes to this point, the ultimate change is you rest in peace. We are dead. Or someone dies. He might rest in peace. We all say that. We want to rest in peace. Even if you are confronting death you want to make peace with everyone, even if you don't believe. You don't want to have trouble between someone and you.

As Socrates died, he said "don't forget to give the chicken to the neighbor," because it is the only thing he was owing someone. He didn't want to die without re-paying his debts. Then he could die in peace. So if we go alongside with this whole knowledge, the only thing I can live from now is really, that most of the things we just don't know. We can imagine the best and try to live in peace. We should strive for the best, to keep this creative life of cycles spinning for good and peace, somehow in this massive chaos. But we are learning I think. I believe we can learn.

Kevin: Yes, we are learning. From chaos comes spontaneous order, and then back into chaos. One catastrophe to true love, an encounter with death, our travel as humans. It is beautiful and it is confusing. Wow. That marks the end. It has been a journey. It has been an honor. It has been a joy philosophizing and inquiring together on this mystery.

Conclusion

We have spent the entirety of this book reflecting on the nature and meaning of sexuality. This journey has taken us from the difference in sexual expression, the emergence of sexual form, worldviews that influence conceptions of sexuality, theories about alternative identity construction in sexuality, the contemporary struggles for masculine sexual identity, nature of emotional suffering in sexuality, coincidence between relations and absolutes in sexuality, paradox in ethics and morality of sexual action, potential future expression of sexuality, and ultimately, the relation between sexuality and love and death.

Is there anything that holds these sexual dimensions all-together? Here I would suggest that there is not "one positive thing" which holds all of these discussions together, there is not "one answer" which holds all of these discussions together, but rather its opposite: there is "one enigma," "mystery," or "impossibility" of sexuality that holds all of these discussions together. In discussing sexuality at the highest philosophical level one finds the self in a strange discursive or epistemological space where it feels like one can keep circling this topic forever and ever and ever, while staying in essentially the same place. In these discussions there is a feeling as if one answer or solution simply opens up a new series of questions and problems that mirror or reduplicate the same old questions and problems that one started with at the beginning.

Take, for example, our first discussion on the nature of sexual difference in form between the masculine and feminine. Before philosophical discussion on the nature of this difference, one simply and spontaneously "acts it out," one simply and unconsciously plays the role of the masculine or the feminine without bringing it to self-reflective attention that "this is what I am doing." After philosophical discussion on the nature of this difference, one still finds oneself in the same structure and the same role, "acting it out," even if with more conscious awareness. However, the point is that whether or not this action is in conscious awareness or not, the same tensions and polarities remain, the same struggle and drive remains.

In other words, the "self-knowledge" was not necessarily a difference that made a difference in the sense that it changes the form, or changes the tensions, or changes the polarity. Instead the "self-knowledge" was simply the bringing to conscious awareness that a difference in the form of a (sexual) enigma, mystery or impossibility, precedes a difference (my historical identity). Thus, in contrast to the contemporary ideology emphasizing the social construction of gendered possibilities, it is almost as if one becomes aware of a deeper metaphysical principle that underlies or governs the structure of constructive sexuation as such.

This is not to say that knowledge of this structure is not important, since one gains the ability to work within the limits of the process, to see what dimensions of the constraints have yet to be exploited or harnessed, for more freedom, power, understanding, truth, beauty and love. However, there is also a sense that in deeply exploring sexuality one hits upon a truth where submission to a "higher" or "deeper" principle is revealed internal to one-self. This is an especially strange experience for a rational, modern, secular, and scientific human being who is not used to submission to a "higher" or "deeper" principle other than one's own self-conscious and rational determination. In other words, the idea that there may be a form of reason that is unconscious, a form of reason which is alien, yet internal, to one's own Self, is something that is alarming, anxiety provoking, and even absolutely terrifying.

Where does that leave us? Well it may leave us in the most interesting possible territory that we can imagine. Take, for example, the idea that we "moderns" (or "postmoderns," if you like), sit in an unfortunate time between two great missed adventures: the adventure of travelling and discovering the world as in our pre-modern ancestors who mapped out the entire Earth as one sphere; and the adventure of travelling and discovering the whole galaxy as in our hypothetical future (transhuman?) offspring who may colonize the rest of the Milky Way. If one takes such a notion to have a high truth value, one may take away the unsettling idea that we just missed out on real adventure and mystery. We postmoderns sit in the unspectacular time when the whole of our world is known and mapped, and at the same time exist just before the time when we, presumably, will start to produce the technologies we need to expand out into a new unknown of the cosmos at large.

This is where the presupposition that marks much of our discourse, the notion of "unconscious sexuality," throws a short-circuit into our conventional way of looking at the world. Far from being stuck in-between two missed adventures, we find ourselves sitting at perhaps one of the most interesting possible horizons in need of collective mapping: the relation between libidinal energy and the heart (love). Consider for a moment that from the perspective of historical spirit, the world has been fully sublated (idealized), but so too has the entire observable universe. In terms of our technological extensions we have already mapped the observable universe, and find it to be totally simple, repetitive, and homogenous, at the largest possible scales of analysis.

Where is the complexity, novelty and heterogenous activity that would provide us with adventure and mystery? Where is the space that calls for sublation (idealization)? Well it may just be in the conscious territory governed by the law of the heart and unconscious energetics of libido. Indeed, on a meta-level that is how one may view this entire *Sexual Trialogues* topic. In a very open-ended form, mediated with lots of authentic feedback, as well as shared control in the hierarchical distribution of labor and attention, Kevin, Daniel and I attempted to use our self-consciousness to bring to light the unconscious energetics of libido, whether that was in relation to its difference in expression, its emergence of form, its ethics of action, or its potential future pathways, and so forth.

Of course, this project is just one of many potential other projects on sexuality that could engage in the same essential philosophical enterprise. How are we to conceive this space and possible collective mapping project on larger scales? Here we can say that the conscious is what we are aware of, what we know (or at least assume) to be true on the terms of sublation (idealization of our shared planet, and the cosmos at large). On the other hand, we can say that the unconscious is what is not-conscious, what we do not know to be true, and yet what surrounds us on all sides, awaiting sublation. At one time our planet and the cosmos were in essence unconscious. Now they have been brought into conscious awareness. What is still in essence unconscious is the essential libidinal drives, motives and aims of the human collective.

In other words, we can say that unconscious sexuality is the "one" enigma, mystery or impossibility around which our collective discourse circulates. This collective discourse is not just a disem-bodied abstraction of a non-human universal necessity (i.e., a map of the Earth or the cosmos). Following the idea of "unconscious sexuality," our collective discourse is rather an embodied abstraction (signifier in the body) that acts in relation to energetic flows which bind and unbind with principles of its own design. The difficulty for our consciousness is that we have to work very hard on ourselves in order to become aware of our heart, to become aware of our own law, to become aware of our own conscience and drive, and to articulate that to the others. Indeed, if the academic path is the path of making the external world known to our conscious awareness, then the spiritual path proper is of making the libidinal drives, motives and aims of the human collective known to conscious awareness.

To confront this dimension, to walk the spiritual path, is very difficult. The only way to really do it may be to accept and embrace a more active relationship to death. Death, far from being an external force that inevitably awaits our being, may in fact best be conceptualized as an internal force that overrides and overdetermines life itself. In the image of Death, Life itself can mobilize new repetitions of libido that gain their creative capacity from allowing one's current concrete identity to die, to push it to its extreme limits, to traverse territory which has never been traversed before. In short, to die differently than anyone who has ever lived before.

In this context, the *Sexual Trialogues* should be re-read from this point of view. The *Sexual Trialogues* should be re-read from the point of view of an internalized death drive. How do you want to die differently than any human who has lived before? What would the law of your own heart determine if it knew itself well enough? If it had been brave enough to live? It is at this moment when the death drive, far from being a desire for the immediate dissolution of one's being back into *Das Nichts*, is in fact the very principle of immortal love internal to the structuring of libido, the death drive is a drive for real love.

This brings us back to the idea that in sexuality we reach a limit that we do not ourselves set, but which we come to recognize through our own self work, on making what is unconscious increasingly conscious, and in the process learning what we really desire and who we really are in this world. Thus, in traversing sexuality ("unconscious energetics of libido") we learn our self so well that we start to know the limits, constraints and obstacles that we *need to work with in order to become our best self*. We learn the limits, constraints and obstacles that we *need to work with in order to constantly transcend what we thought were our limits, constraints and obstacles*. Far from a philosophy that articulates that "anything is possible," and there are "no limitations" or "no obstacles" on our way, such a philosophy empowers us to better understand the truthful relation between, and becoming of, possibility and impossibility. Good luck, with Love!

Cadell Last
October 14 2019

About the Authors

Cadell Last is a historical form of consciousness that has been driven from a young age to questions about origins: of humanity, life, and the cosmos itself. This drive first stimulated a quest to better understand the meaning of metaphysical questions: the creation of reality, why there was something rather than nothing, and whether or not the appearance of something had a deeper meaning than the surface level of day-to-day existence would suggest.

This quest started with an interest in all fields of study, from history and anthropology to biology and physics. He ended up focusing his attention on the origin of humans in his academic practices, specifically studying great ape tool culture, nesting organizations, communication methods; and also with his blog and popular media efforts attempting to bring a general knowledge of human origins to a broader audience. From this work he developed an understanding that the origin of humans was an origin that involved the development of complex culture and technology via the emergence of self-consciousness mediated by symbolic language.

In the process of investigating the origin of humans he became convinced that the complex emergence of self-consciousness, language, culture, and technology would play a causal role in new qualitative transformation in the near-term future. This led him to connect his anthropological knowledge to the study of complex systems and future speculations in the development of his doctoral studies. His doctoral studies focused on the idea of the "Global Brain," which hypothesizes that human civilization is becoming a global superorganism. He finished his doctorate in 2019 and published it in 2020. The thesis attempted to build an evolutionary theory focused on the meaning of self-consciousness, language, culture, and technology for the rest of nature.

Throughout his doctoral studies he became aware that academic knowledge was often disconnected from day-to-day existence. In order to approach this problem, he co-founded the School of Thinking with a few colleagues and led several workshops focused on the nature and methods of meta-reflective thinking (i.e., thinking about thinking). This school has since been transformed into a postgraduate program at multiple institutions and is pioneering work on the nature of thought and its possible future expressions. Such meta-reflective work may become increasingly necessary as our world becomes more complex and it becomes more difficult to make sense of emergent phenomena, novelty, and difference.

He is also continuing his academic research attempting to understand the relationship between general theory and the nature of subjectivity. The nature of subjectivity is the nature of the interior world and its perceptual and conceptual capacities; general theory is the abstract description of universal properties of being. Often times, general theory of being does a poor job of articulating its relationship to the interiority of being, and reconciling these opposites may be important for the future of academic practice and fundamental understanding of essential metaphysical categories, like the meanings of infinity and immortality. He is also a researcher interested in exploring new mediums of artistic and creative expression and is regularly active on social media creating content related to the foundations of philosophy.

Kevin Orosz is the host of "The (R)Evolution" Podcast, a High Performance Coach, Retreat Facilitator, Public Speaker, and Co-Founder of the lifestyle brand "Mystic Misfit."

Primarily, he coaches clients in the weaponization and actualization of their intuition. Developing his clients' spiritual abilities and senses through practical techniques and mindset hacks. People come to him to have radical accountability and wellness applied to their life in the vein of lifestyle science AND mysticism. The "conscious community" and "spiritual world" may seem archaic, silly, unscientific, or even absurd from a Westerner's perspective looking in – however with the synergy of Eastern wisdom and current psychology and neuroscience – there is a balance. Kevin is that bridge. His entrepreneurial work allows him to be a guide in custom coaching programs designed to locate blocks, reveal the doorway, and access the keys to unlocking one's magical potential.

Bridging modern psychology and ancient philosophy, Kevin began his pathway as an undergraduate student driven by mythology, the hero's journey, and masculine initiation as guiding lights. This has been his primary quest in business and art.

He is a flowstate hunter and mixed magical artist, combining transformation in tantra, breathwork, bioenergetics, and ritual. Kevin's training and travels have well equipped him in his tenure as a retreat and mastermind activator internationally.

After a post-graduation spiritual awakening, Kevin left his home tribe in Texas in 2012 and abandoned pursuing his PhD in Psychology. Soon after, his travels led him on a backpacking quest throughout Southeast Asia, Thailand, India, and Nepal. While there, he studied under teachers in the B.K.S. Iyengar yogic style and the Osho meditation and bioenergetics tradition.

As a result of his learnings, he realized a synergy between Eastern and Western mysticism relating to his own personal myth. This led to study and practice in positive masculinity, rites of passage, the archetypes, initiation, and impact entrepreneurship.

Kevin believes powerful habits create our reality. By investing in healthy rituals, optimal lifestyle, and the human body as the gateway to our true potential for healing. Using yogic postures, breathing patterns, and nutritional science, he helps clients transform and craft their lives. Through language, radical honesty, authentic relating, and non-violent communication, Kevin assists his VIP clients with uncovering what authentic expression pioneering to live through them. By exploring their unique story, Kevin helps clients transition across the threshold to the life they desire.

Daniel Dick's life has been full of changes, deep transformations, and personal teachings in his private and profession life.

Daniel was born into a family in which spirituality and medicine have been a daily experience. He has been always in touch with these topics. Extensive travel experiences, especially through South America led him to discover the realms of Shamanism, Alternative Medicine and mystical experiences. Personal relationships and the destiny of life gave him some hard teaching about life and death which empowered his quest of creating meaning in life even more and arise a few times from the ashes. Daniel's professional teachings have been in research and educational institutions related to system science, consciousness research, anthropology, holistic and cross-cultural medicine, consultancy, and sexual pedagogy. Basically, his academic interests have been to make sense about his extraordinary experiences.

Daniel loves life, humans, and meaningful of co-living. This led him to explore various cultures, different spiritual paths, and some holistic healing techniques as well as ways to explore consciousness, such as intuition, meditation, and trance. He explored Buddhist mediations, like Zen and Vipassana, and different kinds of shamanism and guided meditative practices and is trained up to a Reiki Master.

Daniel´s student life has been paralleled by feminist ideas and emancipatory approaches. He got sensitized for socio-political environments as well as empowered by self-organized groups in education, especially in the University.

He worked for business-oriented research, such as for self-exploration software tools, impact assessment and flickering light perception. He has been lecturing at the University of Vienna in Anthropology and in Sociology. Daniel is holding the Young Scientist Bertalanffy Award of the European Meeting of Cybernetics and System Research 2016, worked in institutions, such as the Bertalanffy Center for the Study of Systems Science, the European School of Governance and co-founded the independent Viennese Academy of Consciousness Research in 2015 and the Existential Consciousness Research Institute in 2018. He published articles in academic and popular journals and is editing a book on consciousness research.

After an academic pursuit, the wish to help humankind with compassion and wisdom evolved towards creating a community center for healing and culture in Germany, which is right now his main endeavor.

Being on one hand a curious researcher and the other hand a spiritual inquirer, he loves to enable mutual understanding between people, mindsets, cultures, spirituality, and science. His driving ambitions are to change the current paradigm of health and education to make this world a better place by collaboration, ecological sustainability, and personal growth, which lead to meaningful relationships.
Besides that, he loves the waves of the ocean, the peaks of the mountains, and enjoys music, beauty, friends, and family.

Footnotes

1   Zupančič, A. 2017. *What Is Sex?* The MIT Press.

2   Plato. 2008. *The Symposium*. Cambridge Texts in the History of Philosophy. Howatson, M.C. & Shelffield, F.C.C. (Eds.). Cambridge University Press. p. 22

3   Zupančič, A. 2017. *What Is Sex?* The MIT Press. p. 46.

4   Deacon, T. 2011. *Incomplete Nature: How Mind Emerged from Matter*. W.W. Norton & Company. p. 12.

5   Shakespeare, W. 2009. *As You Like It*. The New Cambridge Shakespeare. Hattaway, M. (Ed.). Cambridge University Press. Act II, Scene VII.

6   Darwin, C. 1859. *On the Origin of Species by Means of Natural Selection or the Preservation of Favoured Races in the Struggle for Life*. New York: D. Appleton and Company. p. 425.

7   Dennett, D. 1996. *Darwin's Dangerous Idea: Evolution and the Meaning of Life*. Simon & Schuster.

8   Butler, J. 1990. *Gender Trouble: Feminism and the Subversion of Identity.* New York: Routledge. p. 6.

9   Ibid. p. 140-1.

10 Tomassi, R. 2013. *The Rational Male.* Counterflow Media LLC. p. 104-5.

11 Lacan, J. 2005. The Signification of the Phallus: *Die Bedeutung des Phallus.* In: *Écrits: The First Complete Edition in English.* Translated by Bruce Fink. New York: Norton. p. 692.

12 Huxley, A. 1947. *The Perennial Philosophy.* London: Chatto & Windus. p. 1.

13 Whitehead, A.N. 1966. *A Key to Whitehead's Process and Reality.* Sherburne, D.W. (Ed.). Chicago: The University of Chicago Press. p. 7.

14 Žižek, S. 2011. *Less Than Nothing: Hegel and the Shadow of Dialectical Materialism.* London: Verso. p. 124.

15 Nietzsche, F. 1989. *On the Genealogy of Morals.* Hollingdale, R.J. (Ed.) Vintage.

16 Freud, S. 2017. *Three Essays on the Theory of Sexuality: The 1905 Edition.* Verso Books.

17 Kurzweil, R. 2005. *The Singularity Is Near.* Penguin Group. p. 25.

18 Ibid. p. 228.

19 Ibid. p. 233, 238 .

Made in the USA
Middletown, DE
09 May 2022